*Marx and Engels
on Law*

LAW, STATE AND SOCIETY SERIES

Editors

Z. BANKOWSKI, *Department of Public Law, University of Edinburgh, U.K.*

M. CAIN, *Department of Sociology, Brunel University, Middlesex, U.K.*

W. CHAMBLISS, *Department of Sociology and Anthropology, University of Delaware, Newark, U.S.A.*

M. MCINTOSH, *Department of Sociology, University of Essex, Colchester, U.K.*

Marx and Engels on Law

MAUREEN CAIN
Department of Sociology, Brunel University, Uxbridge, Middlesex

ALAN HUNT
Assistant Dean of Law, Middlesex Polytechnic, Hendon, London

1979

ACADEMIC PRESS
London · New York · San Francisco
A Subsidiary of Harcourt Brace Jovanovich, Publishers

ACADEMIC PRESS INC. (LONDON) LTD.
24/28 Oval Road,
London NW1

United States Edition published by
ACADEMIC PRESS INC.
111 Fifth Avenue
New York, New York 10003

Library of Congress Catalog Card Number: 78 18678
ISBN Hardback: 0 12 154850 3
ISBN Paperback: 0 12 154852 x

Text set in 11/13 pt VIP Bembo, printed by photolithography,
and bound in Great Britain at the Pitman Press, Bath

For Anita, Leila and Daniel

Acknowledgements

We would like to express our appreciation to Deidre McIlreavy and Helen Lambrias for their assistance with the typing and preparation of this book. We thank Lawrence and Wishart and its staff for their help and for giving copyright permission for the reproduction of the majority of the extracts from the works of Marx and Engels and also Penguin Books for permission to use extracts from the *Grundrisse* and from *The First International and After*.

Contents

Preface

The Task Identified

The object of this book is to make available the writings of Marx and Engels relating to law. Nowhere did either of them take law as a direct object of their study and writing, but as this book establishes, the volume of their writings either on law or directly relevant to an understanding of law is considerable. However, there has been in recent years a very considerable interest in Marxist theories of law and in Marxist analyses of law. It is our hope that this contribution will both stimulate and facilitate that interest.

The growth of concern with Marxism and law is not an isolated phenomenon. During the 1970s there has been a resurgence of interest in Marxism among British social scientists. The concerns which contemporary Marxists largely share are to escape from economic determinism, to escape from the conceptual grip of inevitable historical processes, to reassert the analytic independence of structures from their bearers—from people—and, with a seeming paradox, to insist on the ability of people to change these structures by their concerted action.

This change in mood is epitomized by the speed with which current contributions to Marxist theory and debates are internationally promulgated. The recent contributions of Althusser and Poulantzas, for example, have been translated almost before the ink was dry.[1] Althusser's analyses in particular have been absorbed into the intellectual culture both consciously, in that they have generated major intellectual debates, and unconsciously, in that the issues to which his conceptualizations direct attention can no longer be ignored, even when his work is not explicitly under discussion.[2] But it is not just Althusser and his school[3] who have captured the minds and imaginations of the British intellectual left. Italian Marxism, as represented in particular by Gramsci[4] and Colletti,[5] has also been rediscovered, and it is these latter writers who have had a more immediate impact on practical political thought, pre-eminently in the discussions about the meaning and development of Euro-communism. If the thrust of British Marxism is now to emphasize Marx' adage that "men make history",[6] the question is "how can this be done?"

More specifically, recent students of Marxism have tried to elaborate theories of the instances or levels of structure other than the economic, i.e. theories of the political and ideological levels. The departure involved here is that political and ideological structures are conceived as constitutive of the total social formation, as playing an equal—or an almost equal[7]—part to the economic structure in its constitution. Having acknowledged the contribution to the totality of these other 'levels', the need to theorize or develop a concept of both their structure and their effectivities has also been recognized.[8]

Particular importance has been attached to the analysis of ideology. Ideology has, under the aegis of modern Marxism, emerged from being conceived as merely a passive reflection of reality or a class conspiracy. The writings of Althusser and the subsequent interpretations by Hirst, Laclau, Sumner and others[9] have brought to prominence the need for an elaborated concept and theory. We have ourselves independently emphasized the ideological dimension of law in papers produced in 1974 and 1975.[10] None of the writers on *ideology* was tempted to reduce law simply to an ideological epiphenomenon: rather the tendency was to theorize a new structural importance for both ideology and law. Writers with a primary interest in *law*, however, were not always so sophisticated.

The 'discovery' of law as ideology marked a reaction against the treatments of law which have typified Marxist and radical discussions of the past few decades.[11] The ambience of the more conventional of these discussions was largely provided by the pervasive influence of Lenin's "State and Revolution".[12] Notable exceptions were the contributions of the social democratic Marxist, Karl Renner, and the early Soviet jurist, Evgeny Pashukanis,[13] but the prevailing trend from the 1930s to the 1960s displayed an almost exclusive emphasis on the repressive or coercive character of law, conceived as the direct embodiment of the interests of the ruling class. In this conception law itself is unproblematic: the analysis of legal developments or new legislation has the task merely of exposing the class interests contained in them.

While attempting to break with the 'law as coercion' tradition, at first the discussion of 'law and ideology' remained firmly within it. All that was conceded was that the interests of capital are met as well if not better by sophisticated ideological manipulations as by overt bludgeoning.[14] While the capitalist structure was granted its subtlety, the theory remained crude. The reason was that it was not under-pinned by an adequate political theory. Thus a largely implicit notion of the state as a bourgeois instrumentality was called into play.

There have, of course, been intermittent contributions to a theory of the state, and the instrumentalist view has been explicitly called into question, as has Lenin's contribution.[15] The other component of the political level, the concept of class struggle, has a central place in Marx' own writings on law. But a large part of the reason for this book is that *Marx*-on-law has become suffocated by the mass of more recent Marxisms. In particular, in the context of his and Engels' frequent references to the struggles surrounding the English Factory Acts, he stresses that "it was the first time that in broad daylight the political economy of the middle class succumbed to the political economy of the working class".[16] In Chapter 6 we seek to resuscitate from Marx' and Engels' work a theory of law and political struggle. Such an emphasis is a further corrective to the erstwhile dominant and pessimistic tendency to define law solely as an instrument of capital or, more frequently, as an instrument in the hands of a ruling class.

A seemingly independent growth of the study of 'law in its social context' has also occurred in this decade, and inevitably there has been a reciprocal impact. This Marxist influence is apparent in various collections of papers recently presented or published.[17] These developments hold the promise that social scientists may produce practically relevant contributions based on sound theoretical work, and thus disprove the too common assumption that only a-theoretical 'empirical' studies can yield such results, while 'theory' merely offers the possibility of serendipidous pay-offs at some unspecified future date. Marxist theory suggests, on the contrary, that empiricism yields fundamentally ideological results, because the categories of thought in which these results are expressed are those generated by the everyday experience of social relationships in a class society. Thus, far from being the most useful, empiricist 'findings' may be practically dangerous and compound the errors inherent in judgements based on commonsense or acceptance of phenomena at face value. Conversely, Marxism, insofar as it accepts a separate category of purely 'theoretical' work, suggests that such intellectual efforts construct coherent conceptions which provide the best guidance for practical action.

Such elaborations of a more complex and concrete Marxist theory of law are welcome, but their promise will not be fulfilled if the foundations are unsound. Our task is to help secure these foundations by bringing together the scattered discussions of law to be found in Marx' and Engels' own works, and by showing how they constructed and exposed problems which are still major topics of debate today. In this way we hope to contribute to the development and refinement of a theory of the place of law in capitalist society.

While we share the predominant concern of contemporary writers to expand Marxist theory and their interest in the state, in ideology and in politics, the primary object of our work has been development of an understanding, if not yet an elaborated concept, of 'law'. We have retained this focus throughout this work, so that while theories of the state, ideology and politics are crucial we have considered them and quoted them only insofar as they have a bearing on our more immediate object.

A number of pressures have lent a certain urgency to this undertaking. The first two are related closely to the intellectual movements discussed above. In the first place, we consider that a major justification for attempting a scholarly understanding of law lies in its potential for transforming our society. Each of us has attempted to develop a theory of the state and law which allows for the effectiveness of day-to-day political action.[18] Theories have caused us much anxiety which present the state as monolithic and totally and inevitably bourgeois, law as a production of this bourgeois monolith, and non-bourgeois citizens as largely impotent.[19] The renewed concern with the state, while welcome, enhances this tendency,[20] as do determinist ideologisms which argue that since law is 'mere' ideology, real class struggle and real social change must be going on somewhere else. All theories which deny citizens the power of effective and concerted political action to change the course of events have dangerously nihilist consequences, as well as being false representations of a Marxist position. Politically it is crucial that a theory be developed which, while according primacy to structures, restores to people their dignity by acknowledging that they are capable of changing their world.

Our aim in this collection is to show that many of Marx' and Engels' comments on and discussions of law are not capable of an economic determinist reading, despite the fact their summary statements of their position may give credence to such an interpretation. In part the confusion arises because no theory of law as such is constructed by Marx and Engels: indeed, no concept (theoretical definition) of law is developed, although directions for such an elaboration are suggested. What we do show, from their writings on law and the state, is that they considered political action to be effective and important, and the achieving of legal change to be an appropriate, indeed a crucial, political objective. We show how this position is integrally related to their emergent general theory of law, state and ideology.

Secondly, although a burgeoning of Marxist studies relating to law has been alluded to, it remains true that current jurisprudential theory is in many respects inadequate. Using Marx' and Engels' work we pinpoint more accurately some of these weaknesses. First, travesties of Marx' position which are naïve if not malicious appear in jurisprudence textbooks which are in current use.[21] Here Marx is presented as advancing an 'economic' theory of law, in which law is said to embody and reflect economic interests, inevitably as these are conceived by bourgeois economic science. The other major focus for comment in the standard texts is the notion of the 'withering away of the state', which is immediately classified as Utopian and tersely contrasted with Soviet law.[22] The passages collected here rapidly demonstrate the irrelevance of such crude caricatures.

More importantly, the broad intellectual movement which presses for the study of law as a social phenomenon carries serious theoretical limitations. This tendency has expressed impatience with traditional academic approaches which attempt an *a priori* or an empirically based definition of the phenomenon of 'law', and then treat this construct as an object which can best be studied by those already trained in the allegedly mysterious techniques of academic and professional legal practices. The desire to discuss law in its social context has emerged as an institutionalized set of practices described as the 'sociology of law'. But despite the aspiration of many of its adherents to develop a social and political critique, this has proved a backward-looking radicalism. It has been radical in the sense that the established tradition of legal scholarship has been challenged, but backward-looking in the sense that there has been no fundamental change in that which has to be explained. No theoretical object of law has been constructed. In more familiar words, no theoretical definition of law has been attempted, no definition which constructs a concept of law in relation to a field of articulated concepts constituted in dynamic relationship with each other and with the material world which they represent. While no such conception of law can be found in the works of Marx and Engels, they do develop a field of concepts in which a refined concept of law could usefully be embedded, and as part of the same process, their works do suggest ways of attempting such a theorization. Thus a further reason for collating these extracts is to facilitate constructive criticism of a movement of which in general we are in favour, and which we respect as a set of genuine attempts at understanding.

As teachers we have also had impressed upon us the need for this book from two very different sources. First, the scattered nature of Marx' and Engels' writings on the subject has meant that students can be encouraged to consider only particular sources which contain 'a lot' about law—sufficient in quantitative terms to make their perusal seem worthwhile, and enough to provide some internal context for the discussion of law. Students might therefore read "The German Ideology", or Chapters 27 and 28 of the first volume of *Capital*, or Engels' "Ludwig Feuerbach and the End of Classical German Philosophy". If they read all three they might be in a position to state that there are three different versions of an incipient theory of law in the works of Marx and Engels, but they would not be able to trace the line of development between these productions, or to locate in the authors' broader theories the sources of the inconsistencies they might identify. If only one source were read, a false and uncontroversial interpretation would result.

There has also been a demand for 'radical knowledge' from practitioners. Its organizational base has been the new neighbourhood and community law and advice centres, although teachers in law schools have also played their part in the formulation of the question: "what is the role of the radical lawyer?" People working to promote legal change and to find ways of using the law for the benefit of the underprivileged and for whole communities were uneasily aware of the anomaly in their position created by the determinist and 'bourgeois state' or 'bourgeois ideology' theories which were the only radical perspectives available to them. Their question could be formulated as: "how can we, as practical political activists, live with the incongruity of being theoretically political nihilists? Should we get out of law, into sociology of law maybe?" But even the occupation of Prime Minister would offer no space for political action for those who conceive ordinary citizens as trapped in a monolithic bourgeois state and in monolithic bourgeois modes of thought. The logic of the position would indeed be to sit tight and do nothing and wait for the revolution. Our hope is that in making this set of extracts available we have shown the possibility of a radical theorization which not only allows people to seize their time, but also shows that their time is every day.

The Method

There were three stages in our selection and organization of materials, and our choices were governed by different criteria at each. The themes in terms of which we decided to present the materials are discussed in the next section: a word, however, is due about the processes of collection and elimination.

First, we read comprehensively the works of Marx and Engels available in English, and culled all those passages which explicitly discussed or made reference to law. Our interpretation of our brief at this stage was broad, and subsequently we had to eliminate passages dealing with admittedly crucial and related themes, but in general terms. Thus, for example, discussions of the state were omitted if they did not specifically comment on the relation of law to the state. Similarly, discussions of methodology not touching on the specific substantive area were eliminated, as were discussions of ideology in relation only to religion or philosophy. This initial selection was in part empiricist and nominal as we sought for key cue words; in large part, however, our reading was shaped by our somewhat different theoretical starting points, by our growing concern to locate law in the political and ideological instances, and by our sense of the student and practitioner audiences which we hoped would benefit most from the compilation. To achieve concordance at this stage, many of the materials were read and culled separately by both editors, and all selections were discussed. Thus a more agreed position for the second stage was generated.

After this the total pool of extracts was coded in one chronological and five broad theoretical categories. Each of these six categories was further subdivided. The technique was for each editor separately to code the extract before a final classification was debated and reached. These final classifications were usually in terms of the main line of the argument or topic of the extract. Occasionally a passage was coded to emphasize an important theoretical point which might otherwise have passed unnoticed. For example, the discussion of Thiers' bloody reprisals after the fall of the Paris commune[23] might well have been classified as 'law as coercion'. We felt, however, that what was most interesting about these passages was the demonstration of the manipulation of *constitutional* law to legitimate Thier's position and activities.

In interpreting and so allocating our extracts, we developed and refined the theoretical categories themselves, adding new sub-categories to the classification such as 'punishment'[24] or 'the regulation of labour',[25] establishing the internal consistency of others, e.g. the distinction between the form and content of ideology, and eliminating others. The subcategory 'reformism' was so eliminated when it was found, contrary to expectation, that neither Marx nor Engels develops a distinction between useful and futile attempts to bring about material changes by working for legal changes, although Engels hints at the possibility of doing so.[26] On the other hand, the whole section on historical materialism was added after the work of classifying had been started, when it was realized that some passages dealt with the object of our study—law—too comprehensively for subdivision in terms of emphasis to be possible. We also felt that readers new to the texts would benefit if later extracts could be located in the context of these general statements.

The final stage of the selection was governed by pragmatic considerations. An attempt was made both to include all points and not to duplicate any. This involved distortion. A point made many times for the sake of emphasis by Marx and Engels may appear only once in the collection, and so apparently be given equal status with a point which appears only once in Marx' and Engels' entire *oeuvres*. Given our publisher's strictures as to length, we have tried to overcome this first in our introductions to the sections, and secondly by providing with the extracts references to materials which are similar in content. References to extracts containing new points which none the less we lacked space to present are also listed here.

Themes and Organization

The presentation of extracts in this collection is not in the chronological order of their writing; indeed, different passages from a single work may appear in separate places. Rather, we have organized the work in terms of themes which we claim can be read or identified in the works of Marx and Engels. Some themes recur consistently: the importance and complexities of the workers' struggle for legislation to limit the working day are emphasized and re-emphasized from 1843 to 1885.[27] Other themes are temporarily left in abeyance, but repeatedly re-appear albeit in the contexts of different arguments: discussions of property, of alienation, and of the relationship between the two have this character.[28] Still other themes appear to be abandoned as the authors' life situations change and their thought develops: there are no further discussions of censorship after 1850.[29]

In abstracting themes we have both knowingly imposed Cain and Hunt on the materials and unavoidably been influenced by the specific historical and theoretical context within which we have worked. We make no claim that there was any such division in the minds of Marx and Engels. However, to the limited extent to which it is possible we would wish the texts of Marx and Engels to stand in their own right. The index is intended to facilitate the production of alternative readings.

The guiding rationale for the division into chapters and sections was undoubtedly influenced by Althusser.[30] We collected together in the first chapter Marx' and Engels' earliest writings, and so can show both their different starting points and how their understanding of law was affected by the gathering momentum of their struggle with idealism. So we had to consider the importance of Marx' purported 'epistemological break'. But we have not taken 1844, when Marx and

Engels met (and the "Economic and Philosophic Manuscripts" were produced) as a strict cut-off point, although the reciprocal influence of each on the other is indeed apparent thereafter. Some later pieces dealing with similar themes have been included in the first chapter. Arguments about censorship are the obvious example. But some of the writings from the "Manuscripts" contribute more to an understanding of Marx' developing theorization of property relations, and hence have been included with that discussion in Chapter 3. Similarly, some of Engels' earliest writings have been included in Chapter 5, in the section on crime. In Althusser's own language, this is to say that although we have been sensitive to the issues raised by it, we have not taken 'the break' as an object of our enquiry.

The second organizing principle was the conception of the three instances or levels of structure: the economic, the political and the ideological. While we felt it necessary, as indicated, to present first the general statements of theory and method, the subsequent extracts had to be presented in such a way as to make both theoretical and editorial sense. The comments on and discussions of the place of law in the economic structure are presented first. Apart from the theoretical primacy accorded to this category, its alleged ultimacy as an explicator, this enabled us to reveal at an early stage a contradiction endemic to Marx' and Engels' work. Sometimes—and this is increasingly and predominantly true of Marx—it is capital as such, as it is conceived, which provides this ultimate account in the elaboration of the concept of capitalism itself; at other times—and this occurs in the works of both authors—accounts are presented in terms of the bourgeois classes and their interests. The discussion of property in this chapter spans both conceptions.

In Chapter 4, the contradiction is pointed up more sharply as differing conceptions of ideology are shown to be embedded in the materials. Elaborations of the concept, varying discussions of its autonomy or its mystifying potential, are shown to stem from either the emphasis on structure or the emphasis on its members or bearers. Ideology is discussed second for editorial reasons: its exposition illuminates the even more fragmentary writings on law and politics.

Two chapters are allocated to the discussion of the political level. This is not because we consider it both an important and a neglected area—although we do—but because of the volume of materials, particularly on law and class struggle. Moreover, the materials fell naturally into three sections which Marx and Engels themselves did not attempt to relate. These are writings on the state, writings on crime and writings on class struggle. Any future elaboration must of necessity develop a concept which relates these three. Here, however, we have allowed the fortuitous rather than intended separation to show, for so far from extending their conceptions to include linkages, Marx and Engels give no indication that they realized this as a possibility. As far as crime is concerned they accept a nominal definition, and then theorize about the cause of the activities so unproblematically named. By and large they treat the state in the same way, writing as if there is no problem about what it 'is', the question being why it developed, and the answers predominantly being either that 'it' is functionally necessary for the dominant class or that 'it' is an instrument of ideological and physical repression for the use of the bourgeoisie. They start from the assumption that we all know what we're talking about when we say 'state'.

These two discrete sets of extracts are included together in Chapter 5. We see a theoretical link between them, but must re-affirm that Marx and Engels did not, although sometimes they acknowledge an empirical one along the lines that good states (the Paris Commune) produce fewer criminals because people in them are not driven to crime.

Our final chapter collects the extracts dealing with law and class struggle. Most of these are descriptive, discussing specific constellations of class forces and tactics adopted in specific conjunctures. These descriptions, however, are theoretically based, particularly the later ones. They depend on a theoretical elaboration of the concept of class which the authors had undertaken elsewhere.[31] In one extract,[32] Marx explicitly attempts also to develop a concept of class-political struggle. Facility of comprehension, which the reader will experience with the extracts in this chapter, results from the precision of prior conceptual work: the arguments are not facile although they are easy to understand. Indeed, Engels' earliest discussions of the struggles for the Ten Hours Act present the most difficulty simply because they are at this stage untheorized and presented nominally, that is, in terms of the everyday names of people and of parties.

This last chapter conveys Marx' and Engels' view of people as political animals, deriving their dignity and in part their humanity from so being. The final picture is unfinished; but it is also intellectually exciting and stimulating, revealing and formulating problems which are still new, and hinting at new solutions. We hope the reader will find it as demanding and refreshing as we did to seek a starting point for current work in Marx' and Engels' struggle to create a new theory fit for a new world.

Notes

1. This applies particularly to Althusser's more recent works, such as Althusser, L. (1971) *Lenin and Philosophy and Other Essays*, New Left Books, London, in which appeared the influential paper "Ideology and Ideological State Apparatuses" (pp. 121–173); Althusser, L. (1976) *Essays in Self-Criticism*, New Left Books, London, in which appeared the much discussed "Elements of Self-Criticism" (pp. 100–161); an Althusser, L. (1972, 1977) *Politics and History*, New Left Books, London. The earlier works, which took longer to be translated, are Althusser, L. (1969) *For Marx*, Allen Lane, London; and Althusser, L. and Balibar, E. (1970) *Reading Capital*, New Left Books, London. Poulantzas' writings have followed a similar pattern: Poulantzas, N. (1968) *Political Power and Social Classes*, New Left Books, London; Poulantzas, N. (1974) *Fascism and Dictatorship*, New Left Books, London; and Poulantzas, N. (1975) *Classes in Contemporary Capitalism*, New Left Books, London.
2. In particular the articulation of different levels of structure and the meaning of their 'determination in the last instance' by the economic level, the conception of levels other than the economic being the 'structure in dominance', and the opposition to humanist explanation, have passed as problems into the commonsense of the academic left.
3. In Britain the work of Hindess and Hirst at first marked a continuation of Althusser's project but increasingly broke more sharply from him. See Hindess, B. and Hirst, P. Q. (1975) *Pre-Capitalist Modes of Production*, Routledge and Kegan Paul, London; Hindess, B. and Hirst, P. Q. (1977) *Mode of Production and Social Formation*, Macmillan, London; Cutler, A., Hindess, B., Hirst, P. Q. and Hussain, A. (1977, 1978) *Marx's Capital and Capitalism Today*, 2 vols, Routledge and Kegan Paul, London.
4. Gramsci, A. (1971) *Selections from the Prison Notebooks*, Lawrence and Wishart, London; Gramsci, A. (1977) *Selections from the Political Writings*, Lawrence and Wishart, London.
5. Colletti, L. (1972) *From Rousseau to Lenin*, New Left Books, London.
6. "It [the materialist conception of history] shows that circumstances make men just as much as men make circumstances". From Marx, K. and Engels, F., The German Ideology, *MECW* V, 54. This is Marx' first statement of this position, and it is embedded in a fundamental discussion of materialist theory and methodology which runs from p. 35 to p. 64.
7. Hindess, B. and Hirst, P. Q. (1977) *Pre-Capitalist Modes of Production*,

Routledge and Kegan Paul, London. Here, the contradiction inherent in the concept of relative autonomy is indicated. The problems both of apparent autonomy and of relative autonomy are discussed in Chapter 4 in relation to ideology and in Chapter 5 in relation to the state.

8. Poulantzas in at least two of his major works has tried to conceive a space for political action within the Althusserian structure. This has led to a divergence from Althusser's suggested conception of the state, and also to some internal contradictions in Poulantzas' work: for example, if the state is to be conceived as the site of political action (*see* Poulantzas, N. (1968) *Political Power and Social Classes*, New Left Books, London) then the functional definition offered by him in *Classes in Contemporary Capitalism* (New Left Books, London, 1975) cannot also hold.

9. Hirst, P. Q. (undated, probably 1975) *Problems and Advances in the Theory of Ideology,* Cambridge University Communist Party, Cambridge; Hirst, P. Q. (1976) Althusser and the Theory of Ideology, *Economy and Society* Vol. 5, No. 4; Laclau, E. (1977) *Politics and Ideology in Marxist Theory,* New Left Books, London (especially the essay Fascism and Ideology); Sumner, C. (1979) *Reading Ideologies: an investigation into the Marxist theory of ideology and law,* Academic Press, London and New York; McLennan, G. *et al.* (1977) Althusser's Theory of Ideology, in *Working Papers in Cultural Studies,* 10.

10. Cain, M. (1974) The Main Themes of Marx' and Engels' Sociology of Law, *British Journal of Law and Society* **1,** No. 2, 136–148; Hunt, A. (1978) *The Sociological Movement in Law,* Macmillan, London; Hunt, A. (1976) Law, State, and Class Struggle, *Marxism Today* **20,** 178–187.

11. For example, Turk, A. (1969) *Criminality and Legal Order,* Rand McNally, Chicago; Pritt, D. N. (1970) *Law, Class and Society,* Vols. I–III, Lawrence and Wishart, London; Quinney, R. (1970) *The Social Reality of Crime,* Little Brown, Boston; Chambliss, W. and Seidman, R. (1971) *Law, Order and Power,* Addison–Wesley, Massachusetts; Piven, F. and Cloward, R. (1972) *Regulating the Poor,* Tavistock, London; Lefcourt, R. (1971) *Law Against the People,* Random House, New York.

12. Lenin, V. I. The State and Revolution, *Collected Works,* **25,** pp. 381–481.

13. Renner, K. (1948, 1976) *The Institutions of Private Law and their Social Function,* Routledge and Kegan Paul, London; Pashukanis, E. B. (1978) The General Theory of Law and Marxism, in *Law and Marxism* (C. Arthur, ed.), Ink Links, London.

14. Carson, W. G. (1974) Symbolic and Instrumental Dimensions of Early Factory Legislation, in *Crime, Criminology, and Public Policy: Essays in Honour of Sir Leon Radzinowicz* (R. Hood, ed.), Cambridge University Press, Cambridge.

15. Miliband, R. (1973) *The State in Capitalist Society,* Quartet Books, London; Poulantzas, N., see references in note 1. See also the discussion between Poulantzas, N. and Miliband R. (1969) in issues 58 and 59 of *New Left Review*; Wright, E. O. (1978) *Class, Crisis, and the State,* London, New Left Books; Holloway, J. and Picciotto, S. (1978) *State*

and Capital, Edward Arnold, London. For a summary of recent contributions see "Capital Accumulation, Class Struggle, and the Nation State", University of Essex C.S.E. Group, mimeo, 1977. For a more theoretically eclectic set of papers dealing with these questions, see Littlejohn, G. *et al* (eds) (1978) *Power and the State*, Croom Helm, London.

16. Marx, K. Inaugural Address to the Workingmen's International Association, *MESW* (3) II, 16.

17. Papers by Cain, Collison, McBarnet, Sumner, and others were presented at the British Sociological Association annual conference on "Power and the State" in 1977, all discussing aspects of law. A selection of these papers has appeared as Littlejohn, G. *et al* (eds) (1978) *Power and the State*, Croom Helm, London. In the same year the Conference of Socialist Economists also held a conference on Law and the State. In 1976 Carlen edited a broadly Marxist collection of papers on the sociology of law: Carlen, P. (ed.) *The Sociology of Law*, Sociological Review Monograph 23, University of Keele.

18. Cain, M. (1977) Optimism, Law, and the State: a Plea for the Possibility of Politics, *European Yearbook of Law and Sociology,* Nijhoff, Amsterdam; Hunt, A. (1977) Class structure and political strategy, *Marxism Today,* July 1977.

19. For example, Domhoff, G. (1970) *The Higher Circles*, Random House, New York; Piven, F. and Cloward, R. (1972) *Regulating the Poor*, Tavistock, London; Bankowski, Z. and Mungham, G. (1976) *Images of Law*, Routledge and Kegan Paul, London.

20. Poulantzas, N. *op. cit.* at note 8, is an exception here.

21. Paton, G.W. (1964) *A Text Book of Jurisprudence*, Oxford University Press, Oxford; Stone, J. (1966) *Social Dimensions of Law and Justice*, Stevens, London; Dias, R.W. (1970) *Jurisprudence*, Butterworths, London.

22. Stone, J. *ibid.*, p. 475; Dias, R.W. *ibid.*, pp. 457–465.

23. See discussion on pp. 129–131.

24. This subcategory is discussed and presented on pp. 150–151 and pp. 192–201.

25. This subcategory is discussed and presented on p. 68 and pp. 101–107.

26. Engels, F. The Housing Question, *MESW (3)* II, 314–375; cited on pp. 55–56 and 235–240.

27. Both these contributions were by Engels, F., Letters from London, *MECW* III, 381, and *Anti-Dühring,* 146–147.

28. See, for example, Marx, K., Economic and Philosophic Manuscripts, *MECW* III, 297, cited here on pp. 93–94 and Marx, K. *Grundrisse*, 514 cited here on p. 124 (N).

29. The Class Struggles in France, *MESW (3)* I, 234.

30. Althusser, L. (1969) See references for this author in note 1.

31. In "The German Ideology" the theory of classes, as constitutive of the materialist conception of history, is elaborated most fully. The clearest

exposition is in the first section, on Feuerbach (*MECW* V, 28–93). The most famous treatment must be that in "The Communist Manifesto" *MECW VI,* 482–496. See also Engels, F. Karl Marx, *MESW (3)* III, 84–87.

32. Marx, K. Letter to Bolte, 23.11.1871, *MESC* 328; cited on pp. 211–214.

1 *Young Marx,*
Young Engels

Introduction

> If feuds were settled by *a* and *b*,
> The courts would be swindled out of their fee.[1]

So wrote Marx in 1837 when he was nineteen. It would be possible, but silly, to claim there was an implicit theory of law in this cynical couplet. What can be seen, rather, is an untheorized but critical comment, with court personnel rather than structures as the devils of the piece.

Engels as a young man also expressed himself in rather bad rhymes, "The Insolently Threatened Yet Miraculously Rescued Bible", which was published as a pamphlet in 1842,[2] being the most important of these. Of interest about this irregular doggerel is the running, mocking battle with "The Free"—the Young Hegelians. Both authors engaged separately in this dialogue, although at first they themselves represented the left wing of the same movement. They elaborated their position together after their meeting in 1844. This joint effort resulted finally in the devastating critiques of "The Holy Family" and "The German Ideology", written in 1844 and 1845/6, respectively. In the course of this prolonged encounter, Marx and Engels first elaborated the theory which came to be known as historical materialism, and a view of the place of law within this conception.

But a retrospective reading of the past by those for whom the future is now history can obscure more than it reveals. Marx in particular as a young man was forced to engage intellectually with Hegel's ideas, because these were what he was taught, and these were what the *avant garde* intellectuals of the day were discussing. For a long time Marx, like the Young Hegelians who wrote for the *Rheinische Zeitung* under his editorship, used an Hegelian ethic as the basis of his social criticism. In his more purely philosophical writings he was unable to generate a standpoint outside Hegelianism from which to criticize that body of ideas, although even as a student he was asserting as an insight that analysis should start with the real rather than the essence or spirit.

Engels, although maturing in a similar climate and also forced to take issue with these ideas, incorporated them into his thinking less than Marx. His early writings show a liberal common sense which, although in some respects in advance of his time, was also in tune with it. Engels' ideas on crime and punishment, discussed in Chapter 5, exemplify this. Similar theorizing formed the accepted liberal academic tradition until the early 1960s.

Throughout his life Engels retained a 'humanist' position, that is, one which took man as the starting point of explanation. In this book we adhere to this now conventional use of the word humanist. It is, however, an unfortunate translation from the equivalent French term, for in English, humanism has come to be associated with being humane and tolerant. There is the unfortunate and certainly false implication that those who are opposed to humanism as a mode of explanation are inhumane and intolerant. In Chapter 6 we indicate that, on the contrary, humanism and determinism often go together, although Engels struggled to evade this trap. Explanations in terms of structures leave scope for those structures to be changed by the very men whom they constitute. Certainly a concept of a structure, which is all that is available to knowledge, cannot 'cause' or determine a material change. Thus it is more structural explanations which leave scope for men to seize and shape their futures.

Engels' humanism is most pronounced in his conception of ideology, as is argued in Chapter 4. But although at times he accepted the fundamental category of bourgeois thought, the idea of the *essential individual* (man), he was never comfortable with attempts to explain the social in these humanist reductionist terms. His escape, however, was often to explain in terms of aggregates of men as constituted by social relations: he tended not to offer explanations at the level of structures or relationships in themselves. On the whole, then, Engels' ideas show fewer dramatic changes through time than those of Marx.

Marx and Engels at first shared mainly a sense of social outrage and a growing opposition to the Young Hegelian positions. The juxtaposition of their ideas within the framework of their affection and their common purposes was cataclysmic. What we must remember as we read their earliest works is that they did not know where they were going. We have reduced their writings to an uncertain progression: in this process are lost both the sense of intellectual striving and the importance in precipitating this striving of the particular issues then at stake.

In this chapter we try to show, from a selection of those writings relating to law, first, the emergent ideas of Marx, the student; and second, the growing inability of Hegelianism to found acceptable solutions to social and political issues with which Marx, in his role as editor of the *Rheinische Zeitung* from 1841–1843, was forced to take issue—the Hegelian theory of state and law is here stretched to its limit and found wanting. Our third brief section contrasts Marx' Hegelian social morality with Engels' emergent and still uncertain social humanitarianism. Finally, we present extracts showing their shared early experiences at the 'receiving end' of law, of the censorship which led to Marx' resignation from his first editorship and their joint experience of increasing Government suspicion and increasingly strict censorship legislation when they contributed to the *Neue Rheinische Zeitung*.

Although most of the extracts in this chapter were produced before 1844, the last section includes some discussions written for the new edition of the newspaper as late as 1848. These are similar to the earlier pieces both in subject matter and in method of analysis.

It will be apparent that we have not organized or considered our extracts in relation to the theory of the 'epistemological break', put forward by Louis Althusser.[3] According to this view, "The German Ideology" represents a moment of purification, after which Marx struggles to develop an alternative system of materialist, non-humanist concepts. The discussion has centred largely round the concept of alienation, as elaborated in the "Economic and Philosophic Manuscripts" of 1844.[4] The notion of 'the break' has been found useful as an heuristic device for highlighting significant changes in Marx' ideas. What our extracts show in support of this is the impossibility of thinking the outcomes which both Marx and Engels wanted from an Hegelian starting point. But the struggle to create an alternative continued, now haltingly, now gaining momentum, throughout their lives and continues still.

Marx, the Student

Heinrich Marx' parent's-eye view of his brilliant but extravagant and rather thoughtless son aids us in understanding not only Karl, the object of these affectionate reproofs, not only his youthful theories, but also the typical bourgeois reaction to such a person and to such theorizing. Karl himself found learning the law an unrewarding task. Philosophy was altogether more satisfying. Moreover, he found the study of law impossible without it.

The same long letter to his father in which these views were expressed presents us with a doubly rejected conception of law: rejected shortly after its production and later rendered obsolete by the author's discovery of historical materialism. Marx here argues first for the dialectical development of concrete ideas such as the state and law: they are not abstract concepts merely, but are related to other concretely expressed ideas, and they have a history. This, he claimed, was true of positive law as well. Its rational essence is the core only of a moment-to-moment unity. He then rejected the distinction between form and content in terms of which he had constructed the model set out in the letter, and also the way in which he had constituted the concepts of these properties themselves. This is important as the first evidence of Marx' struggle with idealism, in the course of which the curtain fell, his "holy of holies was rent asunder, and new gods had to be installed" (p. 18). But he had a long way to go before he found the new gods at the centre of the earth, or even before he rejected completely the deity idealism. He had identified their dwelling on the map: what remained was the journey.

The Trial of Hegelianism

As an editor, Marx was forced to engage in a thoughtful, but not in a consciously theoretical, way with the issues of his time. He had to adopt a position on immediate social and political questions. In the course of this engagement Marx became aware of his intellectual purpose.

The first extract in this section is out of the chronological sequence in which the others are presented, having been written several months after Marx resigned his editorship, in 1843. By then Marx had had time to reflect a little on his endeavours, and the Introduction to the "Critique" displays this self-consciousness. The main text of "Contribution to a Critique of Hegel's Philosophy of Law" is not included. It is largely a scholastic internal criticism which contributes little to our understanding of Marx' thought beyond indicating that coming to terms with Hegel was an exercise in which he had to engage. The extract from the Introduction, however, with which this section begins, sets out well the nature of his intellectual enterprise in these early years. He aimed to restore real material man to the centre of the philosophic stage. He wished to escape from the increasingly abstract theorizing and speculation unrelated to the world which characterized the work of many of his contemporaries, but he attempted to do this within the framework of Hegelian idealism and constructed essentialism. As the ensuing extracts show, the framework proved inadequate to the task it had been set.

Marx was necessarily sensitive to the question of press freedom. Censorship, he argued in 1842, contradicts the essential nature of the press, which is to be free: censorship cannot be part of the essence of freedom. This does not mean that the free press is always good, for a free press too *may* not correspond to its essence: a censored press, however, can never so correspond. A censored press is therefore in no sense a press. Thus it can never be good, even if on occasion its productions are. This Hegelian defence did not convince the authorities, who were so unworried that the press did not correspond to its concept as to strengthen the existing censorship laws.

In a later debate, with the leader writer of the *Kolnische Zeitung*, a rival newspaper, Marx developed more fully his position about the nature of the state. This argument involves an application of the principle that the essence of the state is reason. If Christianity is equated with reason, he argues, then all rational states are Christian: conversely, all Christian states will be rational. Yet some of them have been notoriously bad. He points out both the duration and the effectivities of the "philosophies of reason", and indicates that the uniqueness of the Hegelian position lies in the fact that it is social rather than individual reason that characterizes the state, that the philosopher of law starts with and proceeds from an analysis of the whole. Thus "the state (is) the great organism in which legal, moral, and political freedom must be realised".

The same position is brought to bear in Marx' discussions on "The

Law on Thefts of Wood" and the Divorce Bill. However, in the former articles Marx had to confront a problem which was less amenable to the solutions offered by Hegelian jurisprudence. He had to consider the law on thefts of wood, and account for the fact that in effect only the poor would be vulnerable to prosecution under this law. Because of this effect he wanted to argue against the law. This he achieved, not without difficulty, by pointing up a series of contradictions.

The rights of the poor are formless, and therefore contradict the forms constructed by positive law. There is no essentialism in this conception of rights: they are generated out of practices rather than appertaining to men as such. Moreover, in this case the substance of the rights contradicts the specific categories of positive law as it relates to property, for it is by the essential nature of their occupancy right that the poor have, according to this concept, no property. Marx further argues that the state, in criminalizing a wood gatherer, would be acting as a party to the dispute, or on behalf of a category of persons who constituted such a party. In either case the state would not be acting morally, that is, it would not be expressing its true essence. For the nature of the state is to express the whole, and thus the essence of law is never particular or private. Furthermore, the state is a totality which includes also the potential criminal. Thus it harms itself whenever it creates a criminal.

After briefly pointing out that the institutional arrangements for enforcement do not reach the accepted standard of lack of bias or fair play, Marx continues the main argument, reiterating the conflict between particular interest and principles of law, and arguing further that the Provincial Assemblies were so constituted as to be incapable of acting in other than a particular way, of acting other than on behalf of private interests. Thus the legislation of the Provincial Assemblies is inevitably lawless, or contrary to the essentially total and public character of law. So Marx demonstrates the way in which the ideal conception of the state is not realized in Prussia, and with some difficulty explains that in an ideal state the contradictions between the poor and the estates would be resolved. Because state institutions represent particular instrumentalities either the contradictions are exacerbated or in their elimination of the true state is destroyed. As Chapter 5 shows, Marx later came to see this one-sidedness of state institutions as inevitable, and the moment of the elimination of these contradictions by class struggle in concrete material history as the moment of dissolution, or 'absence', of the state. The indebtedness of his later thought to his earlier interpretation of Hegel can be seen clearly if later extracts are read in conjunction with this passage. The celebrated metaphor of head-standing does not seem quite adequate to describe the relationship.

> The mystification which dialectic suffers in Hegel's hands, by no means prevents him from being the first to present its general form of working in a comprehensive and conscious manner. With him it is standing on its head. It must be turned right side up again if you discover the rational kernel within the mystical shell.[5]

In this discussion, then, the tension is starkly apparent between the position which Marx wished to adopt, a position broadly sympathetic to the wood gatherers, and the concepts with which he had to construct his argument. His use of an Hegelian mode of discourse copes fairly adequately with the *general* questions of the state, the law and the constitution; the particular case is more difficult to subsume within these categories. Before passing on the reader must be both cautioned and advised. Most of the "Thefts of Wood" article is relevant to our theme, and, given the very severe editing which has been necessary here, the reader interested in the thinking of the young Marx should turn to the original.

In the Divorce Bill discussion, Marx, using the by now familiar procedure, "set(s) forth the concept of marriage and the consequences of this concept", arguing that it is necessary for the legislator so to identify the essence of marriage. Later he generalizes the argument from the particular question of the day, on the place of religion, maintaining the unity of the world of law and the world of spirit. This unity, however, is the essential nature and totality of things, not an *intellectual* abstraction. Law is at fault, and defying its own nature, if it deals with the latter at the expense of the former.

Here there is no tension. Hegelian logic provides an adequate argument. The only hint of the progression even towards the position cited at the beginning of this section, let alone to fully developed materialism, is the emphasis on the distinction between identifying the real abstract essence of things, and mere intellectual abstraction. The movement was irregular; Marx' thinking lurched forward only when the practical problem he confronted demanded that it should.

The snippet interposed between these two lengthy extracts indicates Marx wrestling in theory with the fact of non-correspondence between law and material reality which, of course, is rendered problematic by Hegelianism. This can be read as a strong statement that law cannot change the world: it can only represent it. This position is far more conservative than that of the later Marx, and again owes more to Hegel than to the kind of materialist theory which Marx ultimately developed. It is important to locate this argument in the context of Marx' early theorizing: it is often attributed but does not belong to the later position.

The contradiction between the ideal and the real is resolved in the early Marx by the proposition, expressed in his discussion about "The Commission of Estates in Prussia", that true material reality corresponds with the ideal. False appearances, which no longer correspond to their concept, do not. Estates are examples of the latter. In this piece at least there seem to be no epistemological problems about recognizing either the empirical or the ideal manifestations of this unity. From this position, then, Marx criticizes the principle of representation by estates. The latter are no longer true institutions of the living state. The dangerous consequences of representation by estates is that the state is thereby cut off from its life force, its constituent members who derive their unity and identity from it. The state thus dissolves itself at the moment of representation which should be the moment of its completion.

Estate representation also renders anomalous the role of the government official. He should not be considered a member of the learned or intellectual estate since his task as an official is to represent the state as such, which by its nature is opposed to all its constituent interests and estates in their particular and separate forms. Under "people's representation" this contradiction for the government official is resolved.

Having introduced this important and still debated and unresolved issue of how to conceive and analyse the position of the state agent, Marx elaborates it further in a series of contributions to the *Rheinische Zeitung* during 1843. Because historical changes have elevated this issue to an even greater importance than it had in Marx' day, we have reproduced these discussions at considerable length. Marx did not return to the topic, so we cannot tell how he would have retheorized the question in the light of his later materialist conception of the state. It is our contention, however, that the ideas presented here are in themselves of immediate substantial interest: for all their idealist underpinning, they enable us to understand state agents better, as well as the development of Marx' ideas.

The passage demonstrates a disjunction between the material and economic conditions in the Mosel region and the bureaucratic construction of this reality. In administrative theory, social conditions which are amenable to change are a consequence of previous administrative efforts. On the other hand, the effort is to reform not the administration itself, but the object administered—the latter being a fiction constructed in the minds of administrators by previous law and administrative activity. If these efforts fail, it is not conceived that they may have been directed towards a falsely constituted object. Rather, the failure is attributed to the inherent character of those administered. Conditions which lie beyond the scope of administrative principles are incurable. The administration is limited by its own predefined scope of activities, and this is exacerbated by the fact that lower officials work within and accept limits set for them by higher officials.

Because the administration is incapable of grasping the real material problem, and because the activities of particular citizens are necessarily affected by private interests, a *political* insight into the nature of the problem and its possible cure is required. Marx argues that the free press can provide this "third element", and create a public opinion, of which it is also the product—a citizen opinion as opposed to a collection of private opinions. While empirically this may have had more truth in the days before mass press advertising, the solution does not seem a happy one. A latter-day Marx or Engels might have argued—and we would argue—that the way out of the *impasse*, and the way to create an alternative conception of the issues, would be through political action, through material pressure rather than self criticism and rational discussion alone. In spite of his analysis, Marx sees his officials and his private persons as being constrained primarily by their modes of thought; despite his argument, his conclusion ignores concrete institutional constraints which restrict as they also necessitate these modes of thought and these patterns of action. Once again, Marx' argument leads him to a point where the application of Hegelian principles of analysis cannot resolve the problem as elaborated, although these principles were also active in the problem's formulation.

On Social Morality and the Early Engels

We have hinted that the development of Engels' thought tended to be continuous while Marx progressed in irregular lurches. But Engels too had to come to terms with an Hegelian heritage. Neither man achieved this intellectual settlement in isolation. It was as a function of their reciprocal ratiocination that they identified the flaws in their earlier positions. Yet as we have shown for Marx, so also Engels, even before their meeting, was struggling free of the web of idealism.

To point up the differences, as well as the parallels, we begin this section with a further article by Marx about the Divorce Bill. After citing Hegel he argues forcefully that a relationship which does not correspond to its essence—as identified in this case in the concept of marriage—is not moral, and, indeed, not a relationship. None the less, real existences must be expected to diverge from their concept. The law must allow the legal dissolution of marriage when real, essential marriage has already ceased to exist—the former case. Dissolution as a matter of particular dissatisfaction, whim, or circumstances should not be possible, since this would be no more than an anticipated divergence of the existence from the real. To modern ears, Marx' very strict moral position on this issue seems strange. It is not, however, our task to judge it as *morality*. What must be noted are first the obeisance to the theory of Hegel, and, following from that and continuing throughout Marx' work, the emphasis on the conceptual and social, the totality as opposed to the individual existential experience. Marx' early morality was *not* humanist, as theorists of 'the break' might argue.

We argue in this work that Engels throughout his life fell easily into the mode of explanation characterized as humanist. For him, social relations are constructed from a multiplicity of human actions, not just empirically, as must be true, but also at the level of analysis. He does not begin with the construction of a social concept, but with people being socially constrained. So he can argue with reference to crime and penal practice (pp. 37, 38 and 175–186) that people are wrong without being culpable. The second element, the culpability of individuals, was never a matter of concern for Marx. Engels was a social humanitarian, with a deep concern for the suffering of mankind. It is a caricature, but one could argue that Marx' concern was for the irrationalities of the system. Consistently enough, Engels was also more influenced by the ideas of classical liberalism.

This last point is nowhere better demonstrated than in the first of the four pieces from Engels which we have included here. In this, he argues for a free market in land. Among other benefits, legislation freeing the land could forestall a revolution, which more reactionary policies could expedite. Thus in 1840 he was advocating straightforward liberal politics.

In 1842 we find him writing in praise of the separation of powers, and in favour also of the jury system. While acknowledging a myriad of other arguments for this, he makes two points. First—and how familiar this sounds—he argues that judges and others who owe their positions to their abilities to interpret "dead abstract law" are opposed to the popular justice of the jury; second, he argues that the release of one proletarian is generalized as evidence of the dangerous social bias of juries. Briefly he summarizes the social humanitarian position about crime: people in desperation are driven to steal by hunger.

Writing "Centralisation and Freedom" for Marx' newspaper later the same year, Engels argues significantly that the English workers are "the standard bearers and representatives of a new principle of right". He contributed to his later friendship with Marx the view that the workers are carriers of history. It is not surprising that this should have provided a meeting point between the two men, for it is in developing this argument that Engels lets his idealist heritage show through his deeply influential British experience.

Our final extract was also written as part of a brief piece for the *Rheinische Zeitung*. Again the theme appears: working people, when they are bad, are not culpable. Their immorality is understandable given their living conditions. Furthermore—and here is a breath of early twentieth century penology—the state by its policies of incarceration exacerbates the problem.

The Experience of Law

The first two extracts in this section relate to the sacking of a member of Marx' *Rheinische Zeitung* staff, after the newspaper had been threatened with closure if he were not dismissed. Marx not only disagreed with the censorship policy, but also felt that in this case the censors had picked on a worthless victim. But it was a strong warning, for four months later he himself resigned from the editorship in protest against the censorship policy, after the paper itself had been banned. The whole of this section indicates that circumstances forced Marx to take the law seriously into account in his early years. Until the time of his exile, engaging with the law was for him far more than a theoretical pastime.

The core of the section is constituted by three early discussions of censorship, and two rather later ones which appeared in Marx' and Engels' second excursion into publishing, the *Neue Rheinische Zeitung*. This paper ran from May 1848 until May 1849, when Marx (who had already resigned his citizenship) was expelled first from Germany and later from Paris in order to silence it. At the end of the chapter we supply some additional references, and Marx' letter of resignation from his first editorial post in 1843.

Marx shows both the internal contradictions of The Censorship Instructions and their theoretical contradictions in his first polemical outcry on behalf of the free press. Such Instructions are contrary to the nature of the state they are protecting. This is elaborated in the subsequent series of debates on press freedom, some of which we have already cited and discussed (p. 20). Marx argues that a press law which regards freedom as the normal state of the press is good: it is in accord with the essential concept of the press. Law, like the state, must be a form of existence of freedom: more, that is, than a simple expression of freedom. Through law, the state compels men to be free.

Censorship law on the other hand is an impossibility. It does not correspond to the concept of that which it seeks to regulate. Censorship thus negates rather than controls the press. In addition, censorship does not accuse the subject of illegality, but of an incorrect opinion. "The censor not only punishes the crime, he *makes* it".[6]

Marx' last argument before his resignation is close to the liberal argument that truth emerges from the free play of ideas—the market analogy. Therefore, he says, it is loyal to criticize the state. But Marx was desperately looking for arguments which would work in the immediate present. Thus, although from these extracts we can abstract some idea of the general pattern of his thinking, it is important also to remember that he sometimes had to argue in the enemy's terms.

Engels and Marx writing together later deploy a different argument in discussing not this time freedom of the press, but freedom of debate. The thrust of their position is that the deputies will inevitably experience pressure as unfreedom and coercion. They have to choose between the people and the Crown. Freedom makes nonsense when there are clearly opposing forces: it then finds its expression in coercion.

In 1848 Marx turned his attention once more to the Prussian Press Bill, the main consequences of which would be, he said, to protect incompetent state officials. Worse, because the press was to be forbidden to report the facts, it would be forced willy nilly to expose itself to the charge of producing hearsay and unsubstantiated reports. Yet the German constitution of the time stated that "the censorship can never be re-established". The unstable power structure at that time, when the bourgeoisie broke its revolutionary alliance with the people but was unable independently to consolidate its position (see Chapter 6), meant that the constitution was both called on to legitimate repression, and simultaneously, as here, was subverted by it.

By this time Marx and Engels, now working together, had identified both their intellectual and their political opponents. This identification lent a force and cogency to their later enterprises which these early contributions lack. The clever casuistry within the dominant paradigm exposed only its weaknesses; the pleas for the underprivileged led to direct repression. The whole social and intellectual order had therefore to be put at bay, and Engels and Marx together did not shirk the task.

Notes

The key to the abbreviations is given on p. 264

1. Marx, K. Mathematical Wisdom, *MECW* I, 545–546.

2. *MECW* II, 313–351.
3. Althusser, L. (1969) Marxism and Humanism, in *For Marx,* pp. 221–247, Penguin, Harmondsworth. *See also* Lewis, J. (1972) The Althusser Case, Parts I and II, *Marxism Today* Jan. and Feb. 1972, Althusser, L. (1976) Reply to John Lewis, in *Essays in Self Criticism*, pp. 35–99, New Left Books, London.
4. *MECW* III, 231–346. *See also* pp. 93–94 of this volume.
5. Afterword to the Second German Edition, *Capital* I, 29.
6. Marx, K. Debates on Freedom of the Press, *MECW* I, 167. Cited on p. 43.

Extracts

Marx, the Student

Letter from Heinrich Marx to his son, Karl Marx, 18–29. 11. 1835, *MECW* I, 646–647.

Your letter, which was barely legible, gave me great joy. Of course, I have no doubt of your good intentions, your diligence, or of your firm resolve to achieve something worth while. However, I am glad that the beginning is pleasant and easy for you and that you are getting a liking for your professional studies.

Nine lecture courses seem to me rather a lot and I would not like you to do more than your body and mind can bear. If, however, you find no difficulty about it, it may be all right. The field of knowledge is immeasurable, and time is short. In your next letter you will surely give me a somewhat larger and more detailed report. You know how greatly I am interested in everything which concerns you closely.

In connection with the lectures on law, you must not demand [. . .] should be touching and poetic. The subject-matter does not allow [. . .] poetic composition, you will have to put up with it and [. . .] find worthy of deep thought. Excuse [. . .] subjects.

. . . .

And so, dear Karl, fare you very well, and in providing really vigorous and healthy nourishment for your mind, do not forget that in this miserable world it is always accompanied by the body, which determines the well-being of the whole machine. A sickly scholar is the most unfortunate being on earth. Therefore, do not study more than your health can bear. With that, daily exercise and abstemiousness, and I hope to find you stronger in mind and body every time I embrace you.

Trier, November 18, 1835
Your faithful father
Marx

Letter from Heinrich Marx to Karl Marx, 28.12.1836, *MECW* I, 665.

Your views on law are not without truth, but are very likely to arouse storms if made into a system and are you not aware how violent storms are among the learned? If what gives offence in this matter itself cannot be entirely eliminated, at least the form must be conciliatory and agreeable.

Letter from Heinrich Marx to Karl Marx, 10.2.1838, *MECW* I, 692.

Only on one point, of course, all transcendentalism is of no avail, and on that you have very wisely found fit to observe an aristocratic silence; I am referring to the paltry matter of money, the value of which for the father of a family you still do not seem to recognise, but I do all the more, and I do not deny that at times I reproach myself with having left you all too loose a rein in this respect. Thus we are now in the fourth month of the law year and you have already drawn 280 talers. I have not yet earned that much this winter.

MARX, Letter to his father, 10–11.11.1837, *MECW* I, 11–19.

Poetry, however, could be and had to be only an accompaniment; I had to study law and above all felt the urge to wrestle with philosophy. The two were so closely linked that, on the one hand, I read through Heineccius, Thibaut and the sources quite uncritically, in a mere school-boy fashion; thus, for instance, I translated the first two books of the Pandect into German, and, on the other hand, tried to elaborate a philosophy of law covering the whole field of law. I prefaced this with some metaphysical propositions by way of introduction and continued this unhappy opus as far as public law, a work of almost 300 pages.

Here, above all, the same opposition between what is and what ought to be, which is characteristic of idealism, stood out as a serious defect and was the source of the hopelessly incorrect division of the subject-matter. First of all came what I was pleased to call the metaphysics of law, i.e., basic principles, reflections, definitions of concepts, divorced from all actual law and every actual form of law, as occurs in Fichte, only in my case it was more modern and shallower. From the outset an obstacle to grasping the truth here was the unscientific form of mathematical dogmatism, in which the author argues hither and thither, going round and round the subject dealt with, without the latter taking shape as something living and developing in a many-sided way. A triangle gives the mathematician scope for construction and proof, it remains a mere abstract conception in space and does not develop into anything further. It has to be put alongside something else, then it assumes other positions, and this diversity added to it gives it different relationships and truths. On the other hand, in the concrete expression of a living world of ideas, as exemplified by law, the state, nature, and philosophy as a whole, the object itself must be studied in its development; arbitrary divisions must not be introduced, the rational character of the object itself must develop as something imbued with contradictions in itself and find its unity in itself.

Next, as the second part, came the philosophy of law, that is to say, according to my views at the time, an examination of the development of ideas in positive Roman law, as if positive law in its conceptual development (I do not mean in its purely finite provisions) could ever be something different from the formation of the concept of law, which the first part, however, should have dealt with.

Moreover, I had further divided this part into the theory of formal law and the theory of material law, the first being the pure form of the system in its sequence and interconnections, its subdivisions and scope, whereas the second, on the other hand, was intended to describe the content, showing how the form becomes embodied in its content. This was an error I shared with Herr v. Savigny, as I discovered later in his learned work on ownership, the only difference being that he applies the term formal definition of the concept to "finding the place which this or that theory occupies in the (fictitious) Roman system", the material definition being "the theory of positive content which the Romans attributed to a concept defined in this way", whereas I understood by form the necessary architectonics of conceptual formulations, and by matter the necessary quality of these formulations. The mistake lay in my belief that matter and form can and must develop separately from each other, and so I obtained not a real form, but something like a desk with drawers into which I then poured sand.

The concept is indeed the mediating link between form and content. In a philosophical treatment of law, therefore, the one must arise in the other; indeed, the form should only be the continuation of the content. Thus I arrived at a division of the material such as could be devised by its author for at most an easy and shallow classification, but in which the spirit and truth of law disappeared. All law was divided into contractual and non–contractual. In order to make this clearer, I take the liberty to set out the plan up to the division of *jus publicum*, which is also treated in the formal part.

I	II
jus privatum	*jus publicum*

I. *jus privatum*

a) Conditional contractual private law.
b) Unconditional non–contractual private law.

A. *Conditional contractual private law*

a) Law of persons; b) Law of things; c) Law of persons in relation to property.

a) Law of persons

I. Commercial contracts; II. Warranties; III. Contracts of bailment.

I. *Commercial contracts*

2. Contracts of legal entities (*societas*). 3. Contracts of casements (*locatio conductio*).

3. *Locatio conductio*

1. Insofar as it relates to *operae*.
    a) *locatio conductio* proper (excluding Roman letting or leasing);
    b) *mandatum*.

2. Insofar as it relates to *usus rei*.
    a) On land: *usus fructus* (also not in the purely Roman sense);
    b) On houses: *habitatio*.

II. *Warranties*

1.   Arbitration or conciliation contract; 2. Insurance contract.

III. *Contracts of bailment*

2. *Promissory contract*

1.   *fide jussio*; 2. *negotiorum gestio*.

3. *Contract of gift*

1.   *donatio*; 2. *gratiae promissum*.

b) *Law of things*

I. *Commercial contracts*

2.   *permutatio stricte sic dicta.*

1.   *permutatio* proper; 2. *mutuum* (*usurae*); 3. *emptio venditio*.

II. *Warranties*

pignus.

III. *Contracts of bailment*

2.   *commodatum*; 3. *depositum.*

But why should I go on filling up pages with things I myself have rejected? The whole thing is replete with tripartite divisions, it is written with tedious prolixity, and the Roman concepts are misused in the most barbaric fashion in order to force them into my system. On the other hand, in this way I did gain a general view of the material and a liking for it, at least along certain lines.

At the end of the section on material private law, I saw the falsity of the whole thing, the basic plan of which borders on that of Kant, but deviates wholly from it in the execution, and again it became clear to me that there could be no headway without philosophy. So with a good conscience I was able once more to throw myself into her embrace, and I drafted a new system of metaphysical principles, but at the conclusion of it I was once more compelled to recognise that it was wrong, like all my previous efforts.

In the course of this work I adopted the habit of making extracts from all the books I read, for instance from Lessing's *Laokoon*, Solger's *Erwin*, Winckelmann's history of art, Luden's German history, and incidentally scribbled down my reflections. At the same time I translated Tacitus' *Germania*, and Ovid's *Tristia*, and began to learn English and Italian by myself, i.e., out of grammars, but I have not yet got anywhere with this. I also read Klein's criminal law and his annals, and all the most recent literature, but this last only by the way. . . .

A curtain had fallen, my holy of holies was rent asunder, and new gods had to be installed.

From the idealism which, by the way, I had compared and nourished with the idealism of Kant and Fichte, I arrived at the point of seeking the idea in reality itself. If previously the gods had dwelt above the earth, now they became its centre. . . .

Shortly after that I pursued only positive studies: the study of Savigny's *Ownership*, Feuerbach's and Grolmann's criminal law, Cramer's *de verborum significatione*, Wenning-Ingenheim's Pandect system, and Mühlenbruch's *Doctrina pandectarum*, which I am still working through, and finally a few titles from Lauterbach, on civil procedure and above all canon law, the first part of which, Gratian's *Concordia discordantium canonum*, I have almost entirely read through in the *corpus* and made extracts from, as also the supplement, Lancelotti's *Institutiones*. Then I translated in part Aristotle's *Rhetoric*, read *de augmentis scientiarum* of the famous Bacon of Verulam, spent a good deal of time on Reimarus, to whose book on the artistic instincts of animals I applied my mind with delight, and also tackled German law, but chiefly only to the extent of going through the capitularies of the Franconian kings and the letters of the Popes to them.

The Trial of Hegelianism

MARX, Introduction to Contribution to a Critique of Hegel's Philosophy of Law, *MECW* III, 181.

The criticism of the *German philosophy of state and law*, which attained its most consistent, richest and final formulation through *Hegel*, is both a critical analysis of the modern state and of the reality connected with it, and the resolute negation of the whole *German political and legal consciousness* as *practised* hitherto, the most distinguished, most universal expression of which, raised to the level of a *science*, is the *speculative philosophy of law* itself. If the speculative philosophy of law, that abstract extravagant *thinking* on the modern state, the reality of which remains a thing of the beyond, if only beyond the Rhine, was possible only in Germany, inversely the *German* thought-image of the modern state which disregards *real man* was possible only because and insofar as the modern state itself disregards *real man* or satisfies the *whole* of man only in imagination. In politics the Germans *thought* what other nations *did*. Germany was their theoretical consciousness. The abstraction and conceit of its thought always kept in step with the one-sidedness and stumpiness of its reality. If therefore the *status quo of German statehood* expresses the *perfection of the ancien régime*, the perfection of the thorn in the flesh of the modern state, the *status quo of German political theory* expresses the *imperfection of the modern state*, the defectiveness of its flesh itself.

See also Contribution to a Critique of Hegel's Philosophy of Law, *MECW* III, 5–129, which is not included in this collection.

An earlier piece in a similar vein is "Philosophical Manifesto of the Historical School of Law", *MECW* I, 208–210.

MARX, Debates on Freedom of the Press, *MECW* I, 158–159.

A free press that is bad does not correspond to its essence. The censored press with it hypocrisy, its lack of character, its eunuch's language, its dog-like tail-wagging, merely realises the inner conditions of its essential nature.

The censored press remains bad even when it turns out good products, for these products are good only insofar as they represent the free press within the censored press, and insofar as it is not in their character to be products of the censored press. The free press remains good even when it produces bad products, for the latter are deviations from the essential nature of the free press. A eunuch remains a bad human being even when he has a good voice. Nature remains good even when she produces monstrosities.

The essence of the free press is the characterful, rational, moral essence of freedom. The character of the censored press is the characterless monster of unfreedom; it is a civilised monster, a perfumed abortion.

Or does it still need to be proved that freedom of the press is in accord with the essence of the press, whereas censorship contradicts it? Is it not self-evident that external barriers to a spiritual life are not part of the inner nature of this life, that they deny this life and do not affirm it?

In order really to justify censorship, the speaker would have had to prove that censorship is part of the essence of freedom of the press; instead he proves that freedom is not part of man's essence. He rejects the whole genus in order to obtain one good species, for is not freedom after all the generic essence of all spiritual existence, and therefore of the press as well? In order to abolish the possibility of evil, he abolishes the possibility of good and realises evil, for only that which is a realisation of freedom can be humanly good.

We shall therefore continue to regard the censored press as a bad press so long as it has not been proved to us that censorship arises from the very essence of freedom of the press.

MARX, Leading article in No. 179 of *Kolnische Zeitung*, *MECW* I, 200–201.

Therefore, you must judge the rightfulness of state constitutions not on the basis of Christianity, but on the basis of the state's own nature and essence, not on the basis of the nature of Christian society, but on the basis of the nature of human society.

The Byzantine state was the real religious state, for in it dogmas were questions of state, but the Byzantine state was the worst of states. The states of the *ancien régime* were the most Christian states of all; nevertheless, they were states dependent on the "will of the court".

There exists a dilemma in the face of which "common" sense is powerless.

Either the Christian state corresponds to the concept of the state as the realisation of rational freedom, and then the state only needs to be a rational state in order to be a Christian state and it suffices to derive the state from the rational character of human relations, a task which philosophy accomplishes; or the state of rational freedom cannot be derived from Christianity, and then you yourself will admit that this derivation is not intended by Christianity, since it does not want a bad state, and a state that is not the realisation of rational freedom is a bad state.

You may solve this dilemma in whatever way you like, you will have to admit that the state must be built on the basis of free reason, and not of religion. Only the crassest ignorance could assert that this theory, the conversion of the concept of the state into an independent concept, is a passing whim of recent philosophers.

.   .   .   .

You wage a polemic, therefore, not against the rational character of recent philosophy, but against the ever new philosophy of reason. Of course, the ignorance which perhaps only yesterday or the day before yesterday discovered for the first time age-old ideas about the state in the *Rheinische* or the *Königsberger Zeitung*, regards these ideas of history as having suddenly occurred to certain individuals overnight, because they are new to it and reached it only overnight; it forgets that it itself is assuming the old role of the doctor of the Sorbonne who considered it his duty to accuse Montesquieu publicly of being so frivolous as to declare that the supreme merit of the state was political, not ecclesiastical, virtue. It forgets that it is assuming the role of Joachim Lange, who denounced Wolff on the ground that his doctrine of predestination would lead to desertion by the soldiers and thus the weakening of military discipline, and in the long run the collapse of the state. Finally, it forgets that Prussian Law was derived from the philosophical school of precisely "this Wolff", and that the French Napoleonic Code was derived not from the Old Testament, but from the school of ideas of Voltaire, Rousseau, Condorcet, Mirabeau, and Montesquieu, and from the French revolution. Ignorance is a demon, we fear that it will yet be the cause of many a tragedy; the greatest Greek poets rightly depicted it as tragic fate in the soul-shattering dramas of the royal houses of Mycenae and Thebes.

Whereas the earlier philosophers of constitutional law proceeded in their account of the formation of the state from the instincts, either of ambition or gregariousness, or even from reason, though not social reason, but the reason of the individual, the more ideal and profound view of recent philosophy proceeds from the idea of the whole. It looks on the state as the great organism, in which legal, moral, and political freedom must be realised, and in which the individual citizen in obeying the laws of the state only obeys the natural laws of his own reason, of human reason. *Sapienti sat.*

See also **MARX**, *ibid.*, 199.

MARX, Debates on the Law on Thefts of Wood, *MECW* I, 232–233.

But whereas these customary rights of the aristocracy are customs which are contrary to the conception of rational right, the customary rights of the poor are rights which are contrary to the customs of positive law. Their content does not conflict with legal form, but rather with its own lack of form. The form of law is not in contradiction to this content, on the contrary, the latter has not yet reached this form. Little thought is needed to perceive how *one-sidedly* enlightened legislation has treated and been compelled to treat the *customary rights of the poor*, of which the various *Germanic* rights can be considered the most prolific source.

In regard to *civil law*, the most liberal legislations have been confined to formulating and raising to a universal level those rights which they found already in existence. Where they did not find any such rights, neither did they create any. They abolished particular customs, but in so doing forgot that whereas the wrong of the estates took the form of arbitrary pretensions, the right of those without social estate appeared in the form of accidental concessions. This course of action was correct in regard to those who, besides right, enjoyed custom, but it was incorrect in regard to those who had only customs without rights. Just as these legislations converted arbitrary pretensions into legal claims, insofar as some rational content of right was to be found in those pretensions, they ought also to have converted accidental concessions into necessary ones. We can make this clear by taking the monasteries as an example. The monasteries were abolished, their property was secularised, and it was right to do so. But the accidental support which the poor found in the monasteries was not replaced by any other positive source of income. When the property of the monasteries was converted into private property and the monasteries received some compensation, the poor who lived by the monasteries were not compensated. On the contrary, a new restriction was imposed on them, while they were deprived of an ancient right. This occurred in all transformations of privileges into rights. A positive aspect of these abuses—which was also an abuse because it turned a right of one side into something accidental—was abolished not by the accidental being converted into a necessity, but by its being left out of consideration.

These legislations were necessarily one-sided, for all customary rights of the poor were based on the fact that certain forms of property were indeterminate in character, for they were not definitely private property, but neither were they definitely common property, being a mixture of private and public right, such as we find in all the institutions of the Middle Ages. For the purpose of legislation, such ambiguous forms could be grasped only by understanding, and understanding is not only one-sided, but has the essential function of making the world one-sided, a great and remarkable work, for only one-sidedness can extract the particular from the unorganised mass of the whole and give it shape. The character of a thing is a product of understanding. Each thing must isolate itself and become isolated in order to be something. By confining each of the contents of the world in a stable definiteness and as it were solidifying the fluid essence of this content, understanding brings out the manifold diversity of the world, for the world would not be many-sided without the many one-sidednesses.

Understanding therefore abolished the hybrid, indeterminate forms of property by applying to them the existing categories of abstract civil law, the model for which was available in Roman law. The legislative mind considered it was the more justified in abolishing the obligations of this indeterminate property towards the class of the very poor, because it also abolished the state privileges of property. It forgot, however, that even from the standpoint of civil law a twofold private right was present here: a private right of the owner and a private right of the non-owner; and this apart from the fact that no legislation abolishes the privileges of property under constitutional law, but merely divests them of their strange character and gives them a civil character. If, however, every medieval form of right, and therefore of property also, was in every respect hybrid, dualistic, split into two, and understanding rightly asserted its principle of unity in respect of this contradictory determination, it nevertheless overlooked the fact that there exist objects of property which, by their very nature, can never acquire the character of predetermined private property, objects which, by their elemental nature and their accidental mode of existence, belong to the sphere of occupation rights, and therefore of the occupation right of that class which, precisely because of these occupation rights, is excluded from all other property and which has the same position in civil society as these objects have in nature.

MARX, *ibid.*, 236–237.

Private interest makes the one sphere in which a person comes into conflict with this interest into this person's whole sphere of life. It makes the law a *rat-catcher*, who wants only to destroy vermin, for he is not a naturalist and therefore regards rats only as vermin. But the state must regard the infringer of forest regulations as something more than a wood-pilferer, more than an *enemy to wood*. Is not the state linked with each of its citizens by a thousand vital nerves, and has it the right to sever all these nerves because this citizen has himself arbitrarily severed *one* of them? Therefore the state will regard even an infringer of forest regulations as a human being, a living member of the state, one in whom its heart's blood flows, a soldier who has to defend his Fatherland, a witness whose voice must be heard by the court, a member of the community with public duties to perform, the father of a family, whose existence is sacred, and, above all, a citizen of the state. The state will not light-heartedly exclude one of its members from all these functions, for the state amputates itself whenever it turns a citizen into a criminal. Above all, the *moral* legislator will consider it a most serious, most painful, and most dangerous matter if an action which previously was not regarded as blameworthy is classed among criminal acts.

Interest, however, is practical, and nothing in the world is more practical than to strike down one's enemy. "Hates any man the thing he would not kill?" we are already told by Shylock. The true legislator should fear nothing but wrong, but the legislative interest knows only fear of the consequences of rights, fear of the evil-doers against whom the laws are made. Cruelty is a characteristic feature of laws dictated by cowardice, for cowardice can be energetic only by being cruel. Private interest, however, is always cowardly, for its heart, its soul, is an external object which can always be wrenched away and injured, and who has not trembled at the danger of losing heart and soul? How could the selfish legislator be human when something inhuman, an alien material essence, is his supreme essence? "*Quand il a peur, il est terrible*," says the *National*, about Guizot. These words could be inscribed as a motto over all *legislation inspired by self-interest*, and therefore by *cowardice*.

. . . .

We see here the enactment of patrimonial jurisdiction. The patrimonial warden is at the same time in part a judge. The valuation is part of the sentence. Hence the sentence is already partly anticipated in the record of the charge. The warden who made the charge sits in the collegium of judges; he is the expert whose decision is binding for the court, he performs a function from which the other judges are excluded by him. It is foolish to oppose inquisitorial methods when there exist even patrimonial gendarmes and denouncers who at the same time act as judges.

Apart from this fundamental violation of our institutions it is obvious from an examination of the qualifications of the warden who makes the charge how little he is objectively able to be at the same time the valuer of the stolen wood.

MARX, *ibid.*, 241.

This claim on the part of private interest, the paltry soul of which was never illuminated and thrilled by thought of the state, is a serious and sound lesson for the latter. If the state, even in a single respect, stoops so low as to act in the manner of private property instead of in its own way, the immediate consequence is that it has to adapt itself in the form of its means to the narrow limits of private property. Private interest is sufficiently crafty to intensify this consequence to the point where private interest in its most restricted and paltry form makes itself the limit and rule for the action of the state. As a result of this, apart from the complete degradation of the state, we have the reverse effect that the most irrational and illegal means are put into operation against the accused; for supreme concern for the interests of limited private property necessarily turns into unlimited lack of concern for the interests of the accused. But if it becomes clearly evident here that private interest seeks to degrade, and is bound to degrade, the state into a means operating for the benefit of private interest, how can it fail to follow that a *body representing private interests,* the estates, will seek to degrade, and is bound to degrade, the state to the thoughts of private interest? Every modern state, however little it corresponds to its concept, will be compelled to exclaim at the first practical attempt at such legislative power: Your ways are not my ways, your thoughts are not my thoughts!

MARX, *ibid.*, 261.

The commission's proposal which we have just examined and the Assembly's vote approving it are the climax to the whole debate, for here the Assembly itself becomes conscious of the *conflict between the interest of forest protection and the principles of law,* principles endorsed by our own laws. The Assembly therefore put it to the vote whether the principles of law should be sacrificed to the interest of forest protection or whether this interest should be sacrificed to the principles of law, and *interest outvoted law.* It was even realised that the whole law was an *exception to the law,* and therefore the conclusion was drawn that *every* exceptional provision it contained was permissible. The Assembly confined itself to drawing consequences that the legislator had neglected. Wherever the legislator had forgotten that it was a question of an exception to the law, and not of a law, wherever he put forward the legal point of view, our Assembly by its activity intervened with confident tactfulness to correct and supplement him, and to make private interest lay down laws to the law where the law had laid down laws to private interest.

The Provincial Assembly, therefore, *completely fulfilled its mission.* In accordance with its *function,* it represented a definite *particular interest* and treated it as the final goal. That in doing so it trampled the law under foot is a *simple consequence of its task,* for interest by its very nature is blind, immoderate, one-sided; in short, it is lawless natural instinct, and can lawlessness lay down laws? Private interest is no more made capable of legislating by being installed on the throne of the legislator than a mute is made capable of speech by being given an enormously long speaking-trumpet.

MARX, Communal Reform, *MECW* I, 273.

Finally, a word about the "separation of town and countryside". Even apart from general grounds, the *law* can only be the ideal, self-conscious image of reality, the *theoretical* expression, made independent, of the practical vital forces. In the *Rhine Province* town and countryside are not separated in reality. Therefore the law cannot decree this separation without decreeing its own nullity.

MARX, The Divorce Bill: Criticism of a Criticism, *MECW* I, 274–276.

The criticism of the Divorce Bill given here has been outlined from the standpoint of *Rhenish* jurisprudence just as the criticism published earlier (see the Supplement to No. 310 of the *Rhein. Ztg.*) was based on the standpoint and practice of old Prussian jurisprudence. A third criticism remains to be made, a criticism from a pre-eminently general point of view, that of the *philosophy of law*. It will no longer suffice to examine the individual reasons for divorce, *pro et contra*. It will be necessary to set forth the concept of marriage and the consequences of this concept. The two articles we have so far published agree in condemning the interference of religion in matters of law, without, expounding to what extent the essence of marriage in and for itself is or is not religious, and without, therefore, being able to explain how the consistent legislator must necessarily proceed if he is guided by the essence of things and cannot be at all satisfied with a mere abstraction of the definition of this essence. If the legislator considers that the essence of marriage is not human morality, but spiritual sanctity, and therefore puts determination from above in the place of self-determination, a supernatural sanction in the place of inner natural consecration, and in the place of loyal subordination to the nature of the relationship puts passive obedience to commandments that stand above the nature of this relationship, can then this religious legislator be blamed if he also subordinates marriage to the church, which has the mission of implementing the demands and claims of religion, and if he places secular marriage under the supervision of the ecclesiastical authorities? Is that not a simple and necessary consequence? It is self-deception to believe that the religious legislator can be refuted by proving that one or other of his rulings is contrary to the secular nature of marriage. The religious legislator does not engage in a polemic against the dissolution of secular marriage; his polemic is rather against the secular essence of marriage, and he seeks partly to purge it of this secularity and partly, where this is impossible, to bring home at all times to this secularity, as a merely tolerated party, its limits and to counteract the sinful defiance of its consequences. Wholly inadequate, however, is the point of view of *Rhenish* jurisprudence, which is shrewdly expounded in the criticism published above. It is inadequate to divide the nature of marriage into two parts, a spiritual essence and a secular one, in such a way that one is assigned to the church and the individual conscience, the other to the state and the citizens' sense of law. The contradiction is not abolished by being divided between two different spheres; on the contrary, the result is a contradiction and an unresolved conflict between these two spheres of life themselves. And can the legislator be obliged to adopt a dualism, a double world outlook? Is not the conscientious legislator who adheres to the religious point of view bound to elevate to the sole authority in the real world and in secular forms that which he recognises as truth itself in the spiritual world and in religious forms, and which he worships as the sole authority? This reveals the basic defect of

Rhenish jurisprudence, its dual world outlook, which, by a superficial separation of conscience and the sense of law, does not solve but cuts in two the most difficult conflicts, which severs the world of law from the world of the spirit, therefore law from the spirit, and hence jurisprudence from philosophy. On the other hand, the opposition to the present Bill reveals even more glaringly the utter lack of foundation of the old Prussian jurisprudence. If it is true that no legislation can decree morality, it is still truer that no legislation can recognise it as binding in law. Prussian law is based on an intellectual abstraction which, being in itself devoid of content, conceived the natural, legal, moral content as external matter which in itself knows no laws and then tried to model, organise and arrange this spiritless and lawless matter in accordance with an external aim. It treats the objective world not in accordance with the latter's inherent laws, but in accordance with arbitrary, subjective ideas and an intention that is extraneous to the matter itself. The old Prussian jurists have shown but little insight into this character of Prussian law. They have criticised not its essence, but only individual external features of its existence. Hence, too, they have attacked not the nature and style of the new Divorce Bill, but its returning tendency. They thought they could find in bad morals proof that the laws were bad. We demand from criticism above all that it should have a critical attitude to itself and not overlook the difficulty of its subject-matter.

MARX, On the Commissions of Estates in Prussia, *MECW* I, 294–297.

These are not conditions which arise from the essence of landownership, but which, from considerations foreign to the latter, add limits that are foreign to it, *restrict* its essence instead of making it more general.

According to the general principle of representation through landownership, there would be no distinction between Jewish and Christian landownership, between landownership by a lawyer and by a merchant, between landownership that is ten years old and one that is one year old. According to this general principle, all these distinctions do not exist. Hence if we ask what the author has shown, we can only reply: the restriction of the general condition of landownership by special conditions which are not part of its nature, by considerations based on the *difference between the estates*.

And the author admits:

> "Closely connected is the complaint heard from many sides that, in regard to these commissions of the estates too, the difference between estates which belongs only to the past has been brought in again and applied as a principle of estate organisation, in alleged contradiction with the present state of our social conditions, and with the demands of the spirit of the time."

The author does not examine whether the general condition of landownership is in contradiction with representation of the estates or even makes it impossible! Otherwise it could hardly have escaped him that, if the estate principle were consistently applied, a condition which forms an essential feature only of the peasant estate could not possibly be made a general condition for the representation of the other estates, whose existence in no way depends on landownership. For the representation of the estates can only be determined by the essential difference between them, and hence not by anything which lies outside this essence. If, therefore, the principle of representation of landownership is annulled because of special estate considerations, then this principle of representation of the estates is annulled because of the general condition of landownership, and neither principle comes into its own. Furthermore, even if a difference between the estates is accepted, the author does not examine whether this difference which is presumed to exist in the institution in question characterises the estates of the past or those of the present. Instead he discusses the difference between the estates in general. We do not demand that in the representation of the people actually existing differences should be left out of account. On the contrary, we demand that one should proceed from the actual differences created and conditioned by the internal structure of the state, and not fall back from the actual life of the state into imaginary spheres which that life has already robbed of their significance. And now take a look at the reality of the Prussian state as it is known and obvious to everyone. The true spheres, in accordance with which the state is ruled, judged, administered, taxed, trained and schooled, the spheres in which its entire movement takes place, are the districts, rural communities, governments, provincial administrations, and military departments, but not the four categories of the estates, which are intermingled in a diverse array among these higher units and owe the distinctions between them not to life itself, but only to dossiers and registers. And those distinctions, which owing to their very essence are dissolved at every moment in the unity of the whole, are free creations of the spirit of the Prussian state, but are by no means raw materials imposed on the present time by blind natural necessity and the dissolution process of a past period! They are members but not parts, they are movements but not states, they are differences of unity but not units of difference. Just as our author will not wish to assert that, for instance, the great movement by which the Prussian state changes daily into a standing army and a militia is the motion of a crude, inorganic mass, so must he not assert this of a representation of the people which is based on similar principles. We repeat once more: we demand only that the Prussian state should not break off its real state life at a sphere which should be the conscious flowering of this state life; we demand only the consistent and comprehensive implementation of the fundamental institutions of Prussia, we demand that the real organic life of the state should not be suddenly abandoned in order to sink back into unreal, mechanical, subordinated, non-state spheres of life. We demand that the state should not dissolve itself in carrying out the act that should be the supreme act of its internal unification. We shall give further criticism of the essay in question in a subsequent article.

It is quite *consistent*, not only with our author's principles, but with those of *estate representation*, for him to convert the question of the right of representation of "intelligence" in the provincial assemblies into the question of the right of representation of the *learned estates*, of the estates which have made a *monopoly* of intelligence, of intelligence which has become an estate. Our author is right to the extent that, given estate representation, it can also only be a question of intelligence that has become an estate. But he is wrong in not acknowledging the right of the learned estates, for where the estate principle prevails all estates must be represented. Just as he errs in excluding clerics, teachers and private men of learning, and does not even mention lawyers, physicians, etc., as possible candidates, he completely misconceives the nature of estate representation when he puts "state servants" belonging to the government on the same footing as the above-mentioned estates of learned men. In a state based on estates, government officials are the representatives of state interests as such, and therefore are hostile towards the representatives of the private interests of the estates. Although government officials are not a contradiction under people's representation, they are very much so under estate representation.

MARX, Justification of the Correspondent from the Mosel, *MECW* I, 345–348.

The higher administrative bodies are bound to have more confidence in *their* officials than in the persons administered, who cannot be presumed to possess the same official understanding. An administrative body, moreover, has its traditions. Thus, as regards the Mosel region too, it has its once and for all established principles, it has its official picture of the region in the Cadastre, it has official data on revenue and expenditure, it has everywhere, alongside the actual reality, a *bureaucratic* reality, which retains its authority however much the times may change. In addition, the two circumstances, namely, the law of the official hierarchy and the principle that there are two categories of citizens—the active, knowledgeable citizens in the administration, and the passive, uninformed citizens who are the object of administration—these two circumstances are mutually complementary. In accordance with the principle that the state possesses conscious and active existence in the administration, every government will regard the condition of a region—insofar as the state aspect of the matter is concerned—as the result of the work of its predecessor. According to the law of hierarchy, this predecessor will in most cases already occupy a higher position, often the one immediately above. Finally, every government is actuated, on the one hand, by the consciousness that the state has laws which it must enforce in the face of all private interests, and, on the other hand, as an individual administrative authority, its duty is not to make institutions or laws, but to apply them. Hence it can try to reform not the administration itself, but only the object administered. It cannot adapt its laws to the Mosel region, it can only try to promote the welfare of the Mosel region *within the limits* of its firmly established rules of administration. *The more zealously* and *sincerely*, therefore, a government endeavours—within the limits of the already established administrative principles and institutions by which it is itself governed—to remove a *glaring state of distress* that embraces perhaps a whole *region*, and the *more stubbornly* the evil resists the measures taken against it and increases despite the *good* administration, *so much the more profound, sincere and decisive will be the conviction* that this is an incurable state of distress, which the administration, i.e., the state, can do nothing to alter, and which requires rather a change on the part of those administered.

Whereas, however, the lower administrative authorities trust the official understanding of those above them that the administrative principles are good, and are themselves ready to answer for their dutiful implementation in each separate case, the higher administrative authorities are fully convinced of the correctness of the general principles and trust the bodies subordinate to them to make the correct official judgment in each case, of which, moreover, they have official proofs.

In this way it is possible for a government *with the best intentions* to arrive at the principle expressed by the government's reporter in Trier in regard to the Mosel region: "*The state will be able to confine itself solely to making the transition as easy as possible for the present population by appropriate measures.*"

If we look now at some of the methods which have transpired and which the government has used to alleviate the distress in the Mosel region, we shall find our argument confirmed at least by the history of the administration which is accessible to all; on the secret history, of course, we cannot pass judgment. We include among these measures: *remission of taxes in bad wine years, the advice to go over to some other cultivation, such as sericulture*, and, finally, the proposal to limit *parcellation of landed property*. The *first* of these measures, obviously, can only alleviate, not remedy. It is a *temporary* measure, by which the state makes an *exception* to its rule, and an exception which does not cost it much. Moreover, it is not the *constant* state of distress which is alleviated, it is likewise an exceptional manifestation of it, not the chronic sickness to which people have become accustomed, but an acute form of it which comes as a surprise.

In regard to the other two measures, the administration goes outside the scope of its own activities. The positive activity which it undertakes here consists partly in instructing the Mosel inhabitants how they *themselves* can come to their own aid, and partly in proposing a *limitation* or even denial of a right they previously possessed. Here, therefore, we find confirmed the train of thought we described above. The administration, which considers that the distressed state of the Mosel region is incurable and due to circumstances lying outside the scope of its principles and its activity, advises the Mosel inhabitants so to arrange their life that it is adapted to the present administrative institutions and that they are able to exist in a tolerable fashion within them. The vinegrower himself is deeply pained by such proposals, even if they only reach him by rumour. He would be thankful if the government carried out experiments at its own expense, but he feels that the advice that he should undertake experiments on himself means that the government is refusing to help him by its own activity. He wants help, not advice. However much he trusts the knowledge possessed by the *administration* in its own sphere, and however confidently he turns to it in such matters, he credits himself just as much with the necessary understanding in his own sphere. But limitation of the parcellation of landed property contradicts his inherited sense of right; he regards it as a proposal to add legal poverty to his physical poverty, for he regards every violation of equality before the law as the distress of right. He feels, sometimes consciously, sometimes unconsciously, that the administration exists for the sake of the country and not the country for the sake of the administration, but that this relationship becomes reversed when the country has to transform its customs, its rights, its kind of work and its property ownership to suit the administration. The Mosel inhabitant, therefore, demands that, if he carries out the work which nature and custom have ordained for him, the state should create conditions for him in which he can grow, prosper, and live. Hence such negative devices come to nought when they encounter the reality not only of the existing conditions, but also of civic consciousness.

[*Rheinische Zeitung* No. 19, January 19, 1843]

What then is the relation of the administration to the distress in the Mosel region? The *distressed state of the Mosel region* is at the same time a *distressed state of the administration*. The *constant* state of distress of part of the country (and a state of distress, which, beginning almost unnoticed more than a decade ago, at first gradually and then irresistibly develops to a climax and assumes ever more threatening dimensions, can well be called *constant*) signifies a *contradiction between reality and administrative principles*, just as, on the other hand, not only the nation, but also the government regards the *well being* of a region as a factual confirmation of good administration. The administration, however, owing to its *bureaucratic* nature, is *capable* of perceiving the reasons for the distress not in the sphere *administered*, but only in the sphere of *nature* and the *private citizen*, which lies outside the sphere administered. The administrative authorities, even *with the best intentions*, the most zealous humanity and the most powerful intellect, *can* find no solution for a conflict that is more than momentary or transient, the constant conflict between reality and the principles of administration, for it is not their official task, nor would it be possible, despite the best intentions, to make a breach in an *essential relation* or, if you like, *fate*. This *essential relation* is the *bureaucratic* one, both within the administrative body itself and in its *relations with the administered body*.

On the other hand, the private vine-grower can no more deny that *his* judgment may be affected, intentionally or unintentionally, by *private interest*, and therefore the correctness of his judgment cannot be assumed absolutely. Moreover, he will realise that there are in the state a multitude of private interests which suffer, and the general principles of administration cannot be abandoned or modified for their sake. Furthermore, if it is asserted that there is distress of a *general* character and that the general well-being is endangered in such a manner and to such an extent that private misfortune becomes a misfortune for the state and its removal a duty which the state owes to *itself*, the rulers regard this assertion of the ruled in relation to them as inappropriate; for the rulers consider they are in the best position to judge how far the welfare of the state is endangered and that they must be presumed to have a deeper insight into the relation between the whole and the parts than the parts themselves have. Furthermore, individuals, even a large number of them, cannot claim that their voice is the voice of the people; on the contrary, their description of the situation always retains the character of a *private* complaint. Finally, even if the conviction held by the complaining private persons were the conviction of the entire Mosel region, the latter, as an individual administrative unit, as an individual part of the country, would be, in relation to its own province as also in relation to the state, in the position of a private person whose convictions and desires should be judged only by their relation to the general conviction and the general desire.

In order to solve this difficulty, therefore, the rulers and the ruled alike are in need of a third element, which would be *political* without being official, hence not based on bureaucratic premises, an element which would be of a *civil* nature without being bound up with private interests and their pressing need. This supplementary element with the *head of a citizen of the state* and the *heart of a citizen* is the *free press*. In the realm of the press, rulers and ruled alike have an opportunity of criticising their principles and demands, and no longer in a relation of subordination, but on terms of equality as *citizens of the state*; no longer as *individuals*, but as *intellectual forces*, as exponents of reason. The "free press", being the product of public opinion, is also the creator of public opinion. It alone can make a particular interest a general one, it alone can make the *distressed state* of the Mosel region an object of general attention and general sympathy on the part of the Fatherland, it alone can mitigate the distress by dividing the feeling of it among all.

See also MARX, Critical Marginal Notes on the Article by a Prussian, *MECW* III, 194–195. This is a similar discussion of the administration of the English Poor Law.

On Social Morality and the Early Engels

MARX, The Divorce Bill, *MECW* I, 307–310.

Cologne, December 18. In regard to the *Divorce Bill* the *Rheinische Zeitung* has adopted *quite a special* position, and so far no proof has been given anywhere that this position is untenable. The *Rheinische Zeitung* agrees with the Bill inasmuch as it considers the hitherto existing Prussian legislation on marriage immoral, the hitherto innumerable and frivolous grounds for divorce impermissible, and the existing procedure not in accord with the dignity of the matter concerned, which, incidentally, can be said of the old Prussian court procedure as a whole. On the other hand, the *Rheinische Zeitung* has put forward the following main objections to the new Bill: 1). Instead of *reform* there has been a mere *revision*, hence Prussian law was retained as the basic law, which has resulted in considerable half-heartedness and uncertainty; 2) the legislation treats marriage not as a *moral*, but as a *religious* and *church* institution, hence the *secular* essence of marriage is ignored; 3) the procedure is very defective and consists of a superficial combination of contradictory elements; 4) it cannot be ignored that there are, on the one hand, severities of a police nature which are contrary to the concept of marriage and, on the other, too great leniency in regard to what are called considerations of fairness; 5) the whole formulation of the Bill leaves much to be desired as regards logical consistency, precision, clarity and comprehensive points of view.

Insofar as opponents of the Bill condemn one or other of these defects, we agree with them; on the other hand, we can by no means approve of their unconditional apologia for the former system. We repeat once more the statement we made previously. "If legislation cannot decree morality, it can still less pronounce immorality to be legally valid." When we ask *these* opponents (who are not opponents of the church conception and of the other shortcomings we have indicated) on what they base their arguments, they always speak to us about the unfortunate position of the husband and wife tied together against their will. They adopt a eudemonic standpoint, they think only of the two individuals and forget about the *family*. They forget that almost every divorce is the break-up of a family and that even from the purely juridical standpoint the children and their property cannot be made to depend on arbitrary will and its whims. If marriage were not the basis of the family, it would no more be the subject of legislation than, for example, friendship is. Thus, the above-mentioned opponents take into account *only* the individual will or, more correctly, the *arbitrary desire* of the married couple, but pay no attention to the *will of marriage*, the moral substance of this relationship. The legislator, however, should regard himself as a naturalist. He does not *make* the laws, he does not invent them, he only formulates them, expressing in conscious, positive laws the inner laws of spiritual relations. Just as one would have to reproach the legislator for the most unbridled arbitrary behaviour if he replaced the essence of the matter by his own notions, so also the legislator is certainly no less entitled to regard it as the most unbridled arbitrariness if private persons seek to enforce their caprices in opposition to the essence of the matter. No one is forced to contract marriage, but everyone who has done so must be compelled to obey the laws of marriage. A person who contracts marriage does not *create* marriage, does not *invent* it, any more than a swimmer creates or invents the nature and laws of water and gravity. Hence marriage cannot be subordinated to his arbitrary wishes; on the contrary, his arbitrary wishes must be subordinated to marriage. Anyone who arbitrarily breaks a marriage thereby asserts that arbitrariness, *lawlessness, is the law of marriage*, for no rational person will have the presumption to consider his actions as privileged, as concerning *him alone*; on the contrary, he will maintain that his actions are legitimate, that they *concern everybody*. But what do you oppose? You oppose the legislation of arbitrariness, but surely you do not want to raise arbitrariness to the level of a law at the very moment when you are accusing the legislator of arbitrariness.

Hegel says: *In itself*, according to the concept, marriage is indissoluble, but *only* in itself, i.e., only according to the concept. This says nothing *specific* about marriage. All moral relations are indissoluble according to *the concept*, as is easily realised if their *truth* is presupposed. A *true* state, a *true* marriage, a *true* friendship are indissoluble, but no state, no marriage, no friendship corresponds fully to its concept, and like real friendship, even in the family, like the real state in world history, so, too, real marriage in the state is *dissoluble*. No moral *existence* corresponds to its *essence* or, at least, it does not *have* to correspond to it. Just as in nature decay and death appear of themselves where an existence has totally ceased to correspond to its function, just as world history decides whether a state has so greatly departed from the idea of the state that it no longer deserves to exist, so, too, the state decides in what circumstances an *existing* marriage has ceased to be a marriage. Divorce is nothing but the statement of the fact that the marriage in question is a *dead* marriage, the existence of which is mere semblance and deception. It is obvious that neither the arbitrary decision of the legislator, nor the arbitrary desire of private persons, but only the *essence of the matter* can decide whether a marriage is dead or not, for it is well known that the *statement* that *death has occurred* depends on the facts, and not on the *desires* of the parties involved. But if, in the case of *physical* death, precise, irrefutable proof is required, is it not clear that the legislator should be allowed to register the fact of a *moral* death only on the basis of the most indubitable symptoms, since preserving the life of moral relationships is not only his right, but also his *duty*, the duty of his self-preservation!

Certainty that the *conditions* under which the *existence* of a moral relationship no longer corresponds to its *essence* are correctly registered, without preconceived opinions, in accordance with the level attained by science and with the generally accepted views—this certainty, of course, can only exist if the law is the conscious expression of the popular will, and therefore originates with it and is created by it. We will add a few words about making divorce easier or more difficult: Can you consider a natural object to be healthy, strong, truly organised, if every external impact, every injury, is capable of destroying it? Would you not feel insulted if someone put forward as an axiom that your friendship could not withstand the slightest accident and *must* be dissolved by any caprice? In regard to marriage, the legislator can only establish when it is *permissible* to dissolve it, that is to say, when in its essence it is *already dissolved*. Juridical dissolution of marriage can only be the registering of its internal dissolution. The standpoint of the legislator is the standpoint of necessity. The legislator, consequently, *gives due honour* to marriage, acknowledges its profound moral essence, if he considers it strong enough to withstand a multitude of collisions without harm to itself. Indulgence of the wishes of individuals would turn into harshness towards the essence of the individuals, towards their moral reason, which is embodied in moral relationships.

Finally, we can only term it undue haste when from many quarters the accusation of *hypocrisy* is levelled against countries with *strict laws on divorce*, among which the Rhine Province is *proud* to be included. Only people whose field of vision does not go beyond the moral corruption around them can dare to make such accusations. In the Rhine Province, for example, these accusations are considered ridiculous and are regarded at most as proof that even the *idea* of moral relationships can be lost, and every moral fact regarded as a *fairy-tale* or a falsehood. This is the direct result of laws that are not dictated by respect for human beings; it is a mistake which is not done away with by contempt for the material nature of man becoming contempt for his ideal nature and blind obedience to a super-moral and supernatural authority being demanded instead of conscious subordination to moral and natural forces.

ENGELS, Ernst Moritz Arndt, *MECW* II, 146–147.

Another thing which Arndt demands of his state is entails, in general an agrarian legislation laying down fixed conditions for landed property. Apart from its general importance, this point also deserves attention because here too the up-to-date reaction already mentioned threatens to put things back on the footing before 1789. How many have been raised to the nobility recently on condition that they institute an entail guaranteeing the prosperity of the family!—Arndt is definitely against the unlimited freedom and divisibility of landed property; he sees as its inevitable consequence the division of the land into plots none of which could support its owner. But he fails to see that complete freeing of the land provides the means of restoring in general the balance which in individual cases it may, of course, upset. While the complicated legislation in most German states and Arndt's equally complicated proposals will never eliminate, but only aggravate anomalies in agrarian relations, they also hinder a voluntary return to the proper order in the event of any dislocation, necessitate extraordinary interference by the state and hinder the progress of this legislation by a hundred petty but unavoidable private considerations. By contrast, freedom of the land allows no extremes to arise, neither the development of big landowners into an aristocracy, nor the splitting up of fields into patches so small as to become useless. If one scale of the balance goes down too far, the content of the other soon becomes concentrated in compensation. And even if landed property were to fly from hand to hand I would rather have the surging ocean with its grand freedom than the narrow inland lake with its quiet surface, whose miniature waves are broken every three steps by a spit of land, the root of a tree, or a stone. It is not merely that the permission to entail means the consent of the state to the formation of an aristocracy; no, this fettering of landed property, like all entails, works directly towards a revolution. When the best part of the land is welded to individual families and made inaccessible to all other citizens, is not that a direct provocation of the people? Does not the right of primogeniture rest on a view of property which has long ceased to correspond to our ideas? As if one generation had the right to dispose absolutely of the property of all future generations, which at the moment it enjoys and administers, as if the freedom of property were not destroyed by so disposing of it that all descendants are robbed of this freedom! As if human beings could thus be tied to the soil for all eternity!

ENGELS, The End of the *Criminalistische Zeitung, MECW* II, 302–303.

Berlin, June 25. On July 1 the local *Criminalistische Zeitung* will "cease to appear for the time being". Hence, its tirades against the jury system do not seem to have found the desired approval of the public. It was a *juste-milieu* paper in the juristic sphere. It favoured public and oral proceedings, but for God's sake no juries. The half-heartedness of such a tendency is fortunately being more and more recognised, and supporters of the jury system multiply daily. The *Criminalistische Zeitung* established the principle that no branch of executive power must be given directly into the hands of the people, hence not judicial office either. That would be all very fine if judicial power were not something quite different from executive power. In all states where the separation of the powers has been really instituted, judicial and executive powers are quite without any connection. This is the case in France, England and America; the mixing of the two leads to the most unholy confusion, and its most extreme consequence would be to unite the chief of police, investigating officer and judge in one person. But it has long been proved, not only in principle but by history, that judicial power is the direct property of the nation, which exercises it through its jurors. I remain silent on the advantages and guarantees offered by the jury system; it would be superfluous to waste words on that. But there are the inveterate jurists, the sticklers for the letter, whose slogan is: *fiat justitia, pereat mundus*! The free jury system naturally does not suit them for not only would they be pushed out of their position as judges, but the sacred letter of the law, dead abstract law, would be jeopardised, and that must not be lost. It is their palladium, and hence the gentlemen cry blue murder when for once a jury in France or England acquits a poor proletarian who, driven to desperation by hunger, has stolen a pennyworth of bread, although the case was proved by witnesses and confession. Then they shout triumphantly: You see, that comes of the jury system, the safety of property, of life itself is undermined, lawlessness is sanctioned, crime and revolution are openly proclaimed!—We hope that for the time being the *Criminalistische Zeitung* will not start again to appear "for the time being".

ENGELS, Centralisation and Freedom, *MECW* II, 356–357.

Centralisation, in the extreme form in which it prevails in France at present, is the state overstepping its bounds, going beyond its essential nature. The state is bounded, on the one hand, by the individual and, on the other hand, by world history. Both of these are harmed by centralisation. By assuming a right which belongs only to history, the state destroys the freedom of the individual. History has eternally had and will always retain the right to dispose of the life, the happiness, the freedom of the individual, for it is the activity of mankind as a whole, it is the life of the species, and as such it is sovereign; no one can revolt against it, for it is absolute right. No one can complain against history, for whatever it allots one, one lives and shares in the development of mankind, which is more than any enjoyment. How ludicrous it would be if the subjects of a Nero or a Domitian were to complain that they had not been born in an age like ours, when beheading or roasting alive does not happen so easily, or if the victims of medieval religious fanaticism were to reproach history because they did not live after the Reformation and under tolerant governments! As if without the suffering of some, the others could have made progress! Thus, the English workers who at present have to suffer bitter hunger, have indeed the right to protest against Sir Robert Peel and the English constitution, but not against history, which is making them the standard-bearers and representatives of a new principle of right. The same thing does not hold good for the state. It is always a particular state and can never claim the right, which mankind as a whole naturally possesses in its activity and the development of history, to sacrifice the individual for the general.

ENGELS, The Condition of the Working Class in England, *MECW* II, 379.

What all this boils down to is that England with her industry has burdened herself not only with a large class of the unpropertied, but among these always a considerable class of paupers which she cannot get rid of. These people have to rough it on their own; the state abandons them, even pushes them away. Who can blame them, if the men have recourse to robbery or burglary, the women to theft and prostitution? But the state does not care whether starvation is bitter or sweet; it locks these people up in prison or sends them to penal settlements, and when it releases them it has the satisfaction of having converted people without work into people without morals. And the curious thing about the whole story is that the sagacious Whig and the "radical" are still unable to understand where Chartism comes from with the country in such a state, and how the Chartists can possibly imagine they have even the slightest chance in England.

See also ENGELS, Polemic against Leo, *MECW* II, 283;
ENGELS, The Internal Crises, *MECW* II, 370–371.

The Experience of Law

MARX, Letter to Arnold Ruge, 30.11.1842, *MECW* I, 393–394.

Dear Friend,

My letter today will be confined to the "confusion" with "The Free".

As you already know, every day the censorship mutilates us mercilessly, so that frequently the newspaper is hardly able to appear. Because of this, a mass of articles by "The Free" have perished. But I have allowed myself to throw out as many articles as the censor, for Meyen and Co. sent us heaps of scribblings, pregnant with revolutionising the world and empty of ideas, written in a slovenly style and seasoned with a little atheism and communism (which these gentlemen have never studied). Because of Rutenberg's complete lack of critical sense, independence and ability, Meyen and Co. had become accustomed to regard the *Rheinische Zeitung* as *their own*, docile organ, but I believed I could not any longer permit this watery torrent of words in the old manner. This loss of a few worthless creations of "freedom", a freedom which strives primarily "to be free from all thought", was therefore the first reason for a darkening of the Berlin sky.

Rutenberg, who had already been removed from the German department (where his work consisted mainly in inserting punctuation marks), and to whom, only *on my application* the. French department was provisionally transferred—Rutenberg, thanks to the monstrous stupidity of our state providence, has had the luck to be regarded as dangerous, although he was not a danger to anyone but the *Rheinische Zeitung* and himself. A categorical demand was made for the removal of Rutenberg.

MARX, Renard's letter to Oberpräsident von Schaper,* *MECW* I, 285, and note at 746.

2. Secondly, as regards Your Excellency's demand for the immediate dismissal of Dr. Rutenberg, I already told Regierungspräsident von Gerlach on February 14 that Dr. Rutenberg was in no way an editor of the *Rheinische Zeitung*, but only did the work of a translator. In response to the threat, conveyed to me through Regierungspräsident von Gerlach, of the immediate suppression of the newspaper if Rutenberg were not at once dismissed, I have yielded to force and have for the time being removed him from any participation in the newspaper. Since, however, I am not aware of any legal provision which would justify this point of the rescript, I request Your Excellency to specify any such provision, and, if necessary, to give a speedy ruling whether the decision reached is to remain in force or not, so that I can claim my legal rights through the appropriate channels.

3. As regards the third point, the submission of an editor for approval, according to the censorship law of October 18, 1819, § [IX], only the supreme censorship authorities are entitled to demand the submission of an editor for approval. I know of no provision which transfers this entitlement to the Oberpräsidents. Therefore I request specification of any such provision or, if necessary, of a censorship ministry decree which orders this. Very willingly, but only in that case, will I submit an editor for approval.

MARX, Comments on the Latest Prussian Censorship Instruction, *MECW* I, 120–121.

The law against a frame of mind is *not a law of the state* promulgated for its *citizens*, but the *law of one party against another party*. The law which punishes tendency abolishes the equality of the citizens before the law. It is a law which divides, not one which unites, and all laws which divide are reactionary. It is not a law, but a *privilege*. One may do what another

* The draft of this letter was written by Marx, but it was sent from Renard, the official manager of the paper.

may not do, not because the latter lacks some objective quality, like a minor in regard to concluding contracts; no, because his good intentions and his frame of mind are under suspicion. The *moral state* assumes its members to have the *frame of mind of the state*, even if they act in *opposition to an organ of the state*, against the *government*. But in a society in which *one* organ imagines itself the sole, exclusive possessor of state reason and state morality, in a government which opposes the people in principle and hence regards *its anti-state frame of mind* as the general, normal frame of mind, the bad conscience of a faction invents laws against tendency, *laws of revenge*, laws against a frame of mind which has its seat only in the government members themselves. Laws against frame of mind are based on an unprincipled frame of mind, on an immoral, material view of the state. They are the involuntary cry of a bad conscience. And how is a law of this kind to be implemented? By a means more revolting than the law itself: by *spies*, or by previous agreement to regard entire literary trends as suspicious, in which case, of course, the trend to which an individual belongs must also be inquired into. Just as in the law against tendency the *legal form contradicts* the *content*, just as the *government* which issues it lashes out against what it is itself, against the anti-state frame of mind, so also in each particular case it forms as it were the *reverse world* to its laws, for it applies a double measuring-rod. What for one side is right, for the other side is wrong. *The very laws issued by the government are the opposite of what they make into law.*

The *new censorship instruction*, too, becomes entangled in this dialectic. It contains the contradiction of itself doing, and making it the censor's duty to do, everything that it condemns as anti-state in the case of the press.

Thus the instruction forbids writers to cast suspicion on the frame of mind of individuals or whole classes, and in the same breath it bids the censor divide all citizens into suspicious and unsuspicious, into well-intentioned and evil-intentioned. The press is deprived of the right to criticise, but criticism becomes the daily duty of the governmental critic. This reversal, however, does not end the matter. Within the press what was anti-state as regards content appeared as something particular, but from the aspect of its form it was something universal, that is to say, subject to universal appraisal.

MARX, Debates on Freedom of the Press, *MECW* I, 158–167.

In order really to justify censorship, the speaker would have had to prove that censorship is part of the essence of freedom of the press; instead he proves that freedom is not part of man's essence. He rejects the whole genus in order to obtain one good species, for is not freedom after all the generic essence of all spiritual existence, and therefore of the press as well? In order to abolish the possibility of evil, he abolishes the possibility of good and realises evil, for only that which is a realisation of freedom can be humanly good.

We shall therefore continue to regard the censored press as a bad press so long as it has not been proved to us that censorship arises from the very essence of freedom of the press.

But even supposing that censorship and the nature of the press come into being together, although no animal, let alone an intelligent being, comes into the world in chains, what follows from that? That freedom of the press, as it exists from the official viewpoint, that is, the censorship, also needs censorship. And who is to censor the governmental press, if not the popular press?

True, another speaker thinks that the evil of censorship would be removed by being tripled, by the local censorship being put under provincial censorship, and the latter in its turn under Berlin censorship, freedom of the press being made one-sided, and the censorship many-sided. So many roundabout ways merely to live! Who is to censor the Berlin censorship? Let us therefore return to *our* speaker.

At the very beginning, he informed us that no light would emerge from the *struggle* between the good and the bad press. But, we may now ask, does he not want to make this *useless* struggle *permanent*? According to his own statement, is not the struggle itself between the censorship and the press a struggle between the good and the bad press?

Censorship does not abolish the struggle, it makes it one-sided, it converts an open struggle into a hidden one, it converts a struggle over principles into a struggle of principle without power against power without principle. The true censorship, based on the very essence of freedom of the press, is *criticism*. This is the tribunal which freedom of the press gives rise to of itself. Censorship is criticism as a monopoly of the government. But does not criticism lose its rational character if it is not open but secret, if it is not theoretical but practical, if it is not above parties but itself a party, if it operates not with the sharp knife of reason but with the blunt scissors of arbitrariness, if it only exercises criticism but will not submit to it, if it disavows itself during its realisation, and, finally, if it is so uncritical as to mistake an individual person for universal wisdom, peremptory orders for rational statements, ink spots for patches of sunlight, the crooked deletions of the censor for mathematical constructions, and crude force for decisive arguments?

. . . .

If, however, a contrast is drawn between the press law and the censorship law, it is, in the first place, not a question of their consequences, but of their basis, not of their individual application, but of their legitimacy in general. Montesquieu has already taught us that despotism is more convenient to apply than legality and Machiavelli asserts that for princes the bad has better consequences than the good. Therefore, if we do not want to confirm the old *Jesuitical* maxim that a good end—and we doubt even the goodness of the end—justifies bad means, we have above all to investigate whether censorship by its essence is a *good* means.

The speaker is right in calling the censorship law a preventive measure, it is a precautionary measure of the police against freedom, but he is wrong in calling the press law a repressive measure. It is the rule of freedom itself which makes itself the yardstick of its own exceptions. The censorship measure is not a law. The press law is not a measure.

In the press law, freedom punishes. In the censorship law, freedom is punished. The censorship law is a law of suspicion against freedom. The press law is a vote of confidence which freedom gives itself. The press law punishes the abuse of freedom. The censorship law punishes freedom as an abuse. It treats freedom as a criminal, or is it not regarded in every sphere as a degrading punishment to be under police supervision? The censorship law has only the *form* of a law. The press law is a *real* law.

The press law is a *real law* because it is the positive existence of freedom. It regards freedom as the *normal* state of the press, the press as the mode of existence of freedom, and hence only comes into conflict with a press offence as an exception that contravenes its own rules and therefore annuls itself. Freedom of the press asserts itself as a press law, against attacks on freedom of the press itself, i.e., against press offences. The press law declares freedom to be inherent in the nature of the criminal. Hence what he has done against freedom he has done against himself and this self-injury appears to him as a *punishment* in which he sees a recognition of his freedom.

The press law, therefore, is far from being a repressive measure against freedom of the press, a mere means of preventing the repetition of a crime through fear of punishment. On the contrary, the *absence of press legislation* must be regarded as an exclusion of freedom of the press from the sphere of legal freedom, for legally recognised freedom exists in the state as *law*. Laws are in no way repressive measures against freedom, any more than the law of gravity is a repressive measure against motion, because while, as the law of gravitation, it governs the eternal motions of the celestial bodies, as the law of falling it kills me if I violate it and want to dance in the air. Laws are rather the positive, clear, universal norms in which freedom has acquired an impersonal, theoretical existence independent of the arbitrariness of the individual. A statute-book is a people's bible of freedom.

Therefore the *press law* is the *legal recognition of freedom of the press*. It constitutes *right*, because it is the positive existence of freedom. It must therefore exist, even if it is never put into application, as in North America, whereas censorship, like slavery, can never become lawful, even if it exists a thousand times over as a law.

There are no actual preventive laws. Law prevents only as a command. It only becomes *effective* law when it is infringed, for it is *true* law only when in it the unconscious natural law of freedom has become conscious state law. Where the law is real law, i.e., a form of existence of freedom, it is the real existence of freedom for man. Laws therefore, cannot prevent a man's actions, for they are indeed the inner laws of life of his action itself, the conscious reflections of his life. Hence law withdraws into the background in the face of man's life as a life of freedom, and only when his actual behaviour has shown that he has ceased to obey the natural law of freedom does law in the form of state law compel him to be free, just as the laws of physics confront me as something alien only when my life has ceased to be the life of these laws, when it has been *struck by illness*. Hence a *preventive law* is a *meaningless contradiction*.

A preventive law, therefore, has within it no *measure*, no *rational rule*, for a rational rule can only result from the nature of a thing, in this instance of freedom. It is *without measure*, for if prevention of freedom is to be effective, it must be as all–embracing as its object, i.e., unlimited. A preventive law is therefore the contradiction of an *unlimited limitation*, and the boundary where it ceases is fixed not by necessity, but by the fortuitousness of arbitrariness, as the censorship daily demonstrates *ad oculos*.

. . . .

What a difference there is between a judge and a censor!

The censor has no law but his superiors. The judge has no superiors but the law. The judge, however, has the duty of interpreting the law, as *he understands* it after conscientious examination, in order to apply it in a particular case. The censor's duty is to understand the law as *officially interpreted* for him in a particular case. The independent judge belongs neither to me nor to the government. The dependent censor is himself a government organ. In the case of the judge, there is involved at most the unreliability of an individual intellect, in the case of the censor the unreliability of an individual character. The judge has a *definite* press offence put before him; confronting the censor is the spirit of the press. The judge judges my act according to a definite law; the censor not only punishes the crime, he *makes* it. If I am brought before the court, I am accused of disobeying an existing law, and for a law to be violated it must indeed exist. Where there is no press law there is no law which can be violated by the press. The censorship does not accuse me of violating an existing law. It condemns my opinion because it is not the opinion of the censor and his superiors. My openly performed act, which is willing to submit itself to the world and its judgment, to the state and its law, has sentence passed on it by a hidden, purely negative power, which cannot give itself the form of law, which shuns the light of day, and which is not bound by any general principles.

A censorship law is an impossibility because it seeks to punish not offences but opinions, because it cannot be anything but a *formula for the censor*, because no state has the courage to put in general legal terms what it can carry out in practice through the agency of the censor. For that reason, too, the operation of the censorship is entrusted not to the courts but to the police.

Even if censorship were in fact the same thing as justice, in the first place this would remain a fact without being a necessity. But, further, freedom includes not only *what* my life is, but equally *how* I live, not only that I do what is free, but also that I do it freely. Otherwise what difference would there be between an architect and a beaver except that the beaver would be an architect with fur and the architect a beaver without fur?

MARX, Marginal Notes to the Accusations of the Ministerial Rescript, *MECW* I, 364.

Even the government has tried to arouse dissatisfaction with the existing legal conditions, for example with the old Prussian marriage situation. All reform and revision of the law, all progress, rests on such dissatisfaction.

Since legal development is not possible without development of the laws, and since development of the laws is impossible without criticism of them, and since every criticism of the laws sets the mind and therefore also the heart of the citizen at variance with the existing laws, and since this variance is experienced as dissatisfaction, it follows that a loyal participation of the press in the development of the state is impossible if it is not permitted to arouse dissatisfaction with the existing legal conditions.

The reproach that the *Rh. Z.* persecutes loyal organs by unworthy ridicule, which is obviously intended to refer to the newspaper controversy, cannot provide grounds for a ban. From all sides, the *Rh. Z.* has been denounced, has had mud cast at it, and been attacked. It was its duty to defend itself. Moreover, there is no *official* press.

MARX/ENGELS, Freedom of Debate in Berlin, *Articles from NRZ*, 129–130.

Why should we not say it? The centre parties certainly were intimidated by the masses on September 7; we leave it open whether their fear was well founded or not.

The right of the democratic popular masses, by their presence, to exert a moral influence on the attitude of constituent assemblies is an old revolutionary right of the people which could not be dispensed with in all stormy periods ever since the English and French revolutions. History owes to this right almost all the energetic steps taken by such assemblies. The only reason why people dwell on the "legal basis" and why the timorous and philistine friends of the "freedom of debate" lament about it is that they do not want any energetic decisions at all.

"Freedom of debate"—there is no emptier phrase than this. The "freedom of debate" is, on the one hand, impaired by the freedom of the press, by the freedom of assembly and of speech, and by the right of the people to take up arms. It is impaired by the existing state power vested in the Crown and its ministers—the army, the police and the so-called independent judges, who depend, however, on every promotion and every political change.

The freedom of debate is always a phrase denoting simply independence of all influences that are not recognised in law. It is only the recognised influences, such as bribery, promotion, private interests and fear of a dissolution of the Assembly, that make the debates really "free". In time of revolution, however, this phrase becomes entirely meaningless. When two forces, two parties in arms confront each other, when a fight may start any moment, the deputies have only this choice:

Either they place themselves *under the protection of the people*, in which case they will put up occasionally with a small lecture;

Or they place themselves *under the protection of the Crown*, move to some small town, deliberate under the protection of bayonets and guns or even a state of siege, in which case they will raise no objections when the Crown and the bayonets dictate their decisions to them.

Intimidation by the unarmed people or intimidation by an armed soldiery—that is the choice before the Assembly.

MARX, The Prussian Press Bill, *The Revolutions of 1848*, 134–137.

We were thinking of amusing our readers once more with the debates of the *Vereinbarungsversammlung*, and in particular of presenting a brilliant speech by deputy Baumstark, but events have prevented this.

Charity begins at home. When the existence of the press is threatened, even deputy Baumstark must be left aside.

Herr Hansemann has laid an interim press law before the Assembly. His fatherly concern for the press demands our immediate consideration.

Before 1848, the Code Napoléon was beautified by the addition of the most edifying sections of the Landrecht. After the revolution, this has changed; now the Landrecht is enriched with the most fragrant blossoms of the Code and the September laws. Duchâtel is naturally no Bodelschwingh.

We have already given the main details of this press bill. We had only just had the opportunity to show that articles 367 and 368 of the Code Pénal stood in the most glaring contradiction with the freedom of the press (by undergoing an investigation for libel), when Herr Hansemann proposed not only to extend it to the whole of the kingdom, but also to make it three times more severe. In the new bill, we find everything we have grown to know and love through practical experience.

We find it prohibited, on pain of three months' to three years' imprisonment, to accuse anyone of an action which is punishable by law, or which merely 'puts him in public contempt'; we find it prohibited to assert the truth of a fact except on the basis of 'completely valid evidence'; in short, we rediscover the most classic characteristics of Napoleon's despotic rule over the press.

One might well say that Herr Hansemann has fulfilled his promise to give the old Prussian provinces a share in the advantages of the laws of the Rhineland!

These measures are crowned by paragraph 10 of the bill: if the libel was committed against *state officials* in relation to their official business, the normal punishment can be *increased by a half*.

Article 222 of the Code Pénal provides for a period of from one month up to two years' imprisonment when an official has received an insult in words (*outrage par parole*) during the performance of, or incidentally (*à l'occasion*) to, the performance of his office. So far, and despite the benevolent endeavours of public prosecutors, this article did not apply to the press, and for good reasons. In order to remedy this abuse, Herr Hansemann transformed article 222 into the above-mentioned paragraph 10. Firstly, 'incidentally' was changed into the more convenient phrase 'in relation to their official business'; secondly, the tiresome 'in word' was changed into 'in writing'; thirdly, the punishment was increased threefold.

From the day when this law comes into force, the Prussian officials will be able to sleep soundly. If Herr Pfuel burns the hands and ears of the Poles with caustic, and the press publishes this: four and a half months to four and a half years in prison! If citizens are thrown into prison by mistake, although it is known that they are not the guilty ones, and the press points this out: four and a half months to four and a half years in prison! If local officials become travelling salesmen of the reaction and collect signatures for royalist addresses, and the press unmasks those gentlemen: four and a half months to four and a half years in prison!

From the day when this law comes into force, the officials will be able, unpunished, to commit any arbitrary, tyrannical, or illegal action; they will be free to flog and order floggings, to arrest and imprison without trial; the only effective control, the press, will have been made ineffective. On the day when this law comes into force, the bureaucracy will be able to celebrate and rejoice: it will be more powerful, more unhindered, and stronger than before March.

Indeed, what is left of the freedom of the press when the press may no longer hold up to the contempt of the public that which *deserves* the contempt of the public?

According to the existing laws, the press could at least present the facts as proofs of its general assertions and accusations. This situation will now come to an end. The press will no longer *report*, it will only be permitted to engage in general phrase-making, so that right-thinking people, from Herr Hansemann down to the simple citizen drinking his pale ale will have the right to say, 'The press merely *grumbles*, it never *brings proof*.' It is precisely for that reason that the bringing of proof is being forbidden.

By the way, we would recommend Herr Hansemann to make an addition to his generous bill. He should declare it a punishable offence to hold up the gentlemen of the bureaucracy, not just to public contempt, but also to public ridicule. This omission will otherwise be painfully felt.

We shall not deal with the paragraphs on obscenity, the regulations relating to confiscation, etc. in any detail. They outdo the cream of the press legislation of the July monarchy and the Restoration. Just one specific point: by paragraph 21, the public prosecutor can demand the confiscation of both the finished publication and the *manuscript handed over for printing*, if the content constitutes a felony or a misdemeanour liable to official prosecution. What broad pastures this opens for philanthropic state prosecutors! What an enjoyable diversion, to go to a newspaper office whenever you wish and have the 'manuscript handed over for printing' presented to you for examination, as it is after all possible that it could constitute a felony or a misdemeanour.

How laughable is the solemn seriousness of that paragraph of the proposed constitution and the 'fundamental rights of the German people' which states that *'the censorship can never be re-established'*, when placed beside this bill!

See also MARX, Comments on the Latest Prussian Censorship Instruction, *MECW* I, 109–131; MARX, On the Critique of the Prussian Laws, *MECW* I, 304–311; MARX, The Ban on the *Leipziger Allemeine Zeitung, MECW* I, 327.

MARX, Announcement, *MECW* I, 374.

The undersigned declares that, owing to the *present conditions of censorship*, he has retired as from today from the editorial board of the *Rheinische Zeitung*.

2 Law in 'Historical Materialism'

This chapter contains a number of formulations by Marx and Engels about 'law in general'. These passages appear in those relatively infrequent contexts in which Marx or Engels advance general formulations of their theoretical position, which have subsequently come to be identified as 'historical materialism'. Engels, particularly in his later writings in which he sought to give a more accessible and popular presentation of Marxist theory, advances more of these general or metatheoretical formulations than did Marx, and it was he who coined the label 'historical materialism'.

The most famous and oft quoted of these passages occurs in the 1859 Preface to "A Contribution to the Critique of Political Economy". Here is to be found the classic presentation of the base/superstructure thesis in which the economic structure or base constitutes "the real foundation on which rises a legal and political superstructure".[1] In this and other passages the superstructure (legal–political and ideological) is conceived as an 'expression' or a 'reflection' of the base.

These formulations are frequently in marked contrast to many of the passages that appear in our later chapters. Where Marx, in particular, and Engels engage in historical or substantive analysis of specific legal phenomena, they do not make use of such a direct or simple relation posited between base and superstructure.

The extent to which these formulations of a determinant relation between base and superstructure can be regarded as an adequate précis of the full richness of Marx' theoretical position is itself an important area of controversy within Marxist theory.[2] Marx himself spoke of these formulations somewhat tentatively as the "guiding thread for my studies".[3] The elaboration of 'historical materialism' by Engels and the early generation of post-Marx writers turned the formulae of the Preface into canon law.

The 'base/superstructure' formulation is, it must be insisted, a *metaphor*. It transposes from the arena of physical and spatial relations to the phenomenon of society. As with all metaphors there is both illumination and, at the same time, a forcing of the phenomenon to which it is applied into terms appropriate to the objects from which the metaphor derives. Both Marx and Engels were greatly influenced in both thoughts and language by the concepts of Newtonian physics; this has its impact both upon their own concepts and upon their conception of science.

The base/superstructure metaphor gives rise to a number of related problems. These can only be sketched here but they are of central importance not only to their treatment of law but for Marxist social theory as a whole. First, the spatial content of the metaphor induces us to think of the elements of society as structures—'things'—existing as discrete objects in spatial relations. Note how so much of the language of both Marxist and non-Marxist social theory, for example 'elements', 'structures', makes use of concepts derived from the physical sciences forcing us to think of social phenomena as 'things'. This makes it difficult to 'think' society, as Marx is at great pains to insist we should, as an "ensemble of social relations", as a totality which is not simply the sum of independently existing elements.

The second problem concerns the closely related issues of whether the general formulations of the 1859 Preface imply or require Marxist theory to be understood as positing a *determinism* or a *reductionism*. 'Determinism' is a difficult and slippery term.[4] In its strongest sense, determinism imports a unidirectional causality in which one element (superstructure) is a necessary consequence of another (base); the base or economy 'rules'. Law, in these terms, is to be explained and understood as a product of, or as a reflection of, changes in the economic base. It is this conception of determinism that gives rise to the problem of reductionism. If the base 'determines' the superstructure, then all knowledge of the superstructure can be 'reduced' to, or derived from, or read off from, the base. Thus to explain a change in legislation we would only have to examine changes in the economic base to give a sufficient causal account of changes in law.

These problems are inherent in the base/superstructure metaphor. They are clearly present in the general passages about law that appear in this chapter. Law is frequently cited by both Marx and Engels, not only as a constituent part of the superstructure, but as an example of the superstructure. It is important to stress that one of the peculiarities of the base/superstructure metaphor is that it is rarely invoked by Marx in either his substantive theoretical writings or in his political writing. As the passages collected in the subsequent chapters clearly show, Marx' and Engels' discussion of law is not constrained within the limitations and simplifications of the base/superstructure metaphor.

The provisional nature of these most general formulations emerges in some of Engels' later letters in which he insists that "Marx and I are ourselves partly to blame for the fact that the younger people sometimes lay more stress on the economic side than is due to it. We had to emphasize the main principle vis-à-vis our adversaries, who denied it".[5] In these letters he advances the concept of the 'relative autonomy' of the superstructure. This has important repercussions in his treatment of law as can be seen particularly clearly in his letter to Schmidt in which he emphasizes that "law must not only correspond to the general economic condition and be its *internally coherent* expression which does not, owing to internal conflicts, contradict itself".[6] However, it is necessary to pose the question: to what extent does the concept of 'relative autonomy' of the superstructure overcome or resolve the problem of determinism referred to above? Engels insists that the economic base is determinant "in the last instance" or "in the final analysis". This raises the difficulty, which needs to be considered in relation to the discussion of law, of how this ultimate causal determination is to be understood: under what conditions does the economic finally impose itself upon the superstructure which has undergone relatively autonomous development? While the 'relative autonomy' concept is not without its own difficulties, it provides a valuable context within which the texts and passages relating to law should be considered.

The majority of the general passages in this chapter do not go beyond a rather more general, and less problematic, emphasis upon the *dependence of law*. Law is presented as dependent upon the level of economic development or the form of property relations. Law is "the official recognition of fact",[7] or is "the reflex of the real economic relations".[8] It is important to place the persistence of these formulations in their context. They are expressions of their protracted confrontation with idealist theory. Within the idealist tradition, especially within historical theories of law, which Marx' early legal studies made him familiar with, law is conceived as an autonomous principle playing a causal role in the historical process. It is against this tradition that Marx stresses that "revolutions are not made by law".[9] This general assertion of the 'the dependence of law' is not simply to be equated with the more specific and problematic base/superstructure formulations.

Notes

1. Marx, K. *MESW (3)* I, 503.
2. See for valuable general discussion of base/superstructure, Williams, R. (1973) Base and Superstructure, *New Left Review* **82,** 3–16; Hall, S. (1977) Rethinking the 'Base-and-Superstructure' Metaphor, in *Class, Hegemony and Party* (J. Bloomfield, ed.), Lawrence and Wishart, London.
3. Marx, K. *MESW (3)* I, 503.
4. See for useful general discussion Williams, R. (1977) *Marxism and Literature*, pp. 83–89, Oxford University Press, London.
5. Engels, F. Letter to Bloch 21.9.1890, *MESC*, 396.
6. Engels, F. Letter to Schmidt 27.10.1890, *MESC*, 399 (Engels' emphasis).
7. Marx, K. The Poverty of Philosophy, *MECW* VI, 50.
8. Marx, K. *Capital* I, 88.
9. Marx, K. *ibid.*, 750.

Extracts

MARX, Preface to a Contribution to the Critique of Political Economy, *MESW (3)* I, 503–504.

The general result at which I arrived and which, once won, served as a guiding thread for my studies, can be briefly formulated as follows: In the social production of their life, men enter into definite relations that are indispensable and independent of their will, relations of production which correspond to a definite stage of development of their material productive forces. The sum total of these relations of production constitutes the economic structure of society, the real foundation, on which rises a legal and political superstructure and to which correspond definite forms of social consciousness. The mode of production of material life conditions the social, political and intellectual life process in general. It is not the consciousness of men that determines their being, but, on the contrary, their social being that determines their consciousness. At a certain stage of their development, the material productive forces of society come in conflict with the existing relations of production, or—what is but a legal expression for the same thing—with the property relations within which they have been at work hitherto. From forms of development of the productive forces these relations turn into their fetters. Then begins an epoch of social revolution. With the change of the economic foundation the entire immense superstructure is more or less rapidly transformed. In considering such transformations a distinction should always be made between the material transformation of the economic conditions of production, which can be determined with the precision of natural science, and the legal, political, religious, aesthetic or philosophic—in short, ideological forms in which men become conscious of this conflict and fight it out.

See also ENGELS, Socialism: Utopian and Scientific, *MESW (3)* III, 132; MARX/ENGELS, The German Ideology, *MECW* V, 36.

MARX, *Capital* III, 793.

Since the direct producer is not the owner, but only a possessor, and since all his surplus-labour *de jure* actually belongs to the landlord, some historians have expressed astonishment that it should be at all possible for those subject to enforced labour, or serfs, to acquire any independent property, or relatively speaking, wealth, under such circumstances. However, it is evident that tradition must play a dominant role in the primitive and undeveloped circumstances on which these social production relations and the corresponding mode of production are based. It is furthermore clear that here as always it is in the interest of the ruling section of society to sanction the existing order as law and to legally establish its limits given through usage and tradition. Apart from all else, this, by the way, comes about of itself as soon as the constant reproduction of the basis of the existing order and its fundamental relations assumes a regulated and orderly form in the course of time. And such regulation and order are themselves indispensable elements of any mode of production, if it is to assume social stability and independence from mere chance and arbitrariness. These are precisely the form of its social stability and therefore its relative freedom from mere arbitrariness and mere chance. Under backward conditions of the production process as well as the corresponding social relations, it achieves this form by mere repetition of their very reproduction. If this has continued on for some time, it entrenches itself as custom and tradition and is finally sanctioned as an explicit law.

See also MARX, *Grundrisse*, 469–470.

MARX/ENGELS, The German Ideology, *MECW* V, 90–92.

Since the state is the form in which the individuals of a ruling class assert their common interests, and in which the whole civil society of an epoch is epitomised, it follows that all common institutions are set up with the help of the state and are given a political form. Hence the illusion that law is based on the will, and indeed on the will divorced from its real basis—on *free* will. Similarly, justice is in its turn reduced to statute law.

Civil law develops simultaneously with private property out of the disintegration of the natural community. With the Romans the development of private property and civil law had no further industrial and commercial consequences, because their whole mode of production did not alter. With modern people, where the feudal community was disintegrated by industry and trade, there began with the rise of private property and civil law a new phase, which was capable of further development. The very first town which carried on an extensive maritime trade in the Middle Ages, Amalfi, also developed maritime law. As soon as industry and trade developed private property further, first in Italy and later in other countries, the highly developed Roman civil law was immediately adopted again and raised to authority. When later the bourgeoisie had acquired so much power that the princes took up its interests in order to overthrow the feudal nobility by means of the bourgeoisie, there began in all countries—in France in the sixteenth century—the real development of law, which in all countries except England proceeded on the basis of the Roman code of laws. In England, too, Roman legal principles had to be introduced to further the development of civil law (especially in the case of movable property). (It must not be forgotten that law has just as little an independent history as religion.)

In civil law the existing property relations are declared to be the result of the general will. The *jus utendi et abutendi** itself asserts on the one hand the fact that private property has become entirely independent of the community, and on the other the illusion that private property itself is based solely on the private will, the arbitrary disposal of the thing. In practice, the *abuti* has very definite economic limitations for the owner of private property, if he does not wish to see his property and hence his *jus abutendi* pass into other hands, since actually the thing, considered merely with reference to his will, is not a thing at all, but only becomes a thing, true property, in intercourse, and independently of the law (*a relationship*, which the philosophers call an idea). This juridical illusion, which reduces law to the mere will, necessarily leads, in the further development of property relations, to the position that a man may have a legal title to a thing without really having the thing. If, for instance, the income from a piece of land disappears owing to competition, then the proprietor has certainly his legal title to it along with the *jus utendi et abutendi*. But he can do nothing with it: he owns nothing as a landed proprietor if he has not enough capital elsewhere to cultivate his land. This illusion of the jurists also explains the fact that for them, as for every code, it is altogether fortuitous that individuals enter into relations among themselves (e.g., contracts); it explains why they consider that these relations [can] be entered into or not at will, and that their content [rests] purely on the individual free will of the contracting parties.

Whenever, through the development of industry and commerce, new forms of intercourse have been evolved (e.g., insurance companies, etc.), the law has always been compelled to admit them among the modes of acquiring property.

[12. FORMS OF SOCIAL CONSCIOUSNESS]

The influence of the division of labour on science.

The role of *repression* with regard to the state, law, morality, etc.

It is precisely because the bourgeoisie rules as a class that in the law it must give itself a general expression.

Natural science and history.

There is no history of politics, law, science, etc., of art, religion, etc.

Why the ideologists turn everything upside-down.

Clerics, jurists, politicians.

Jurists, politicians (statesmen in general), moralists, clerics.

For this ideological subdivision within a class: 1) *The occupation assumes an independent existence owing to division of labour.* Everyone believes his craft to be the true one. Illusions regarding the

---

* The right of use and of disposal.—*Ed.*

connection between their craft and reality are the more likely to be cherished by them because of the very nature of the craft. In consciousness—in jurisprudence, politics, etc.—relations become concepts; since they do not go beyond these relations, the concepts of the relations also become fixed concepts in their mind. The judge, for example, applies the code, he therefore regards legislation as the real, active driving force. Respect for their goods, because their craft deals with general matters.

Idea of law. Idea of state. The matter is turned upside-down in *ordinary* consciousness.

ENGELS, The Housing Question, *MESW (3)*, 365–366.

At a certain, very primitive stage of the development of society, the need arises to bring under a common rule the daily recurring acts of production, distribution and exchange of products, to see to it that the individual subordinates himself to the common conditions of production and exchange. This rule, which at first is custom, soon becomes *law*. With law organs necessarily arise which are entrusted with its maintenance—public authority, the state. With further social development, law develops into a more or less comprehensive legal system. The more intricate this legal system becomes, the more is its mode of expression removed from that in which the usual economic conditions of the life of society are expressed. It appears as an independent element which derives the justification for its existence and the substantiation of its further development not from the economic relations but from its own inner foundations or, if you like, from "the concept of the will." People forget that their right derived from their economic conditions of life, just as they have forgotten that they themselves derive from the animal world. With the development of the legal system into an intricate, comprehensive whole a new social division of labour becomes necessary; an order of professional jurists develops and with these legal science comes into being. In its further development this science compares the legal systems of various peoples and various times not as a reflection of the given economic relationships, but as systems which find their substantiations in themselves. The comparison presupposes points in common, and these are found by the jurists compiling what is more or less common to all these legal systems and calling it *natural right*. And the stick used to measure what is natural right and what is not is the most abstract expression of right itself, namely, *justice*. Henceforth, therefore, the development of right for the jurists, and for those who take their word for everything, is nothing more than a striving to bring human conditions, so far as they are expressed in legal terms, ever closer to the ideal of justice, *eternal* justice. And always this justice is but the ideologised, glorified expression of the existing economic relations, now from their conservative, and now from their revolutionary angle. The justice of the

Greeks and Romans held slavery to be just; the justice of the bourgeois of 1789 demanded the abolition of feudalism on the ground that it was unjust. For the Prussian Junker even the miserable District Ordinance is a violation of eternal justice. The conception of eternal justice, therefore, varies not only with time and place, but also with the persons concerned, and belongs among those things of which Mülberger correctly says, "everyone understands something diffcrent." While in everyday life, in view of the simplicity of the relations discussed, expressions like right, wrong, justice, and sense of right are accepted without misunderstanding even with reference to social matters, they create, as we have seen, the same hopeless confusion in any scientific investigation of economic relations as would be created, for instance, in modern chemistry if the terminology of the phlogiston theory were to be retained. The confusion becomes still worse if one, like Proudhon, believes in this social phlogiston, "justice", or if one, like Mülberger, avers that the phlogiston theory is as correct as the oxygen theory.

ENGELS, Letter to J. Bloch, 21.9.1890, *MESC*, 394–395.

According to the materialist conception of history, the *ultimately* determining factor in history is the production and reproduction of real life. Neither Marx nor I have ever asserted more than this. Hence if somebody twists this into saying that the economic factor is the *only* determining one, he transforms that proposition into a meaningless, abstract, absurd phrase. The economic situation is the basis, but the various elements of the superstructure—political forms of the class struggle and its results, such as constitutions established by the victorious class after a successful battle, etc., juridical forms, and especially the reflections of all these real struggles in the brains of the participants, political, legal, philosophical theories, religious views and their further development into systems of dogmas—also exercise their influence upon the course of the historical struggles and in many cases determine their *form* in particular. There is an interaction of all these elements in which, amid all the endless host of accidents (that is, of things and events whose inner interconnection is so remote or so impossible of proof that we can regard it as non-existent and neglect it), the economic movement is finally bound to assert itself. Otherwise the application of the theory to any period of history would be easier than the solution of a simple equation of the first degree.

ENGELS, Letter to Conrad Schmidt, 27.10.1890, *MESC*, 399–402.

The retroaction of the state power upon economic development can be of three kinds: it can proceed in the same direction, and then things move more rapidly; it can move in the opposite direction, in which case nowadays it [the state] will go to pieces in the long run in every great people; or it can prevent the economic development from proceeding along certain lines, and prescribe other lines. This case ultimately reduces itself to one of the two previous ones. But it is obvious that in cases two and three the political power can do great damage to the economic development and cause extensive waste of energy and material.

Then there is also the case of the conquest and brutal destruction of economic resources, as a result of which, in certain circumstances, the entire economic development in a particular locality or in a country could be ruined in former times. Nowadays such a case usually has the opposite effect, as least with great peoples: in the long run the vanquished often gains more economically, politically and morally than the victor.

Similarly with law. As soon as the new division of labour which creates professional lawyers becomes necessary, another new and independent sphere is opened up which, for all its general dependence on production and trade, has also a specific capacity for reacting upon these spheres. In a modern state, law must not only correspond to the general economic condition and be its expression, but must also be an *internally coherent* expression which does not, owing to internal conflicts, contradict itself. And in order to achieve this, the faithful reflection of economic conditions suffers increasingly. All the more so the more rarely it happens that a code of law is the blunt, unmitigated, unadulterated expression of the domination of a class—this in itself would offend the "conception of right". Even in the *Code Napoléon* the pure, consistent conception of right held by the revolutionary bourgeoisie of 1792–96 is already adulterated in many ways, and, in so far as it is embodied in the Code, has daily to undergo all sorts of attenuations owing to the rising power of the proletariat. This does not prevent the *Code Napoléon* from being the statute book which serves as the basis of every new code of law in every part of the world. Thus to a great extent the course of the "development of law" simply consists in first attempting to eliminate contradictions which arise from the direct translation of economic relations into legal principles, and to establish a harmonious system of law, and then in the repeated breaches made in this system by the influence and compulsion of further economic development, which involves it in further contradictions. (I am speaking here for the moment only of civil law.)

The reflection of economic relations in the form of legal principles is likewise bound to be inverted: it goes on without the person who is acting being conscious of it; the jurist imagines he is operating with *a priori* propositions, whereas they are really only economic reflections; everything is therefore upside down. And it seems to me obvious that this inversion, which, so long as it remains unrecognised, forms what we call *ideological outlook*, influences in its turn the economic basis and may, within certain limits, modify it. The basis of the right of inheritance is an economic one, provided the level of development of the family is the same. It would, nevertheless, be difficult to prove, for instance, that the absolute liberty of the testator in England and the severe and very detailed restrictions imposed upon him in France are due to economic causes alone. But in their turn they exert a very considerable effect on the economic sphere, because they influence the distribution of property.

. . . .

Hence if Barth alleges that we altogether deny that the political, etc., reflections of the economic movement in their turn exert any effect upon the movement itself, he is simply tilting at windmills. He should only look at Marx's *Eighteenth Brumaire*, which deals almost exclusively with the *particular* part played by political struggles and events, of course within their *general* dependence upon economic conditions. Or *Kapital*, the section on the working day, for instance, where legislation, which is surely a political act, has such a drastic effect. Or the section on the history of the bourgeoisie. (Chapter XXIV.) And why do we fight for the political dictatorship of the proletariat if political power is economically impotent? Force (that is, state power) is also an economic power!

ENGELS, Letter to W. Borgius (Starkenburg), 25.1.1894, *MESC*, 441–442.

Dear Sir,

Here is the answer to your questions:

1. By economic relations, which we regard as the determining basis of the history of society, we understand the manner in which men in a given society produce their means of subsistence and exchange the products (in so far as division of labour exists). They comprise therefore the *entire technique* of production and transport. According to our conception this technique also determines the mode of exchange and, further more, of the distribution of products and hence, after the dissolution of gentile society, also the division into classes, and consequently the relations of lordship and servitude and consequently the state, politics, law, etc.

. . . .

2. We regard economic conditions as that which ultimately determines historical development. But race is itself an economic factor. In this context, however, two points must not be overlooked:

a) Political, legal, philosophical, religious, literary, artistic, etc., development is based on economic development. But all these react upon one another and also upon the economic basis. One must think that the economic situation is *cause, and solely active*, whereas everything else is only passive effect. On the contrary, interaction takes place on the basis of economic necessity, which *ultimately* always asserts itself.

MARX, *Grundrisse*, 98.

Laws may perpetuate an instrument of production, e.g. land, in certain families. These laws achieve economic significance only when large-scale landed property is in harmony with the society's production, as e.g. in

England. In France, small-scale agriculture survived despite the great landed estates, hence the latter were smashed by the revolution. But can laws perpetuate the small-scale allotment? Despite these laws, ownership is again becoming concentrated. The influence of laws in stabilizing relations of distribution, and hence their effect on production, requires to be determined in each specific instance.

MARX, The Poverty of Philosophy, *MECW* VI, 147.

Truly, one must be destitute of all historical knowledge not to know that it is the sovereigns who in all ages have been subject to economic conditions, but they have never dictated laws to them. Legislation, whether political or civil, never does more than proclaim, express in words, the will of economic relations.

MARX, *ibid.*, 150

To make "every commodity acceptable in exchange, if not in fact then at least in law," on the basis of the role of gold and silver is, then, to misunderstand this role. Gold and silver are acceptable in law only because they are acceptable in fact; and they are acceptable in fact because the present organisation of production needs a universal agent of exchange. Law is only the official recognition of fact.

MARX, *Capital* I, 88–89.

It is plain that commodities cannot go to market and make exchange of their own account. We must, therefore, have recourse to their guardians, who are also their owners. Commodities are things, and therefore without power of resistance against man. If they are wanting in docility he can use force; in other words, he can take possession of them. In order that these objects may enter into relation with each other as commodities, their guardians must place themselves in relation to one another, as persons whose will resides in those objects, and must behave in such a way that each does not appropriate the commodity of the other, and part with his own, except by means of an act done by mutual consent. They must, therefore, mutually recognise in each other the rights of private proprietors. This juridical relation, which thus expresses itself in a contract, whether such contract be part of a developed legal system or not, is a relation between two wills, and is but the reflex of the real economic relation between the two. It is this economic relation that determines the subject-matter comprised in each such juridical act.* The

* Proudhon begins by taking his ideal of justice, of "justice éternelle," from the juridical relations that correspond to the production of commodities; thereby, it may be noted he proves to the consolation of all good citizens, that the production of commodities is a form of production as everlasting as justice. Then he turns round and seeks to reform the actual production of commodities and the actual legal system corresponding thereto, in accordance with this ideal.

persons exist for one another merely as representatives of, and, therefore, as owners of, commodities. In the course of our investigation we shall find, in general, that the characters who appear on the economic stage are but the personifications of the economic relations that exist between them.

MARX, *ibid.,* 337.

If, in a society with capitalist production, anarchy in the social division of labour and despotism in that of the workshop are mutual conditions the one of the other, we find, on the contrary, in those earlier forms of society in which the separation of trades has been spontaneously developed, then crystallised, and finally made permanent by law, on the one hand, a specimen of the organisation of the labour of society, in accordance with an approved and authoritative plan, and on the other, the entire exclusion of division of labour in the workshop, or at all events a mere dwarf-like or sporadic and accidental development of the same.

MARX, *ibid.*, 702–703.

"At present, all the wealth of society goes first into the possession of the capitalist . . . he pays the landowner his rent, the labourer his wages, the tax and tithe gatherer their claims, and keeps a large, indeed the largest, and a continually augmenting share, of the annual produce of labour for himself. The capitalist may now be said to be the first owner of all the wealth of the community, though no law has conferred on him the right to this property . . . this change has been effected by the taking of interest on capital . . . and it is not a little curious that all the law-givers of Europe endeavoured to prevent this by statutes, viz., statutes against usury. . . . The power of the capitalist over all the wealth of the country is a complete change in the right of property, and by what law, or series of laws, was it effected?"* The author should have remembered that revolutions are not made by laws.

ENGELS, Letter to K. Kautsky, 26.6.1884, *MESC*, 451–452.

Dear Kautsky,

The Anti-Rodbertus manuscript goes back tomorrow by registered mail. I found few remarks to make; jotted down some pencil comments. In addition the following:

1) Roman law was the consummate law of *simple*, i.e. precapitalist, *commodity production*, which however included most of the legal relations of the capitalist period. Hence precisely what our city burghers *needed* at the time of their rise and did *not* find in the local law of custom.

* "The Natural and Artificial Rights of Property Contrasted." London., 1832, pp. 98–99. Author of the anonymous work: "Th. Hodgskin."

MARX/ENGELS, The German Ideology, *MECW* V, 365.

The hitherto existing production relations of individuals are bound also to be expressed as political and legal relations. Within the division of labour these relations are bound to acquire an independent existence over against the individuals. All relations can be expressed in language only in the form of concepts. That these general ideas and concepts are looked upon as mysterious forces is the necessary result of the fact that the real relations, of which they are the expression, have acquired independent existence. Besides this meaning in everyday consciousness, these general ideas are further elaborated and given a special significance by politicians and lawyers, who, as a result of the division of labour, are dependent on the cult of these concepts, and who see in them, and not in the relations of production, the true basis of all real property relations.

3 Law and Economic Relations

Introduction

A general characteristic of Marx' treatment of law is the insistence on establishing its class character and class specificity. This is the most pronounced theme in those passages that directly refer to law in the context of either theoretical or historical treatment of questions of political economy. However, these passages cannot, as we have seen from the previous chapter, be read as presenting a simple economic reductionist view of law, as the passive reflection of economic conditions and relations. The general character of Marx' treatment contains a dual orientation. On the one hand, there is the basic simplification that asserts the class character of law as a controlled instrument used to protect and further the interests of the dominant class. On the other hand, there is present a more complex and sophisticated analysis in which law emerges having a specific effectivity and is an integral part of economic relations themselves which cannot be reduced to a direct 'class interest' account. This more complex analysis appears in a form that is not fully theorized, partly because questions concerning law did not form an object of inquiry for Marx, but also because outside the great theoretical labour of *Capital*, he was writing as a direct intervention in contemporary politics.

The important and difficult question is to assess the implications of these two aspects or levels of theory that are present in Marx' writings. We do not hold the view that these amount to a contradiction or incoherence within Marx' theoretical position. Rather, the initial discovery achieved by Marx lies in the 'simple' identification of the class character of law. However, his much greater achievement was to go beyond this by achieving an analysis in which the specific effects of the elements of the social formation and, in particular, of the superstructure, is established. The source of the major problem in the history of Marxist theory has been and remains the tendency to elevate the simple class reductionist thesis into the substance of Marxist social theory.

The problem that remains is the fact that the elaboration of an analysis going beyond the basic simplification of class analysis remained in Marx' work in what Althusser describes as its 'practical state'. The theorization and conceptualization of the more sophisticated level remained either unelaborated or only partially elaborated. What exists in the texts of Marx, and to a lesser extent of Engels, are a number of analyses, concepts and lines of thought that are rife with potential. It is important to stress that this overview is one which necessarily rejects a view of Marxism as a completed project which is available and can thus be appropriated and applied; rather it sees Marxism as a continuing project with rich seams to be opened up and developed.

The specific regional problem which underlies this chapter can be posed as revolving around the *specificity of law*. If law cannot be reduced to a simple or direct expression of economic relations and processes, then we must enquire as to the impact or effectivity of law and legislation in the development and transformation of the economic process. Nowhere is the approach more important than in the opening section which is concerned with the role of law in the transition from feudalism to capitalism. The emergence of a capitalist mode of production requires not only a generalized system of commodity production with circulation based on exchange value. This element by itself is perfectly consistent with the classical model of primitive accumulation. It is important to emphasize that Marx insisted that the development of capitalism was not, in this sense, 'natural'; that it was not simply a result of extension of commodity relations plus primitive accumulation. Thus capitalism cannot be accounted for as a process of the internal and necessary evolution consequent upon the decline of the feudal mode of production.[1]

In addition to the extension of commodity relations, a second process is also required, namely, the creation of 'free labour' or the separation of agricultural workers from the land in such a way that they become 'available' for industrial employment. The role of law in this process can be approached through an examination of the contention advanced by Hindess and Hirst (1977), who argue that law is one of the 'conditions of existence' of the development and reproduction of the capitalist mode of production. Law is conceived not as an agent or bearer of a process whose determination resides in the unfolding of an economic process. Rather it is a necessary, indispensable and independent presence which has specific effects or consequences which are a precondition of the transition from feudalism to capitalism. The effectivity of law is two-fold; first legislation shatters the remnants of feudal relations, expropriates the agricultural labourers and through the coercion of the landless poor creates a potential labour force available for capitalist production. Second, laws provide the necessary contractual framework within which labour-power itself is transformed into a commodity.

However, the utilization of the concept 'conditions of existence' is not without serious problems and major consequences for Marxist social theory. Marxist theory has always claimed some priority for the economic level; the form of nature of that priority is variously interpreted, whether it be as a primary 'causation', a 'determinant' (whether in the first or the last instance), or a methodological priority. Implicit in the analysis by Hindess and Hirst is a repudiation of the *priority of the economic*, whatever the form of that priority.[2] The question that needs to be resolved is whether the abolition of the priority of the economic leads to a fundamental rupture with Marxist theory itself. This requires an answer to the question of whether the conceptualization of 'conditions of existence' as independent of autonomous elements within social processes does not inevitably lead back to an empiricism in which there is an infinite number of potential variables whose 'weight' can only be determined within a positivist mode of enquiry. These problems are clearly of great importance and go to the very heart of Marxist theory.

The texts selected provide no definitive answer to these questions. They draw heavily from Chapters 27 and 28 of *Capital* I concerning the expropriation of the agricultural population. What stands out is the complex manner in which legislation, stretching from the fifteenth to the nineteenth century, plays a determinant role in a generalized historical process. But this legislation cannot be reduced to a general strategy conceived in advance. The individual legislative acts have their own specific historical context and incorporate both contradictory features and effects, in that while they facilitate rural expropriation, they often expressly recognize the traditional rights of the rural population. Legislation is both an active agency in historical processes and, at the same time, it records and encapsulates the balance between social forces at particular historical moments and the ideological forms in which these struggles are fought out.

While each piece of legislation is specific in its historical genesis, the process of land enclosure and clearance goes hand in hand with the growing severity of laws against vagrancy; they combine in their effects to drive the expropriated population towards the labour market and to induce the forms of labour discipline requisite for the capitalist organization of production.[3] It emerges from some of the passages that legislation may have no necessary consequences or impact, and thereby indicates the limits of legal effectivity. This recognition poses as a problem in any historical analysis of the effectivity of legislation the question of the necessary conditions for specific effects to be realized, and of the wider problem that these effects are to be identified at all levels whether economic, social, political or ideological. Law is not confined in its effectivity to the level to which its appears to relate.

A comment should be made at this stage about the work of Karl Renner, the Austrian Marxist. His book, *The Institutions of Private Property and Their Social Function*,[4] has for a long time had an important status as a text on the Marxist theory of law; its status has largely derived from the fact that it was one of the very few works available in English which attempted to approach law from a Marxist perspective. He deals not only with the transition from feudalism, but also with the transformation of industrial capitalism. His primary thesis is that the transition was effected without a fundamental rupture of the substantive law. The legal regulation of commodity relations was effected through the application of a substantive law developed within the feudal period. He points to a 'functional transformation' in the role of the substantive law that occurs without any outward change in the legal norms themselves; this transformation is effected by an extension of the contractual form and, in particular, of the contract of employment. The position that he advances, while apparently staying close to Marx' method of exposition in *Capital*, is much closer to functionalist social theory than it is to Marxism in that his starting point is the trans-historical proposition that legal institutions fulfil "one function which comprises all others, that of the preservation of the species".[5] This tendency calls into question Renner's unquestioned status as a leading exponent of the Marxist theory of law.

The second section of this chapter is more diverse but it seeks to capture the complex relationship between law and bourgeois economic interests. The most important feature emerges in the passages which concern the factory legislation in nineteenth-century England; here we see the application of a full analysis which extends and builds upon the basic class thesis. This legislation embodies basic contradictions that are important not only for the specific historical analysis, which is the most extensive and thorough analysis that Marx provides of the genesis and impact of legislation; but it is also important with reference to the general relations between law and the class struggle.[6] On the one hand legislation governing the hours of labour emerges as an historically imposed necessity for the *general* conditions of existence of the capitalist mode of production. The expansion of surplus value through the physical intensification and duration of labour runs into conflict with the general necessity of reproducing a healthy labour force. The necessity for legislative protection of labour is a requirement of the capitalist class *as a whole*, but it is resisted and evaded by many individual capitalists and by sections of the capitalist class. This interplay determines the extent and the form of the evasion of the legislation by employers and the skewing of its enforcement through the courts; the effectivity of the legislation stems not from its content alone but from the conditions of its application. The legislation had an important, albeit unintended consequence; it facilitated and accelerated the process of development of factory production as against the manufacturing system which could not survive once it was no longer able to drive its workers for longer and longer hours. In other words the Factory Acts facilitated the pace of development and rationalization of capitalist production.

The third section concerns law and property relations. It should be stressed that this section is not intended to cover the very considerable volume of writing by both Marx and Engels on property relations. Marx and Engels both wrote extensively on the question of property. As a consequence, we have not been able nor felt it desirable to include anything other than the barest sample. Thus we start with the "Economic and Philosophic Manuscripts" in which private property is the expression of estrangement or alienation, but where it is also important to stress that emphasis is laid firmly upon the social character and forms of such relations. A very large body of their writing on property has an historical and developmental point of reference; this is particularly true of the *Grundrisse* and of "Origin of the Family." While boundaries are often inflexible we have kept our primary object as the writings of Marx and Engels on law.

In extracting from the writings on property, our intention has been to focus on a central question for a Marxist theory of law, namely the nature of the connection between 'economic relations' and the legal form of 'property relations'. The nature of the relationship between forms of property, what we may designate as 'real economic relations' and the legal form of property relations, 'juridical relations', is not systematically explored by Marx and Engels. It will be recalled that in the 1859 Preface, Marx makes reference to "the existing relations of production, or—what is but a legal expression for the same thing—with property relations".[7] The equation of 'economic relations' and 'juridical relations' is not always present in their writing. For example, while the above formulation suggests that law merely gives expression to existing economic relations, in the passage from *Grundrisse* (p. 94) law is presented as having an effectivity in the fixing and fossilizing of a particular distribution of property. This and other passages give hints towards the necessity of a more rigorous analysis of the relation between 'economic' and 'juridical relations'. In particular it points to the need to explore the non-isomorphic relationship between these relations; such an examination has importance for the concepts of 'ownership' and 'possession'. Thus in their discussion of property, the dualism is repeated between an interpretation of legal relations as constitutive of the economic level and legal relations as a consequence of economic relations.[8]

The general feature which emerges from Marx' and Engels' discussion of property is their emphasis upon the social origin and character of property and property relations. The continuing historical clash with the idealist tradition, taken up later in a different form in the polemics against Proudhon, made it imperative to rebut the conception of property as an independent or abstract emergent principle. Thus they rejected taking legal forms, conceived as relations of volition, as the starting point; instead they focus on property relations as social relations located within specific production relations. Law not only reflects these *real* social relations but it also represents them in specific forms. Here the overlap with the discussion of law and ideology in Chapter 4 should be noted. The focus is upon the ideological process through which law both hides and universalizes real relations, or in the language of the early writings, objectivizes estranged or alienated relations.

The final section concerns the regulation of labour. It collects together a number of passages, generally of a descriptive character, concerning the use of systems of 'private law', embodied in factory disciplinary codes used in the control and regulation of labour. This treatment is not linked to the discussion of public or legislative regulations of labour discussed above, except for the comment that the legal fiction of equality in the contract of employment conceals the oppression of labour inherent within the factory system, as epitomized in the employers' 'private law'.

Notes

1. See the classical debate on the transition to capitalism in Hilton, R. (ed.) (1976) *The Transition from Feudalism to Capitalism*, New Left Books, London; and the more recent intervention by Hindess, B. and Hirst, P. (1975) *Pre-Capitalist Modes of Production*, Routledge and Kegan Paul, London (in particular Chapter 6).
2. See for the most explicit presentation of this position Hindess, B. and Hirst, P. (1977) *Mode of Production and Social Formation*, Macmillan, London.
3. The contradictory nature of the intervention of law in this process, full of unexpected and unintended consequences, is brilliantly brought out in Thompson, E. P. (1975) *Whigs and Hunters: The Origin of the Black Acts*, Allen Lane, London; and in the companion volume, Hay, D. *et al.* (1975) *Albion's Fatal Tree*, Allen Lane, London.
4. Renner, K. (1948, 1976) *The Institutions of Private Property and their Social Function*. Routledge and Kegan Paul, London.
5. Renner, K. *ibid.*, 70.
6. See for fuller discussion of this relationship, Hunt, A. (1976) Law, State and Class Struggle, *Marxism Today* **20**, 178–187.
7. *MESW (2)*, I, 503–504.
8. See the recent discussion by Bettleheim, C. (1976) *Economic Calculation and Forms of Property*, Routledge and Kegan Paul, London; and Cutler, A., Hindess, B., Hirst, P. and Hussain, A. (1977) *Marx's 'Capital' and Capitalism Today*, Routledge and Kegan Paul, London (in particular Chapters 10 and 11).

Extracts

Law and the Transition to Capitalism

MARX, *Grundrisse*, 508–509.

The other circumstances which e.g. in the sixteenth century increased the mass of circulating commodities as well as that of money, which created new needs and thereby raised the exchange value of indigenous products etc., raised prices etc., all of these promoted on one side the dissolution of the old relations of production, sped up the separation of the worker or non-worker but able-bodied individual from the objective conditions of his reproduction, and thus promoted the transformation of money into capital. There can therefore be nothing more ridiculous than to conceive this *original formation* of capital as if capital had stockpiled and created the *objective conditions of production*—necessaries, raw materials, instrument—and then offered them to the worker, who was *bare* of these possessions. Rather, monetary wealth in part helped to *strip* the labour powers of able-bodied individuals from these conditions; and in part this process of divorce proceeded without it. When the formation of capital had reached a certain level, monetary wealth could place itself as mediator between the objective conditions of life, thus liberated, and the liberated but also *homeless* and *empty-handed* labour powers, and buy the latter with the former. But now, as far as the *formation of money-wealth* itself is concerned, this belongs to the prehistory of the bourgeois economy. Usury, trade, urbanization and the treasury rising with it play the main roles here. So, too, *hoarding* by tenants, peasants etc.; although to a lesser degree.—This shows at the same time that the development of exchange and of exchange value, which is everywhere mediated through trade, or whose mediation may be termed trade—money achieves an independent existence in the merchant estate, as does circulation in trade—brings with it both the dissolution of *labour's relations of property in its* conditions of existence, in one respect, and at the same time the dissolution of *labour* which is itself *classed as one of the objective conditions of production*; all these are relations which express a predominance of use value and of production directed towards use value, as well as of a real community which is itself still directly present as a presupposition of production. Production based on exchange value and the community based on the exchange of these exchange values—even though they seem, as we saw in the previous chapter on money, to posit property as the outcome of *labour* alone, and to posit private property over the product of one's own labour as condition—and labour as general condition of wealth, all presuppose and produce the separation of labour from its objective conditions. This exchange of equivalents proceeds; it is only the surface layer of a production which rests on the appropriation of alien labour *without exchange*, but with the *semblance of exchange*.

MARX, *ibid.*, 769–770.

The forcible transformation of the greater part of the population into wage labourers, and the discipline which transforms their existence into that of mere labourers, correspond to the first form. Throughout a period of 150 years, e.g. from Henry VII on, the annals of English legislation contain the bloody handwriting of coercive measures employed to transform the mass of the population, after they had become propertyless and free, into free wage labourers. The dissolution of the monastic orders, the confiscation of church lands, the abolition of the guilds and confiscation of their property, the forcible ejection of the population from the land through the transformation of tillage into pasture, enclosures of commons etc., had posited the labourers as mere labour capacities. But they now of course preferred vagabondage, beggary etc. to wage labour, and had still to be accustomed forcibly to the latter. This is repeated in a similar fashion with the introduction of large industry, of factories operating with machines.

Only at a certain stage of the development of capital does *the exchange of capital and labour become in fact formally free*. One can say that wage labour is completely realized in form in England only at the end of the eighteenth century, with the repeal of the law of apprenticeship.

See also MARX, *ibid.*, 507.

MARX, *Capital* I, 672–693.

The prelude of the revolution that laid the foundation of the capitalist mode of production, was played in the last third of the 15th, and the first decade of the 16th century. A mass of free proletarians was hurled on the labour-market by the breaking-up of the bands of feudal retainers, who, as Sir James Steuart well says, "everywhere uselessly filled house and castle." Although the royal power, itself a product of bourgeois development, in its strife after absolute sovereignty forcibly hastened on the dissolution of these bands of retainers, it was by no means the sole cause of it. In insolent conflict with king and parliament, the great feudal lords created an incomparably larger proletariat by the forcible driving of the peasantry from the land, to which the latter had the same feudal right as the lord himself, and by the usurpation of the common lands. The rapid rise of the Flemish wool manufactures, and the corresponding rise in the price of wool in England, gave the direct impulse to these evictions. The old nobility had been devoured by the great feudal wars. The new nobility was the child of its time, for which money was the power of all powers. Transformation of arable land into sheepwalks was, therefore, its cry. Harrison, in his "Description of England, prefixed to Holinshed's Chronicles," describes how the expropriation of small peasants is ruining the country. "What care our great encroachers?" The dwellings of the peasants and the cottages of the labourers were razed to the ground or doomed to decay. "If," says Harrison, "the old records of euerie manour be sought . . . it will soon appear that in some manour seventeene, eighteene, or twentie houses are shrunk . . . that England was neuer less furnished with people than at the present. . . . Of cities and townes either utterly decaied or more than a quarter or half diminished, though some one be a little increased here or there; of townes pulled downe for sheepe-walks, and no more but the lordship now standing in them. . . . I could saie somewhat." The complaints of these old chroniclers are always exaggerated, but they reflect faithfully the impression made on contemporaries by the revolution in the conditions of production. A comparison of the writings of Chancellor Fortescue and Thomas More reveals the gulf between the 15th and 16th century. As Thornton rightly has it, the English working-class was precipitated without any transition from its golden into its iron age.

Legislation was terrified at this revolution. It did not yet stand on that height of civilisation where the "wealth of the nation" (*i.e.*, the formation of capital, and the reckless exploitation and impoverishing of the mass of the people) figure as the *ultima Thule* of all state-craft. In his history of Henry VII., Bacon says: "Inclosures at that time (1489) began to be more frequent, whereby arable land (which could not be manured without people and families) was turned into pasture, which was easily rid by a few herdsmen; and tenancies for years, lives, and at will (whereupon much of the yeomanry lived) were turned into demesnes. . . . An Act of Henry VII., 1489, cap. 19, forbad the destruction of all "houses of husbandry" to which at least 20 acres of land belonged. By an Act, 25 Henry VIII., the same law was renewed. It recites, among other things, that many farms and large flocks of cattle, especially of sheep, are concentrated in the hands of a few men, whereby the rent of land has much risen and tillage has fallen off, churches and houses have been pulled down, and marvellous numbers of people have been deprived of the means wherewith to maintain themselves and their families. The Act, therefore, ordains the rebuilding of the decayed farm-steads, and fixes a proportion between corn land and pasture land, &c. An Act of 1533 recites that some owners possess 24,000 sheep, and limits the number to be owned to 2,000. The cry of the people and the legislation directed, for 150 years after Henry VII., against the expropriation of the small farmers and peasants, were alike fruitless. The secret of their inefficiency Bacon, without knowing it, reveals to us. "The device of King Henry VII.," says Bacon, in his "Essays, Civil and Moral," Essay 29, "was profound and admirable, in making farms and houses of husbandry of a standard; that is, maintained with such a proportion of land unto them as may breed a subject to live in convenient plenty, and no servile condition, and to keep the plough in the hands of the owners and not mere hirelings." What the capitalist system demanded was, on the other hand, a degraded and almost servile condition of the mass of the people, the transformation of them into mercenaries, and of their means of labour into capital. During this transformation period, legislation also strove to retain the 4 acres of land by the cottage of the agricultural wage-labourer, and forbad him to take lodgers into his cottage. In the reign of James I., 1627, Roger Crocker of Front Mill, was condemned for having built a cottage on the manor of Front Mill without 4 acres of land attached to the same in perpetuity. As late as Charles I.'s reign, 1638, a royal commission was appointed to enforce the carrying out of the old laws, especially that referring to the 4 acres of land. Even in Cromwell's time, the building of a house within 4 miles of London was forbidden unless it was endowed with 4 acres of land. As late as the first half of the 18th century complaint is made if the cottage of the agricultural labourer has not an adjunct of one or two acres of land. Nowadays he is lucky if it is furnished with a little garden, or if he may rent, far away from his cottage a few roods. "Landlords and farmers," says Dr. Hunter, "work here hand in hand. A few acres to the cottage would make the labourers too independent."

The process of forcible expropriation of the people received in the 16th century a new and frightful impulse from the Reformation, and from the consequent colossal spoliation of the church property. . . . The legally guaranteed property of the poorer folk in a part of the church's tithes was tacitly confiscated. "Pauper ubique jacet," cried Queen Elizabeth, after a journey through England. In the 43rd year of her reign the nation was obliged to recognize pauperism officially by the introduction of a poor-rate. "The authors of this law seem to have been ashamed to state the grounds of it, for [contrary to traditional usage] it has no preamble whatever." By the 16th of Charles I., ch. 4, it was declared perpetual, and in fact only in 1834 did it take a new and harsher form.* These immediate results of the Reformation were not its most lasting ones. The property of the church formed the religious bulwark of the traditional conditions of landed property. With its fall these were no longer tenable.

---

* The "spirit" of Protestantism may be seen from the following, among other things. In the south of England certain landed proprietors and well-to-do farmers put their heads together and propounded ten questions as to the right interpretation of the poor-law of Elizabeth. These they laid before a celebrated jurist of that time, Sergeant Snigge (later a judge under James I.) for his opinion. "Question 9—Some of the more wealthy farmers in the parish have devised a skilful mode by which all the trouble of executing this Act (the 43rd of Elizabeth) might be avoided. They have proposed that we shall erect a prison in the parish, and then give notice to the neighbourhood, that if any persons are disposed to farm the poor of this parish, they do give in sealed proposals, on a certain day, of the lowest price at which they will take them off our hands; and that they will be authorised to refuse to any one unless he be shut up in the aforesaid prison. The proposers of this plan conceive that there will be found in the adjoining counties, persons, who, being unwilling to labour

Even in the last decade of the 17th century, the yeomanry, the class of independent peasants, were more numerous than the class of farmers. They had formed the backbone of Cromwell's strength, and, even according to the confession of Macaulay, stood in favourable contrast to the drunken squires and to their servants, the country clergy, who had to marry their masters' cast-off mistresses. About 1750, the yeomanry had disappeared, and so had, in the last decade of the 18th century, the last trace of the common land of the agricultural labourer. We leave on one side here the purely economic causes of the agricultural revolution. We deal only with the forcible means employed.

After the restoration of the Stuarts, the landed proprietors carried, by legal means, an act of usurpation, effected everywhere on the Continent without any legal formality. They abolished the feudal tenure of land, *i.e.*, they got rid of all its obligations to the State, "indemnified" the State by taxes on the peasantry and the rest of the mass of the people, vindicated for themselves the rights of modern private property in estates to which they had only a feudal title, and, finally, passed those laws of settlement, which *mutatis mutandis*, had the same effect on the English agricultural labourer, as the edict of the Tartar Boris Godunof on the Russian peasantry.

The "glorious Revolution" brought into power, along with William of Orange, the landlord and capitalist appropriators of surplus-value.

---

and not possessing substance or credit to take a farm or ship, so as to live without labour, may be induced to make a very advantageous offer to the parish. If any of the poor perish under the contractor's care, the sin will lie at his door, as the parish will have done its duty by them. We are, however, apprehensive that the present Act (43rd of Elizabeth) will not warrant a prudential measure of this kind; but you are to learn that the rest of the freeholders of the county, and of the adjoining county of B, will very readily join in instructing their members to propose an Act to enable the parish to contract with a person to lock up and work the poor; and to declare that if any person shall refuse to be so locked up and worked, he shall be entitled to no relief. This, it is hoped, will prevent persons in distress from wanting relief, and be the means of keeping down parishes." (R. Blakey: "The History of Political Literature from the Earliest Times." Lond., 1855. Vol. II., pp. 84–85.) In Scotland, the abolition of serfdom took place some centuries later than in England. Even in 1698, Fletcher of Saltoun, declared in the Scotch parliament, "The number of beggars in Scotland is reckoned at not less than 200,000. The only remedy that I, a republican on principle, can suggest, is to restore the old state of serfdom, to make slaves of all those who are unable to provide for their own subsistence." Eden, l. c., Book 1., ch. 1, pp. 60–61, says, "The decrease of villenage seems necessarily to have been the era of the origin of the poor. Manufactures and commerce are the two parents of our national poor." Eden, like our Scotch republican on principle, errs only in this: not the abolition of villenage, but the abolition of the property of the agricultural labourer in the soil made him a proletarian, and eventually a pauper. In France, where the expropriation was effected in another way, the ordonnance of Moulins, 1566, and the Edict of 1656, correspond to the English poor-laws.

They inaugurated the new era by practising on a colossal scale thefts of state lands, thefts that had been hitherto managed more modestly. These estates were given away, sold at a ridiculous figure, or even annexed to private estates by direct seizure. All this happened without the slightest observation of legal etiquette. The Crown lands thus fraudulently appropriated, together with the robbery of the Church estates, as far as these had not been lost again during the republican revolution, form the basis of the to-day princely domains of the English oligarchy. The bourgeois capitalists favoured the operation with the view, among others, to promoting free trade in land, to extending the domain of modern agriculture on the large farm-system, and to increasing their supply of the free agricultural proletarians ready to hand. Besides, the new landed aristocracy was the natural ally of the new bankocracy, of the newly-hatched *haute finance*, and of the large manufacturers, then depending on protective duties. . . . .

We have seen how the forcible usurpation of this, generally accompanied by the turning of arable into pasture land, begins at the end of the 15th and extends into the 16th century. But, at that time, the process was carried on by means of individual acts of violence against which legislation, for a hundred and fifty years, fought in vain. The advance made by the 18th century shows itself in this, that the law itself becomes now the instrument of the theft of the people's land, although the large farmers make use of their little independent methods as well. The parliamentary form of the robbery is that of Acts for enclosures of Commons, in other words, decrees by which the landlords grant themselves the people's land as private property, decrees of expropriation of the people. Sir F. M. Eden refutes his own crafty special pleading, in which he tries to represent communal property as the private property of the great landlords who have taken the place of the feudal lords, when he, himself, demands a "general Act of Parliament for the enclosure of Commons" (admitting thereby that a parliamentary *coup d'état* is necessary for its transformation into private property), and moreover calls on the legislature for the indemnification for the expropriated poor.

In the 19th century, the very memory of the connexion between the agricultural labourer and the communal property had, of course, vanished. To say nothing of more recent times, have the agricultural population received a farthing of compensation for the 3,511,770 acres of common land which between 1801 and 1831 were stolen from them and by parliamentary devices presented to the landlords by the landlords?

The last process of wholesale expropriation of the agricultural population from the soil is, finally, the so-called clearing of estates, *i.e.*, the sweeping men off them. All the English methods hitherto considered culminated in "clearing." As we saw in the picture of modern conditions given in a former chapter, where there are no more independent peasants to get rid of, the "clearing" of cottages begins; so that the agricultural labourers do not find on the soil cultivated by them even the spot necessary for their own housing. But what "clearing of estates" really and properly signifies, we learn only in the promised land of modern romance, the Highlands of Scotland. There the process is distinguished by its systematic character, by the magnitude of the scale on which it is carried out at one blow (in Ireland landlords have gone to the length of sweeping away several villages at once; in Scotland areas as large as German principalities are dealt with), finally by the peculiar form of property, under which the embezzled lands were held.

The Highland Celts were organised in clans, each of which was the owner of the land on which it was settled. The representative of the clan, its chief or "great man," was only the titular owner of this property, just as the Queen of England is the titular owner of all the national soil. When the English government succeeded in suppressing the intestine wars of these "great men," and their constant incursions into the Lowland plains, the chiefs of the clans by no means gave up their time-honoured trade as robbers; they only changed its form. On their own authority they transformed their nominal right into a right of private property, and as this brought them into collision with their clansmen, resolved to drive them out by open force. . . . In the 18th century the hunted-out Gaels were forbidden to emigrate from the country, with a view to driving them by force to Glasgow and other manufacturing towns. As an example of the method obtaining in the 19th century, the "clearing" made by the Duchess of Sutherland will suffice here. This person, well instructed in economy, resolved, on entering upon her government, to effect a radical cure, and to turn the whole country, whose population had already been, by earlier processes of the like kind, reduced to 15,000, into a sheep-walk. From 1814 to 1820 these 15,000 inhabitants, about 3,000 families, were systematically hunted and rooted out. All their villages were destroyed and burnt, all their fields turned into pasturage. British soldiers enforced this eviction, and came to blows with the inhabitants. One old woman was burnt to death in the flames of the hut, which she refused to leave. Thus this fine lady appropriated 794,000 acres of land that had from time immemorial belonged to the clan. She assigned to the expelled inhabitants about 6,000 acres on the sea-shore—2 acres per family. The 6,000 acres had until this time lain waste, and brought in no income to their owners. The Duchess, in the nobility of her heart, actually went so far as to let these at an average rent of 2s. 6d. per acre to the clansmen, who for centuries had shed their blood for her family. The whole of the stolen clanland she divided into 29 great sheep farms, each inhabited by a single family, for the most part imported English farm-servants. In the year 1835 the 15,000 Gaels were already replaced by 131,000 sheep. The remnant of the aborigines flung on the sea-shore, tried to live by catching fish. They became amphibious and lived, as an English author says, half on land and half on water, and withal only half on both.

But the brave Gaels must expiate yet more bitterly their idolatry, romantic and of the mountains, for the "great men" of the clan. The smell of their fish rose to the noses of the great men. They scented some profit in it, and let the sea-shore to the great fishmongers of London. For the second time the Gaels were hunted out.

The spoliation of the church's property, the fraudulent alienation of the State domains, the robbery of the common lands, the usurpation of feudal and clan property, and its transformation into modern private property under circumstances of reckless terrorism, were just so many idyllic methods of primitive accumulation. They conquered the field for capitalistic agriculture, made the soil part and parcel of capital, and created for the town industries the necessary supply of a "free" and outlawed proletariat.

CHAPTER XXVIII

BLOODY LEGISLATION AGAINST THE EXPROPRIATED, FROM THE END OF THE 15TH CENTURY. FORCING DOWN OF WAGES BY ACTS OF PARLIAMENT

The proletariat created by the breaking up of the bands of feudal retainers and by the forcible expropriation of the people from the soil, this "free" proletariat could not possibly be absorbed by the nascent manufactures as fast as it was thrown upon the world. On the other hand, these men, suddenly dragged from their wonted mode of life, could not as suddenly adapt themselves to the discipline of their new condition. They were turned *en masse* into beggars, robbers, vagabonds, partly from inclination, in most cases from stress of circumstances. Hence at the end of the 15th and during the whole of the 16th century, throughout Western Europe a bloody legislation against vagabondage. The fathers of the present working-class were chastised for their enforced transformation into vagabonds and paupers. Legislation treated them as "voluntary" criminals, and assumed that it depended on their own good will to go on working under the old conditions that no longer existed.

In England this legislation began under Henry VII.

Henry VIII. 1530: Beggars old and unable to work receive a beggar's licence. On the other hand, whipping and imprisonment for sturdy vagabonds. They are to be tied to the cart-tail and whipped until the blood streams from their bodies, then to swear an oath to go back to their birthplace or to where they have lived the last three years and to "put themselves to labour." What grim irony! In 27 Henry VIII. the former statute is repeated, but strengthened with new clauses. For the second arrest for vagabondage the whipping is to be repeated and half the ear sliced off; but for the third relapse the offender is to be executed as a hardened criminal and enemy of the common weal.

Edward VI.: A statute of the first year of his reign, 1547, ordains that if anyone refuses to work, he shall be condemned as a slave to the person who had denounced him as an idler. The master shall feed his slave on bread and water, weak broth and such refuse meat as he thinks fit. He has the right to force him to do any work, no matter how disgusting, with whip and chains. If the slave is absent a fortnight, he is condemned to slavery for life and is to be branded on forehead or back with the letter S; if he runs away thrice, he is to be executed as a felon. The master can sell him, bequeath him, let him out on hire as a slave, just as any other personal chattell or cattle. If the slaves attempt anything against the masters, they are also to be executed. Justices of the peace, on information, are to hunt the rascals down. If it happens that a vagabond has been idling about for three days, he is to be taken to his birthplace, branded with a redhot iron with the letter V on the breast and be set to work, in chains, in the streets or at some other labour. If the vagabond gives a false birthplace, he is then to become the slave for life of this place, of its inhabitants, or its corporation, and to be branded with an S. All persons have the right to take away the children of the vagabonds and to keep them as apprentices, the young men until the 24th year, the girls until the 20th. If they run away, they are to become up to this age the slaves of their masters, who can put them in irons, whip them, &c., if they like. Every master may put an iron ring round the neck, arms or legs of his slave, by which to know him more easily and to be more certain of him. The last part of this statute provides, that certain poor people may be employed by a place or by persons, who are willing to give them food and drink and to find them work. This kind of parish-slaves was kept up in England until far into the 19th century under the name of "roundsmen."

Elizabeth, 1572: Unlicensed beggars above 14 years of age are to be severely flogged and branded on the left ear unless some one will take them into service for two years; in case of a repetition of the offence, if they are over 18, they are to be executed, unless some one will take them into service for two years; but for the third offence they are to be executed without mercy as felons. Similar statutes: 18 Elizabeth. c. 13. and another of 1597.

James I: Any one wandering about and begging is declared a rogue and a vagabond. Justices of the peace in petty sessions are authorised to have them publicly whipped and for the first offence to imprison them for 6 months, for the second for 2 years. Whilst in prison they are to be whipped as much and as often as the justices of the peace think fit. . . . Incorrigible and dangerous rogues are to be branded with an R on the left shoulder and set to hard labour, and if they are caught begging again, to be executed without mercy. These statutes, legally binding until the beginning of the 18th century, were only repealed by 12 Anne, c. 23.

Similar laws in France, where by the middle of the 17th century a kingdom of vagabonds (truands) was established in Paris. Even at the beginning of Louis XVI.'s reign (Ordinance of July 13th, 1777) every man in good health from 16 to 60 years of age, if without means of subsistence and of practising a trade, is to be sent to the galleys. Of the same nature are the statute of Charles V. for the Netherlands (October, 1537), the first edict of the States and Towns of Holland (March 10, 1614), the "Plakaat" of the United Provinces (June 26, 1649), &c.

Thus were the agricultural people, first forcibly expropriated from the soil, driven from their homes, turned into vagabonds, and then whipped, branded, tortured by laws grotesquely terrible, into the discipline necessary for the wage system.

It is not enough that the conditions of labour are concentrated in a mass, in the shape of capital, at the one pole of society, while at the other are grouped masses of men, who have nothing to sell but their labour-power. Neither is it enough that they are compelled to sell it voluntarily. The advance of capitalist production develops a working-class, which by education, tradition, habit, looks upon the conditions of that mode of production as self-evident laws of Nature. The organisation of the capitalist process of production, once fully developed, breaks down all resistance. The constant generation of a relative surplus-population keeps the law of supply and demand of labour, and therefore keeps wages, in a rut that corresponds with the wants of capital. The dull compulsion of economic relations completes the subjection of the labourer to the capitalist. Direct force, outside economic conditions, is of course still used, but only exceptionally. In the ordinary run of things, the labourer can be left to the "natural laws of production," *i.e.*, to his dependence on capital, a dependence springing from, and guaranteed in perpetuity by, the conditions of production themselves. It is otherwise during the historic genesis of capitalist production. The bourgeoisie, at its rise, wants and uses the power of the state to "regulate" wages, *i.e.*, to force them within the limits suitable for surplus-value making, to lengthen the working-day and to keep the labourer himself in the normal degree of dependence. This is an essential element of the so-called primitive accumulation.

.   .   .   .

Legislation on wage-labour (from the first, aimed at the exploitation of the labourer and, as it advanced, always equally hostile to him), is started in England by the Statute of Labourers, of Edward III., 1349.

.   .   .   .

The Statute of Labourers was passed at the urgent instance of the House of Commons. A Tory says naïvely: "Formerly the poor demanded such *high* wages as to threaten industry and wealth. Next, their wages are so *low* as to threaten industry and wealth equally and perhaps more, but in another way." A tariff of wages are fixed by law for town and country, for piece-work and day-work. The agricultural labourers were to hire themselves out by the year, the town ones "in open market." It was forbidden, under pain of imprisonment, to pay higher wages than those fixed by the statute, but the taking of higher wages was more severely punished than the giving them. [So also in Section 18 and 19 of the Statute of Apprentices of Elizabeth, ten days' imprisonment is decreed for him that pays the higher wages, but twenty-one days for him that receives them.] A statute of 1360 increased the penalties and authorised the masters to extort labour at the legal rate of wages by corporal punishment. All combinations, contracts, oaths, &c., by which masons and carpenters reciprocally bound themselves, were declared null and void. Coalition of the labourers is treated as a heinous crime from the 14th century to 1825, the year of the repeal of the laws against Trades' Unions. The spirit of the Statute of Labourers of 1349 and of its offshoots, comes out clearly in the fact, that indeed a maximum of wages is dictated by the State, but on no account a minimum.

In the 16th century, the condition of the labourers had, as we know, become much worse. The money wage rose, but not in proportion to the depreciation of money and the corresponding rise in the prices of commodities. Wages, therefore, in reality fell. Nevertheless, the laws for keeping them down remained in force, together with the ear-clipping and branding of those "whom no one was willing to take into service." By the Statute of Apprentices 5 Elizabeth, c. 3, the justices of the peace were empowered to fix certain wages and to modify them according to the time of the year and the price of commodities. James I. extended these regulations of labour also to weavers, spinners, and all possible categories of workers.* George II. extended the laws against coalitions of labourers to manufacturers. In the manufacturing period *par excellence*, the capitalist mode of production had become sufficiently strong to render legal regulation of wages as impracticable as it was unnecessary; but the ruling classes were unwilling in case of necessity to be without the weapons of the old arsenal. Still, 8 George II. forbade a higher day's wage than 2s. 7½d. for journeymen tailors in and around London, except in cases of general mourning; still, 13 George III., c. 68, gave the regulation of the wages of silk-weavers to the justices of the peace; still, in 1706, it required

---

* From a clause of Statute 2 James 1., c. 6, we see that certain clothmakers took upon themselves to dictate, in their capacity of justices of the peace, the official tariff of wages in their own shops. In Germany, especially after the Thirty Years' War, statutes for keeping down wages were general. "The want of servants and labourers was very troublesome to the landed proprietors in the depopulated districts. All villagers were forbidden to let rooms to single men and women; all the latter were to be reported to the authorities and cast into prison if they were unwilling to become servants, even if they were employed at any other work, such as sowing seeds for the peasants at a daily wage, or even buying and selling corn. (Imperial privileges and sanctions for Silesia, I., 25.) For a whole century in the decrees of the small German potentates a bitter cry goes up again and again about the wicked and impertinent rabble that will not reconcile itself to its hard lot, will not be content with the legal wage; the individual landed proprietors are forbidden to pay more than the State had fixed by a tariff. And yet the conditions of service were at times better after the war than 100 years later; the farm servants of Silesia had, in 1652, meat twice a week, whilst even in our century, districts are known where they have it only three times a year. Further, wages after the war were higher than in the following century." (G. Freytag.)

two judgments of the higher courts to decide, whether the mandates of justices of the peace as to wages held good also for non-agricultural labourers; still, in 1799, an act of Parliament ordered that the wages of the Scotch miners should continue to be regulated by a statute of Elizabeth and two Scotch acts of 1661 and 1671. How completely in the meantime circumstances had changed, is proved by an occurrence unheard-of before in the English Lower House. In that place, where for more than 400 years laws had been made for the maximum, beyond which wages absolutely must not rise, Whitbread in 1796 proposed a legal minimum wage for agricultural labourers. Pitt opposed this, but confessed that the "condition of the poor was cruel." Finally, in 1813, the laws for the regulation of wages were repealed. They were an absurd anomaly, since the capitalist regulated his factory by his private legislation, and could by the poor-rates make up the wage of the agricultural labourer to the indispensable minimum. . . . .

The barbarous laws against Trades' Unions fell in 1825 before the threatening bearing of the proletariat. Despite this, they fell only in part. Certain beautiful fragments of the old statute vanished only in 1859. Finally, the act of Parliament of June 29, 1871, made a pretence of removing the last traces of this class of legislation by legal recognition of Trades' Unions. But an act of Parliament of the same date (an act to amend the criminal law relating to violence, threats, and molestation), re-established, in point of fact, the former state of things in a new shape. By the Parliamentary escamotage the means which the labourers could use in a strike or lock-out were withdrawn from the laws common to all citizens, and placed under exceptional penal legislation, the interpretation of which fell to the masters themselves in their capacity as justices of the peace. Two years earlier, the same House of Commons and the same Mr. Gladstone in the well-known straightforward fashion brought in a bill for the abolition of all exceptional penal legislation against the working-class. But this was never allowed to go beyond the second reading, and the matter was thus protracted until at last the "great Liberal party," by an alliance with the Tories, found courage to turn against the very proletariat that had carried it into power. Not content with this treachery, the "great Liberal party" allowed the English judges, ever complaisant in the service of the ruling classes, to dig up again the earlier laws against "conspiracy," and to apply them to coalitions of labourers. We see that only against its will and under the pressure of the masses did the English Parliament give up the laws against Strikes and Trades' Unions, after it had itself, for 500 years, held, with shameless egoism, the position of a permanent Trades' Union of the capitalists against the labourers.

During the very first storms of the revolution, the French bourgeoisie dared to take away from the workers the right of association but just acquired. By a decree of June 14, 1791, they declared all coalition of the workers as "an attempt against liberty and the declaration of the rights of man," punishable by a fine of 500 livres, together with deprivation of the rights of an active citizen for one year. This law which, by means of State compulsion, confined the struggle between capital and labour within limits comfortable for capital, has outlived revolutions and changes of dynasties. Even the Reign of Terror left it untouched. It was but quite recently struck out of the Penal Code. Nothing is more characteristic than the pretext for this bourgeois *coup d'état*. "Granting," says Chapelier, the reporter of the Select Committee on this law, "that wages ought to be a little higher than they are, . . . that they ought to be high enough for him that receives them, to be free from that state of absolute dependence due to the want of the necessaries of life, and which is almost that of slavery," yet the workers must not be allowed to come to any understanding about their own interest, nor to act in common and thereby lessen their "absolute dependence, which is almost that of slavery;" because, forsooth, in doing this they injure "the freedom of their cidevant masters, the present entrepreneurs," and because a coalition against the despotism of the quondam masters of the corporations is—guess what!—is a restoration of the corporations abolished by the French constitution.

See also MARX/ENGELS, The German Ideology, *MECW* V, 68–69; MARX, *Capital* III, 196; ENGELS, *Anti-Dühring*, 226–228.

MARX, The Poverty of Philosophy, *MECW* VI, 188.

The automatic workshop opened its career with acts which were anything but philanthropic. Children were kept at work by means of the whip; they were made an object of traffic and contracts were undertaken with the orphanages. All the laws on the apprenticeship of workers were repealed, because, to use M. Proudhon's phraseology, there were no further need of *synthetic* workers. Finally, from 1825 onwards, almost all the new inventions were the result of collisions between the worker and the employer who sought at all costs to depreciate the worker's specialised ability. After each new strike of any importance, there appeared a new machine. So little indeed did the worker see in the application of machinery a sort of rehabilitation, *restoration*—as M. Proudhon would say—that in the eighteenth century he resisted for a very long time the incipient domination of automation.

MARX, The Bill Proposing the Abolition of Feudal Obligations, *Articles from NRZ*, 71–76.

Cologne, July 29. If any Rhinelander should have forgotten what he owes to the "foreign rule", to "the yoke of the Corsican tyrant", he ought to read the Bill providing for the abolition without compensation of various services and dues. The Bill has been submitted by Herr Hansemann in this year of grace 1848 for the "consideration" of his conciliators.

Liegedom, allodification rent, death dues, heriot, protection money, legal dues and fines, signet money, tithes on live-stock, bees, etc.—what a strange, what a barbaric ring these absurd terms have for our ears, which have been civilised by the French Revolution's destruction of feudalism and by the Code Napoléon. How incomprehensible to us is this farrago of medieval duties and taxes, this collection of musty junk from an antediluvian age.

Reading the Bill, it seems to you at first glance that our Minister of Agriculture Herr *Gierke*, on the orders of Herr Hansemann, has brought off a terrifically "bold stroke", has done away with the Middle Ages by a stroke of the pen, and of course quite gratuitously.

But when one looks at the Bill's *motivation*, one discovers that it sets out straight away to prove that *no* feudal obligations *whatever* ought to be abolished without compensation, that is to say, it starts with a bold assertion which directly contradicts the "bold stroke".

The minister's practical timidity now manoeuvres warily and prudently between these two bold postures. On the left "the general welfare" and "the demands of the spirit of our time"; on the right the "established rights of the lords of the manor"; in the middle the "praiseworthy idea of a freer development of rural relations" represented by Herr Gierke's shamefaced embarrassment—what a picture!

In short, Herr Gierke fully recognises that feudal obligations in general ought to be abolished only against compensation. Thus the most onerous, the most widespread, the principal obligations are to *continue* or, seeing that the peasants have in fact already done away with them, they are to be *reimposed*.

.   .   .   .

The revolution in the countryside consisted in the actual elimination of all feudal obligations. The government of action, which recognises the revolution, recognises it in the countryside by destroying it underhandedly. It is quite impossible to restore the old status quo completely; the peasants would promptly kill their feudal lords—even Herr Gierke realises that. An impressive list of insignificant feudal obligations existing only in a few places is therefore abolished, but the principal feudal obligation epitomised in the simple term *corvée* is revived.

.   .   .   .

As a result of all the rights that are to be abolished, the aristocracy will sacrifice less than 50,000 thaler a year, but will thereby save several million. Indeed the minister hopes that they will thus placate the peasants and even gain their votes at future parliamentary elections. This would really be a very good deal, provided Herr Gierke does not miscalculate.

In this way the objections of the peasants would be eliminated, and so would those of the aristocrats, in so far as they correctly understand their position. There remains the Chamber, the scruples of the inflexible legalists and radicals. The distinction between obligations that are to be abolished and those that are to be retained—which is simply the distinction between practically worthless obligations and very valuable obligations—must be based as regards the Chamber on some semblance of legal and economic justification. Herr Gierke must prove that the obligations to be abolished 1. have an insufficient inner justification, 2. are incompatible with the general welfare, 3. are incompatible with the demands of the spirit of our time, and 4. that their abolition is fundamentally no infringement of property rights, i.e., no expropriation without compensation.

In order to prove the insufficient justification of these dues and services Herr Gierke delves into the darkest recesses of feudal law. He invokes the entire, "originally very slow development of the Germanic states over a period of a thousand years". But what good will it do? The deeper he digs, the more he rakes up the stagnant mire of feudal law, the more does that feudal law prove that the obligations in question have, not an insufficient justification, but from the feudal point of view, a very solid justification. The hapless minister merely causes general amusement when he tries his hardest to induce feudal law to make cryptic pronouncements in the style of modern civil law, or to let the feudal lord of the twelfth century think and judge like a bourgeois of the nineteenth century.

.   .   .   .

It is hardly necessary to add that for the sake of consistency Herr Gierke constantly insinuates modern legal concepts into feudal legal regulations, and in an extremity he always invokes them. But if Herr Gierke evaluates some of these obligations in terms of the modern ideas of law, then it is incomprehensible why the same should not be done with all obligations. In that case, however, the corvée, faced with the freedom of the individual and of property, would certainly come off badly.

But there is another difficulty. Both in previous commutations of the obligations now to be abolished and in all other commutations, the peasants were flagrantly cheated in favour of the aristocracy by corrupt commissions. The peasants now demand the revision of all commutation agreements concluded under the previous government, and they are quite justified in doing so.

But Herr Gierke will have nothing to do with this, since "formal right and law are opposed" to it; such an attitude is altogether opposed to any progress, since every new law nullifies some old formal right and law.

.   .   .   .

It cannot be denied that, though the abolished obligations are quite insignificant, Herr Gierke, by abolishing them, secures "advantages to those under obligations by means that run counter to the eternal legal principles" and this is "directly opposed to formal right and law"; he "undermines the entire legal framework of landed property" and attacks the very foundation of the "most indubitable" rights.

Really, Herr Gierke, was it worth while to go to all this trouble and commit such a grievous sin in order to achieve such paltry results?

Herr Gierke does indeed *attack property*—that is quite indisputable—but it is feudal property he attacks, not modern, bourgeois property. By destroying feudal property he *strengthens* bourgeois property which arises on the ruins of feudal property. The only reason he does not want the commutation agreements revised is because by means of these contracts feudal ownership relations were converted into *bourgeois* ones, and consequently he cannot revise them without at the same time formally infringing bourgeois property. Bourgeois property is, of course, as sacred and inviolable as feudal property is vulnerable and—depending on the requirements and courage of the ministers—violable.

See also **MARX**, The Bourgeoisie and the Counter-revolution, *Articles from NRZ*, 179–180.

MARX, The Bourgeoisie and the Counter-revolution, *Articles from NRZ*, 183.*

The revolutions of 1648 and 1789 were not *English* and *French* revolutions, they were revolutions in the *European* fashion. They did not represent the victory of a *particular* social class over the *old political system*; they *proclaimed the political system of the new European society*. The bourgeoisie was victorious in these revolutions, but the *victory of the bourgeoisie* was at that time the *victory of a new social order*, the victory of bourgeois ownership over feudal ownership, of nationality over provincialism, of competition over the guild, of partitioning of the land over primogeniture, of the rule of the landowner over the domination of the owner of the land, of enlightenment over superstition, of the family over the family name, of industry over heroic idleness, of bourgeois law over medieval privileges.

Law and Bourgeois Economic Interests

ENGELS, Principles of Communism, *MECW* VI, 345–346.

Wherever large-scale industry replaced manufacture, the industrial revolution developed the bourgeoisie, its wealth and its power, to the highest degree and made it the first class in the land. The result was that wherever this happened, the bourgeoisie obtained political power and ousted the hitherto ruling classes—the aristocracy, the guild-burghers and the absolute monarchy representing both. The bourgeoisie annihilated the power of the aristocracy, the nobility, by abolishing entails or the ban on the sale of landed property, and all privileges of the nobility. It destroyed the power of the guild-burghers by abolishing all guilds and craft privileges. In place of both it put free competition, that is, a state of society in which everyone has the right to engage in any branch of

---

* For the full context of this extract, see pp. 220–221.

industry he likes, and where nothing can hinder him in carrying it on except lack of the necessary capital. The introduction of free competition is therefore the public declaration that henceforward the members of society are only unequal in so far as their capital is unequal, that capital has become the decisive power and therefore the capitalists, the bourgeois, have become the first class in society. But free competition is necessary for the beginning of large-scale industry since it is the only state of society in which large-scale industry can grow. The bourgeoisie having thus annihilated the social power of the nobility and the guild-burghers, annihilated their political power as well. Having become the first class in society, the bourgeoisie proclaimed itself also the first class in the political sphere. It did this by establishing the representative system, which rests upon bourgeois equality before the law and the legal recognition of free competition, and which in European countries was introduced in the form of constitutional monarchy. Under these constitutional monarchies those only are electors who possess a certain amount of capital, that is to say, the bourgeois; these bourgeois electors elect the deputies, and these bourgeois deputies, by means of the right to refuse taxes, elect a bourgeois government.

MARX, *Capital* I, 442–453.

The cheapening of labour-power, by sheer abuse of the labour of women and children, by sheer robbery of every normal condition requisite for working and living, and by the sheer brutality of over-work and night-work, meets at last with natural obstacles that cannot be overstepped. So also, when based on these methods, do the cheapening of commodities and capitalist exploitation in general. So soon as this point is at last reached—and it takes many years—the hour has struck for the introduction of machinery, and for the thenceforth rapid conversion of the scattered domestic industries and also of manufactures into factory industries. . . . .

The revolution in the industrial methods which is the necessary result of the revolution in the instruments of production is effected by a medley of transition forms. . . . .

The system actually prevalent in England is, that the capitalist concentrates a large number of machines on his premises, and then distributes the produce of those machines for further manipulation amongst the domestic workers. The variety of the transition forms, however, does not conceal the tendency to conversion into the factory system proper. . . . .

This industrial revolution which takes place spontaneously, is artificially helped on by the extension of the Factory Acts to all industries in which women, young persons and children are employed. The compulsory regulation of the working-day as regards its length, pauses, beginning and end, the system of relays of children, the exclusion of all children under a certain age, &c., necessitate on the one hand more machinery and the substitution of steam as a motive power in the place of muscles. On the other hand, in order to make up for the loss of time, an expansion occurs of the means of production used in common, of the furnaces, buildings, &c., in one word, greater concentration of the means of production and correspondingly greater concourse of workpeople. The chief objection, repeatedly and passionately urged on behalf of each manufacture threatened with the Factory Act, is in fact this, that in order to continue the business on the old scale a greater outlay of capital will be necessary. But as regards labour in the so-called domestic industries and the intermediate forms between them and Manufacture, so soon as limits are put to the working-day and to the employment of children, those industries go to the wall. Unlimited exploitation of cheap labour-power is the sole foundation of their power to compete. . . . .

Wherever there is a working-day without restriction as to length, wherever there is night-work and unrestricted waste of human life, there the slighest obstacle presented by the nature of the work to a change for the better is soon looked upon as an everlasting barrier erected by Nature. No poison kills vermin with more certainty than the Factory Act removes such everlasting barriers. . . . .

It is evident that the English legislature, which certainly no one will venture to reproach with being overdosed with genius, has been led by experience to the conclusion that a simple compulsory law is sufficient to enact away all the so-called impediments, opposed by the nature of the process, to the restriction and regulation of the working-day. Hence, on the introduction of the Factory Act into a given industry, a period varying from six to eighteen months is fixed within which it is incumbent on the manufacturers to remove all technical impediments to the working of the Act. . . . .

But though the Factory Acts thus artificially ripen the material elements necessary for the conversion of the manufacturing system into the factory system, yet at the same time, owing to the necessity they impose for greater outlay of capital, they hasten on the decline of the small masters, and the concentration of capital.

Besides the purely technical impediments that are removable by technical means, the irregular habits of the workpeople themselves obstruct the regulation of the hours of labour. This is especially the case where piece-wage predominates, and where loss of time in one part of the day or week can be made good by subsequent over-time, or by night-work, a process which brutalises the adult workman, and ruins his wife and children. . . . .

In the same way as technical impediments, so, too, those "usages which have grown with the growth of trade" were and still are proclaimed by interested capitalists as obstacles due to the nature of the work. This was a favourite cry of the cotton lords at the time they were first threatened with the Factory Acts. Although their industry more than any other depends on navigation, yet experience has given them the lie. Since then, every pretended obstruction to business has been treated by the Factory inspectors as a mere sham. . . . .

Factory legislation, that first conscious and methodical reaction of society against the spontaneously developed form of the process of production, is, as we have seen, just as much the necessary product of modern industry as cotton yarn, self-actors, and the electric telegraph. Before passing to the consideration of the extension of that legislation in England, we shall shortly notice certain clauses contained in the Factory Acts, and not relating to the hours of work. . . . .

What could possibly show better the character of the capitalist mode of production, than the necessity that exists for forcing upon it, by Acts of Parliament, the simplest appliances for maintaining cleanliness and health? . . . .

At the same time, this portion of the Act strikingly shows that the capitalist mode of production, owing to its very nature, excludes all rational improvement beyond a certain point. It has been stated over and over again that the English doctors are unanimous in declaring that where the work is continuous, 500 cubic feet is the very least space that should be allowed for each person. Now, if the Factory Acts, owing to their compulsory provisions, indirectly hasten on the conversion of small workshops into factories, thus indirectly attacking the proprietary rights of the smaller capitalists, and assuring a monopoly to the great ones, so, if it were made obligatory to provide the proper space for each workman in every workshop, thousands of small employers would, at one full swoop, be expropriated directly! The very root of the capitalist mode of production, *i.e.*, the self-expansion of all capital, large or small, by means of the "free" purchase and consumption of labour-power, would be attacked. Factory legislation is therefore brought to a dead-lock before these 500 cubic feet of breathing space. The sanitary officers, the industrial inquiry commissioners, the factory inspectors, all harp, over and over again, upon the necessity for those 500 cubic feet, and upon the impossibility of wringing them out of capital. They thus, in fact, declare that consumption and other lung diseases among the workpeople are necessary conditions to the existence of capital.

MARX, *ibid*., 464.

What strikes us, then, in the English legislation of 1867, is, on the one hand, the necessity imposed on the parliament of the ruling classes, of adopting in principle measures so extraordinary, and on so great a scale, against the excesses of capitalistic exploitation; and on the other hand, the hesitation, the repugnance, and the bad faith, with which it lent itself to the task of carrying those measures into practice.

The Inquiry Commission of 1862 also proposed a new regulation of the mining industry, an industry distinguished from others by the exceptional characteristic that the interests of landlord and capitalist there join hands. The antagonism of these two interests had been favourable to Factory legislation, while on the other hand the absence of that antagonism is sufficient to explain the delays and chicanery of the legislation on mines.

MARX, *ibid.*, 472.

If the general extension of factory legislation to all trades for the purpose of protecting the working-class both in mind and body has become inevitable, on the other hand, as we have already pointed out, that extension hastens on the general conversion of numerous isolated small industries into a few combined industries carried on upon a large scale; it therefore accelerates the concentration of capital and the exclusive predominance of the factory system. It destroys both the ancient and the transitional forms, behind which the dominion of capital is still in part concealed, and replaces them by the direct and open sway of capital; but thereby it also generalises the direct opposition to this sway. While in each individual workshop it enforces uniformity, regularity, order, and economy, it increases by the immense spur which the limitation and regulation of the working-day give to technical improvement, the anarchy and the catastrophies of capitalist production as a whole, the intensity of labour, and the competition of machinery with the labourer. By the destruction of petty and domestic industries it destroys the last resort of the "redundant population," and with it the sole remaining safety-valve of the whole social mechanism. By maturing the material conditions, and the combination on a social scale of the processes of production, it matures the contradictions and antagonisms of the capitalist form of production, and thereby provides, along with the elements for the formation of a new society, the forces for exploding the old one.

See also ENGELS, The Housing Question, *MESW (3)* II, 324; MARX, Letter to Engels, 22.6.1867, *MESC*, 176–177.

ENGELS, The Condition of the Working Class in England, *MECW* IV, 568–569.

Down to the present hour, the property-holding class in Parliament still struggles against the better feelings of those not yet fallen a prey to egotism, and seeks to subjugate the proletariat still further. One piece of common land after another is appropriated and placed under cultivation, a process by which the general cultivation is furthered, but the proletariat greatly injured. Where there were still commons, the poor could pasture an ass, a pig, or geese, the children and young people had a place where they could play and live out of doors; but this is gradually coming to an end. The earnings of the worker are less, and the young people, deprived of their play-ground, go to the beer-shops. A mass of acts for enclosing and cultivating commons is passed at every session of Parliament. When the Government determined during the session of 1844 to force the all monopolising railways to make travelling possible for the workers by means of charges proportionate to their means, a penny a mile, and proposed therefore to introduce such a third class train upon every railway daily, the "Reverend Father in God", the Bishop of London, proposed that Sunday, the only day upon which working-men in work *can* travel, be exempted from this rule, and travelling thus be left open to the rich and shut off from the poor. This proposition was, however, too direct, too undisguised to pass through Parliament, and was dropped. I have no room to enumerate the many concealed attacks of even one single session upon the proletariat.

ENGELS, *ibid.*, 578.

I hope that after this picture of the New Poor Law and its results, no word which I have said of the English bourgeoisie will be thought too stern. In this public measure, in which it acts *in corpore* as the ruling power, it formulates its real intentions, reveals the animus of those smaller transactions with the proletariat, of which the blame apparently attaches to individuals. And that this measure did not originate with any one section of the bourgeoisie, but enjoys the approval of the whole class, is proved by the Parliamentary debates of 1844. The Liberal party had enacted the New Poor Law; the Conservative party, with its Prime Minister Peel at the head, defends it, and only alters some pettifogging trifles in the Poor Law Amendment Bill of 1844. A Liberal majority carried the bill, a Conservative majority approved it, and the "Noble Lords" gave their consent each time. Thus is the expulsion of the proletariat from State and society outspoken, thus is it publicly proclaimed that proletarians are not human beings, and do not deserve to be treated as such. Let us leave it to the proletarians of the British Empire to reconquer their human rights.

MARX, The Class Struggles in France, *MESW (3)* I, 275.

The country folk—over two-thirds of the total French population—consist for the most part of so-called free *landowners*. The first generation, gratuitously freed by the revolution of 1789 from its feudal burdens, had paid no price for the soil. But the following generations paid, under the form of the *price of land*, what their semi-serf forefathers had paid in the form of rent, tithes, *corvée*, etc. The more, on the one hand, the population grew and the more, on the other hand, the partition of the soil increased, the higher became the price of the parcels, for the demand for them increased with their smallness. But in proportion as the price which the peasant paid for his parcel rose, whether he bought it directly or whether he had it accounted as capital by his coheirs, necessarily also rose the *indebtedness of the peasant*, that is, the *mortgage*. The claim to a debt encumbering the land is termed a *mortgage*, a pawn-ticket in respect of the land. Just as *privileges* accumulated on the medieval estate, *mortgages* accumulate on the modern small allotment.

See also MARX, The Eighteenth Brumaire of Louis Bonaparte, *MESW (3)* I, 480–483.

MARX, *Capital* III, 626–627.

We are referring to ground-rent in countries with developed capitalist production. Among English tenants, for instance, there are a number of small capitalists who are destined and compelled by education, training, tradition, competition, and other circumstances to invest their capital as tenants in agriculture. They are forced to be satisfied with less than the average profit, and to turn over part of it to the landlords as rent. This is the only condition under which they are permitted to invest their capital in the land, in agriculture. Since landlords everywhere exert considerable, and in England even overwhelming, influence on legislation, they are able to exploit this situation for the purpose of victimising the entire class of tenants. For instance, the Corn Laws of 1815—a bread tax, admittedly imposed upon the country to secure for the idle landlords a continuation of their abnormally increased rentals during the anti-Jacobin war—had indeed the effect, excluding cases of a few extraordinarily rich harvests, of maintaining prices of agricultural products above the level to which they would have fallen had corn imports been unrestricted. But they did not have the effect of maintaining prices at the level decreed by the lawmaking landlords to serve as normal prices in such manner as to constitute the legal limit for imports of foreign corn. But the leaseholds were contracted in an atmosphere created by these normal prices. As soon as the illusion was dispelled, a new law was passed, containing new normal prices, which were as much the impotent expression of a greedy landlord's fantasy as the old ones. In this way, tenants were defrauded from 1815 up to the thirties. Hence the standing problem of agricultural distress during this entire period. Hence the expropriation and the ruin of a whole generation of tenants during this period and their replacement by a new class of capitalists.

See also MARX, Irish Tenant Rights, in MARX/ENGELS, *On Ireland*, 59–61.

MARX, *Capital* II, 180.

Legislation has everywhere drawn a distinction, in leases of houses and other objects which represent fixed capital to their owners and are leased as such, between normal depreciation, which is the result of time, the action of the elements, and normal wear on the one hand and on the other those occasional repairs which are required from time to time for maintenance during the normal life of the house and during its normal use. As a rule, the former are borne by the owner, the latter by the tenant. Repairs are further divided into ordinary and substantial ones. The last-named are partly a renewal of the fixed capital in its bodily form, and they fall likewise on the shoulders of the owner, unless the lease explicitly states the contrary. Take for instance the English law: "A tenant from year to year, on the other hand, is not bound to do more than keep the premises wind and watertight, when that can be done without 'substantial' repairs; and generally to do repairs coming fairly under the head 'ordinary.' Even with respect to those parts of the premises which are the subject of 'ordinary' repairs, regard must be had to their age and general state, and condition, when he took possession, for he is not bound to replace old and worn-out materials with new ones, nor to make good the inevitable depreciation resulting from time and ordinary wear and tear." (Holdsworth, *Law of Landlord and Tenant*, pp. 90 and 91.)

MARX, *ibid.*, 373–375.

Machinery also revolutionises out and out the contract between the labourer and the capitalist, which formally fixes their mutual relations. Taking the exchange of commodities as our basis, our first assumption was that capitalist and labourer met as free persons, as independent owners of commodities; the one possessing money and means of production, the other labour-power. But now the capitalist buys children and young persons under age. Previously, the workman sold his own labour-power, which he disposed of nominally as a free agent. Now he sells wife and child. He has become a slave-dealer. The demand for children's labour often resembles in form the inquiries for negro slaves, such as were formerly to be read among the advertisements in American journals. "My attention," says an English factory inspector, "was drawn to an advertisement in the local paper of one of the most important manufacturing towns of my district, of which the following is a copy: Wanted, 12 to 20 young persons, not younger than what can pass for 13 years. Wages, 4 shillings a week. Apply &c." The phrase "what can pass for 13 years," has reference to the fact, that by the Factory Act, children under 13 years may work only 6 hours. A surgeon officially appointed must certify their age. The manufacturer, therefore, asks for children who look as if they were already 13 years old. The decrease, often by leaps and bounds in the number of children under 13 years employed in factories, a decrease that is shown in an astonishing manner by the English statistics of the last 20 years, was for the most part, according to the evidence of the factory inspectors themselves, the work of the certifying surgeons, who overstated the age of the children, agreeably to the capitalist's greed for exploitation, and the sordid trafficking needs of the parents. In the notorious district of Bethnal Green, a public market is held every Monday and Tuesday morning, where children of both sexes from 9 years of age upwards, hire themselves out to the silk manufacturers.

"The usual terms are 1s. 8d. a week (this belongs to the parents) and '2d. for myself and tea.' The contract is binding only for the week. The scene and language while this market is going on are quite disgraceful." It has also occurred in England, that women have taken "children from the workhouse and let any one have them out for 2s. 6d. a week." In spite of legislation, the number of boys sold in Great Britain by their parents to act as live chimney-sweeping machines (although there exist plenty of machines to replace them) exceeds 2,000. The revolution effected by machinery in the juridical relations between the buyer and the seller of labour-power, causing the transaction as a whole to lose the appearance of a contract between free persons, afforded the English Parliament an excuse, founded on juridical principles, for the interference of the state with factories. Whenever the law limits the labour of children to 6 hours in industries not before interfered with, the complaints of the manufacturers are always renewed. They allege that numbers of the parents withdrew their children from the industry brought under the Act, in order to sell them where "freedom of labour" still rules, i.e., where children under 13 years are compelled to work like grown-up people, and therefore can be got rid of at a higher price. But since capital is by nature a leveller, since it exacts in every sphere of production equality in the conditions of the exploitation of labour, the limitation by law of children's labour, in one branch of industry, becomes the cause of its limitation in others.

MARX, *Capital* III, 89–90.

Factories. Under this heading there is covered the disregard for safety measures to ensure the security, comfort, and health of labourers also in the actual factories. It is to blame for a large portion of the casualty lists containing the wounded and killed industrial workers (cf. the annual factory reports). Similarly, lack of space, ventilation, etc.

As far back as October 1855, Leonard Horner complained about the resistance of very many manufacturers to the legal requirements concerning safety devices on horizontal shafts, although the danger was continually emphasised by accidents, many of them fatal, and although these safety devices did not cost much and did not interfere with production. (Reports of Insp. of Fact., October 1855, p. 6.) In their resistance against these and other legal requirements the manufacturers were openly seconded by the unpaid justices of the peace, who were themselves mostly manufacturers or friends of manufacturers, and handed down their decisions accordingly. What sort of verdicts these gentlemen handed down was revealed by Superior Judge Campbell, who said with reference to one of them, against which an appeal had been made to him: "It is not an interpretation of the Act of Parliament, it is a repeal of the Act of Parliament" (*loc. cit.*, p. 11). . . . The manufacturer had a trades union at the time to oppose factory legislation, the so-called National Association for the Amendment of the Factory Laws which had been organised in 1854 for the express purpose of opposing the law which prescribed such protection. The manufacturers had not paid the least heed to it during the whole period from 1844 to 1854. When the factory inspectors, at instructions from Palmerston, then informed the manufacturers that the law would be enforced in earnest, the manufacturers instantly founded their association, many of whose most prominent members were themselves justices of the peace and in this capacity were supposed to enforce the law. When in April 1855 the new Minister of the Interior, Sir George Grey, offered a compromise under which the government would be content with practically nominal safety appliances the Association indignantly rejected even this. In various law-suits the famous engineer William Fairbairn threw the weight of his reputation behind the principle of economy and in defence of the freedom of capital which had been violated. The head of factory inspection, Leonard Horner, was persecuted and maligned by the manufacturers in every conceivable manner.

But the manufacturers did not rest until they obtained a writ of the Court of Queen's Bench, according to which the Law of 1844 did not prescribe protective devices for horizontal shafts installed more than seven feet above the ground and, finally, in 1856 they succeeded in securing an Act of Parliament entirely satisfactory to them in the circumstances, through the services of the bigot Wilson Patten, one of those pious souls whose display of religion is always ready to do the dirty work for the knights of the money-bag. This Act practically deprived the labourers of all special protection and referred them to the common courts for compensation in the event of industrial accidents (sheer mockery in view of the excessive cost of English lawsuits), while it made it almost impossible for the manufacturer to lose the lawsuit by providing in a finely-worded clause for expert testimony. The result was a rapid increase of accidents.

See also ENGELS, The Condition of the Working Class in England, MECW IV, 539; ENGELS, The Housing Question, MESW (3), 345–346.

Law and Property Relations

MARX, Economic and Philosophic Manuscripts, MECW III, 297.

It is easy to see that the entire revolutionary movement necessarily finds both its empirical and its theoretical basis in the movement of *private property*—more precisely, in that of the economy.

This *material*, immediately *perceptible* private property is the material perceptible expression of *estranged human* life. Its movement—production and consumption—is the *perceptible* revelation of the movement of all production until now, i.e., the realisation or the reality of man. Religion, family, state, law, morality, science, art, etc., are only *particular* modes of production, and fall under its general law. The positive transcendence of *private property*, as the appropriation of *human* life, is therefore the positive transcendence of all estrangement—that is to say, the return of man from religion, family, state, etc., to his *human*, i.e., *social*, existence. Religious estrangement as such occurs only in the realm of *consciousness*, of man's inner life, but economic estrangement is that of *real life*; its transcendence therefore embraces both aspects.

See also MARX, *ibid.*, 246–247; MARX, *ibid.*, 279–280; MARX, *Grundrisse*, 497–499; ENGELS, Origin of the Family, Private Property and the State, *MESW (3)* III, 280–281.

MARX, *Grundrisse*, 96.

As regards whole societies, distribution seems to precede production and to determine it in yet another respect, almost as if it were a pre-economic fact. A conquering people divides the land among the conquerors, thus imposes a certain distribution and form of property in land, and thus determines production. Or it enslaves the conquered and so makes slave labour the foundation of production. Or a people rises in revolution and smashes the great landed estates into small parcels, and hence, by this new distribution, gives production a new character. Or a system of laws assigns property in land to certain families in perpetuity, or distributes labour [as] a hereditary privilege and thus confines it within certain castes. In all these cases, and they are all historical, it seems that distribution is not structured and determined by production, but rather the opposite, production by distribution.

MARX, *ibid.*, 485–489.

The main point here is this: In all these forms— in which landed property and agriculture form the basis of the economic order, and where the economic aim is hence the production of use values, i.e. the *reproduction of the individual* within the specific relation to the commune in which he is its basis—there is to be found: (1) Appropriation not through labour, but presupposed to labour; appropriation of the natural conditions of labour, of the *earth* as the original instrument of labour as well as its workshop and repository of raw materials. The individual relates simply to the objective conditions of labour as being his; [relates] to them as the inorganic nature of his subjectivity, in which the latter realizes itself; the chief objective condition of labour does not itself appear as a *product* of labour, but is already there as *nature*; on one side the living individual, on the other the earth, as the objective condition of his reproduction; (2) but this *relation* to land and soil, to the earth, as the property of the labouring individual—who thus appears from the outset not merely as labouring individual, in this abstraction, but who has an *objective mode of existence* in his ownership of the land, an existence *presupposed* to his activity, and not merely as a result of it, a presupposition of his activity just like his skin, his sense organs, which of course he also reproduces and develops etc. in the life process, but which are nevertheless presuppositions of this process of his reproduction—is instantly mediated by the naturally arisen, spontaneous, more or less historically developed and modified presence of the individual as *member of a commune*—his naturally arisen presence as member of a tribe etc. An isolated individual could no more have property in land and soil than he could speak. He could, of course, live off it as substance, as do the animals. The relation to the earth as property is always mediated through the occupation of the land and soil, peacefully or violently, by the tribe, the commune, in some more or less naturally arisen or already historically developed form. The individual can never appear here in the dot-like isolation [*Punktualität*] in which he appears as mere free worker. If the objective conditions of his labour are presupposed as belonging to him, then he himself is subjectively presupposed as member of a commune, through which his relation to land and soil is mediated. His relation to the objective conditions of labour is mediated through his presence as member of the commune: at the same time, the real presence of the commune is determined by the specific form of the individual's property in the objective conditions of labour. Whether this property mediated by commune-membership appears as *communal property*, where the individual is merely the possessor and there is no private property in land and soil—or whether property appears in the double form of state and private property alongside one another, but so that the latter appears as posited by the former, so that only the citizen is and must be a private proprietor, while his property as citizen has a separate, particular existence at the same time—or whether, finally, the communal property appears only as a complement to individual property, with the latter as the base, while the commune has no existence for-itself except in the *assembly* of the commune members, their coming-together for common purposes—these different forms of the commune or tribe members' relation to the tribe's land and soil—to the earth where it has settled—depend partly on the natural inclinations of the tribe, and partly on the economic conditions in which it relates as proprietor to the land and soil in reality, i.e. in which it appropriates its fruits through labour, and the latter will itself depend on climate, physical make-up of the land and soil, the physically determined mode of its exploitation, the relation with hostile tribes or neighbour tribes, and the modifications which migrations, historic experiences etc. introduce. . . . In all these forms, the *reproduction of presupposed* relations—more or less naturally arisen or historic as well, but become traditional—or the individual to his commune, together with a *specific, objective* existence, *predetermined* for the individual, of his relations both to the conditions of labour and to his co-workers, fellow tribesmen etc.—are the foundation of development, which is therefore from the outset *restricted*, but which signifies decay, decline and fall once this barrier is suspended. . . . For the encounter with the objective conditions of labour as separate from him, as *capital* from the worker's side, and the encounter with the *worker* as propertyless, as an abstract worker from the capitalist's side—the exchange such as takes place between value and living labour, presupposes a *historic process*, no matter how much capital and labour themselves reproduce this relation and work out its objective scope, as well as its depth—a historic process, which, as we saw, forms the history of the origins of capital and wage labour. In other words: the *extra-economic origin* of property means nothing else than the *historic origin* of the bourgeois economy, of the forms of production which are theoretically or ideally expressed by the categories of political economy. But the fact that pre-bourgeois history, and each of its phases, also has its own *economy* and an *economic foundation* for its movement, is at bottom only the tautology that human life has since time immemorial rested on production, and, in one way or another, on *social* production, whose relations we call, precisely, economic relations.

See also MARX, *ibid.*, 472–473; MARX/ENGELS, The German Ideology, *MECW* V, 32–35 and 354–357; MARX, Contribution to the Critique of Hegel's Philosophy of Law, *MECW* III, 101–102 and 110–111.

MARX, *Grundrisse*, 491–493.
Property thus originally means no more than a human being's relation to his natural conditions of production as belonging to him, as his, as *presupposed* along with *his own being*; relations to them as *natural presuppositions* of his self, which only form, so to speak, his extended body. He actually does not relate to his conditions of production, but rather has a double existence, both subjectively as he himself, and objectively in these natural non-organic conditions of his existence. The forms of these *natural conditions of production* are double: (1) his existence as a member of a community; hence the existence of this community, which in its original form is a *clan* system, a more or less modified *clan* system; (2) the relation to *land and soil* mediated by the community, as *its own*, as communal landed property, at the same time *individual possession* for the individual, or in such a way that only the fruits are divided, but the land itself and the labour remain common. (However, *residences* etc., even if only the Scythians' wagons, always appear in individual possession.) A natural condition of production for the living individual is his belonging to a *naturally arisen, spontaneous society*, clan etc. This is e.g. already a condition for his language etc. His own productive existence is possible only on this condition. His subjective existence is thereby conditioned as such, just as it is conditioned by his relation to the earth as his workshop. (Property is, it is true, originally *mobile*, for mankind first seizes hold of the ready-made fruits of the earth, among whom belong e.g. the animals, and for him especially the ones that can be tamed.

Nevertheless even this situation—hunting, fishing, herding, gathering fruits from trees etc.—always presupposes appropriation of the earth, whether for a fixed residence, or for roaming, or for animal pasture etc.)

Property therefore means *belonging to a clan* (community) (having subjective-objective existence in it); and, by means of the relation of this community to the land and soil, [relating] to the earth as the individual's inorganic body; his relation to land and soil, to the external primary condition of production—since the earth is raw material, instrument and fruit all in one—as to a presupposition belonging to his individuality, as modes of his presence. *We reduce this property to the relation to the conditions of production.* Why not to consumption, since the production of the individual is originally restricted to the reproduction of his own body through the appropriation of ready objects prepared by nature itself for consumption? Even where the only task is to *find* and to *discover*, this soon requires exertion, labour—as in hunting, fishing, herding—and production (i.e. development) of certain capacities on the part of the subject. Then also, situations in which it is possible to seize hold of the things available without any instruments whatever (i.e. products of labour destined for production), without alteration of form (which already takes place for herding) etc., are themselves transitional and in no case to be regarded as normal; nor as normal original situations. The original conditions of production, incidentally, of course include substances consumable directly, without labour; thus the consumption fund appears as a component part of the *original production fund.*

The fundamental condition of property resting on the clan system (into which the community originally resolves itself)—to be a member of the clan—makes the clan conquered by another clan *propertyless* and throws it among the *inorganic conditions* of the conqueror's reproduction, to which the conquering community relates as its own. Slavery and serfdom are thus only further developments of the form of property resting on the clan system. They necessarily modify all of the latter's forms. They can do this least of all in the Asiatic form. In the self-sustaining unity of manufacture and agriculture, on which this form rests, conquest is not so necessary a condition as where *landed property, agriculture* are exclusively predominant. On the other hand, since in this form the individual never becomes a proprietor but only a possessor, he is at bottom himself the property, the slave of him in whom the unity of the commune exists, and slavery here neither suspends the conditions of labour nor modifies the essential relation.

It is now clear, further, that:

Property, in so far as it is only the conscious relation—and posited in regard to the individual by the community, and proclaimed and guaranteed as law—to the conditions of production as *his own*, so that the producer's being appears also in the objective conditions *belonging to him*—is only realized by production itself. The real appropriation takes place not in the mental but in the real, active relation to these condi-

tions—in their real positing as the conditions of his subjective activity.
See also MARX, *ibid.*, 494–495 and 500–501.

MARX, Letter to Annenkov, 28.12.1846. *MESC,* 33–34.

Mr. Proudhon surpasses himself when he allows competition, monopoly, taxes or police, balance of trade, credit and property to develop
inside his head in the order in which I have mentioned them. Almost the
whole of the credit system had been developed in England by the
beginning of the eighteenth century, before the invention of machinery.
Government loans were only a fresh method of increasing taxation and
satisfying the new demands created by the rise of the bourgeoisie to
power. Finally, the last category in Mr. Proudhon's system is *property*. In
the real world, on the other hand, division of labour and all Mr.
Proudhon's other categories are social relations forming in their entirety
what is today known as *property*; outside these relations bourgeois
property is nothing but a metaphysical or legal illusion. The property of
some other epoch, feudal property, develops under entirely different
social relations. By presenting property as an independent relation, Mr.
Proudhon commits more than a mistake in method: he clearly shows that
he has not grasped the bond which holds together all forms of *bourgeois*
production, that he has not understood the *historical* and *transitory*
character of the forms of production in a particular epoch. Mr.
Proudhon, who does not regard our social institutions as historical
products, who is unable to understand either their origin or their
development, can only produce dogmatic criticism of them.

MARX, *Theories of Surplus Value* I, 346.

Society itself—the fact that man lives in society and not as an independent, self-supporting individual—is the root of property, of the laws
based on it and of the inevitable slavery.

See also MARX/ENGELS, The German Ideology, *MECW* V, 230–231;
MARX, The Poverty of Philosophy, *MECW* VI, 197.

MARX, Letter to Schweitzer, 24.1.1865, *MESC,* 143–144.

Thus history itself had expressed its criticism upon past *property relations*.
What Proudhon was actually dealing with was *modern bourgeois property*
as it exists today. The question of what this is could have only been
answered by a critical analysis of *"political economy"*, embracing the
totality of these *property relations*, considering not their *legal* aspect as
relations of volition but their real form, that is, as *relations of production*. But
as Proudhon entangled the whole of these economic relations in the
general legal concept of *"property"*, he could not get beyond the answer
which, in a similar work published before 1789, *Brissot* had already given
in the same words: "Property is theft."

The upshot is at best that the bourgeois legal conceptions of *"theft"* apply equally well to the *"honest"* gains of the bourgeois himself. On the other hand, since *"theft"* as a forcible violation of property *presupposes the existence of property*, Proudhon entangled himself in all sorts of fantasies, obscure even to himself, about *true bourgeois property*.

ENGELS, Origin of the Family, Private Property and the State, *MESW* *(3)*, 317.

Whatever was produced and used in common was common property: the house, the garden, the long boat. Here, and only here, then, do we find the "earned property" which jurists and economists have falsely attributed to civilised society—the last mendacious legal pretext on which modern capitalist property rests.

See also MARX, *Theories of Surplus Value* I, 365–367; ENGELS, *Anti-Dühring*, 242–243; MARX, *Capital* I, 547–548; MARX/ENGELS, The Holy Family, *MECW* IV, 31–33.

MARX, The Duchess of Sutherland and Slavery, *Articles on Britain*, 148.

If of any property it ever was true that it was *robbery*, it is literally true of the property of the British aristocracy. Robbery of Church property, robbery of commons, fraudulent transformation, accompanied by murder, of feudal and patriarchal property into private property—these are the titles of British aristocrats to their possessions. And what services in this latter process were performed by a servile class of lawyers, you may see from an English lawyer of the last century, Dalrymple, who, in his *History of Feudal Property*, very naïvely proves that every law or deed concerning property was interpreted by the lawyers, in England, when the middle class rose in wealth, in favour of the *middle class*—in Scotland, where the nobility enriched themselves, in favour of the *nobility*—in either case it was interpreted in a sense hostile to the *people*.

MARX, *Capital* I, 550–551

So long as the laws of exchange are observed in every single act of exchange the mode of appropriation can be completely revolutionised without in any way affecting the property rights which correspond to commodity production. These same rights remain in force both at the outset, when the product belongs to its producer, who, exchanging equivalent for equivalent, can enrich himself only by his own labour, and also in the period of capitalism, when social wealth becomes to an ever-increasing degree the property of those who are in a position to appropriate continually and ever afresh the unpaid labour of others.

This result becomes inevitable from the moment there is a free sale, by the labourer himself, of labour-power as a commodity. But it is also only from then onwards that commodity production is generalised and becomes the typical form of production; it is only from then onwards that, from the first, every product is produced for sale and all wealth produced goes through the sphere of circulation. Only when and where wage-labour is its basis does commodity production impose itself upon society as a whole; but only then and there also does it unfold all its hidden potentialities. To say that the supervention of wage-labour adulterates commodity production is to say that commodity production must not develop if it is to remain unadulterated. To the extent that commodity production, in accordance with its own inherent laws, develops further, into capitalist production, the property laws of commodity production change into the laws of capitalist appropriation.

MARX, *Capital* III, 757.

The mere legal ownership of land does not create any ground-rent for the owner. But it does, indeed, give him the power to withdraw his land from exploitation until economic conditions permit him to utilise it in such a manner as to yield him a surplus, be it used for actual agricultural or other production purposes, such as buildings, etc. He cannot increase or decrease the absolute magnitude of this sphere, but he can change the quantity of land placed on the market. Hence, as Fourier already observed, it is a characteristic fact that in all civilised countries a comparatively appreciable portion of land always remains uncultivated.

MARX, *ibid.*, 614–618.

The form of landed property which we shall consider here is a specifically historical one, a form *transformed* through the influence of capital and of the capitalist mode of production, either of feudal landownership, or of small-peasant agriculture as a means of livelihood, in which the *possession* of the land and the soil constitutes one of the prerequisites of production for the direct producer, and in which his *ownership* of land appears as the most advantageous condition for the prosperity of *his* mode of production. Just as the capitalist mode of production in general is based on the expropriation of the conditions of labour from the labourers, so does it in agriculture presuppose the expropriation of the rural labourers from the land and their subordination to a capitalist, who carries on agriculture for the sake of profit. . . . .

Landed property is based on the monopoly by certain persons over definite portions of the globe, as exclusive spheres of their private will to the exclusion of all others. With this in mind, the problem is to ascertain the economic value, that is, the realisation of this monopoly on the basis of capitalist production. With the legal power of these persons to use or misuse certain portions of the globe, nothing is decided. The use of this power depends wholly upon economic conditions, which are independent of their will. The legal view itself only means that the landowner can do with the land what every owner of commodities can do with his commodities. And this view, this legal view of free private ownership of land, arises in the ancient world only with the dissolution of the organic order of society, and in the modern world only with the development of capitalist production. . . . .

One of the major results of the capitalist mode of production is that, on the one hand, it transforms agriculture from a mere empirical and mechanical self-perpetuating process employed by the least developed part of society into the conscious scientific application of agronomy, in so far as this is at all feasible under conditions of private property; that it divorces landed property from the relations of dominion and servitude, on the one hand, and, on the other, totally separates land as an instrument of production from landed property and landowner—for whom the land merely represents a certain money assessment which he collects by virtue of his monopoly from the industrial capitalist, the capitalist farmer; it dissolves the connection between landownership and the land so thoroughly that the landowner may spend his whole life in Constantinople, while his estates lie in Scotland. Landed property thus receives its purely economic form by discarding all its former political and social embellishments and associations, in brief all those traditional accessories, which are denounced, as we shall see later, as useless and absurd superfluities by the industrial capitalists themselves, as well as their theoretical spokesmen, in the heat of their struggle with landed property.

See also MARX, *ibid.*, 751.

Regulation of Labour

ENGELS, The Condition of the Working Class in England, *MECW* IV, 467–471.

Further, the slavery in which the bourgeoisie holds the proletariat chained, is nowhere more conspicuous than in the factory system. Here ends all freedom in law and in fact. The operative must be in the mill at half-past five in the morning; if he comes a couple of minutes too late, he is fined; if he comes ten minutes too late, he is not let in until breakfast is over, and a quarter of the day's wages is withheld, though he loses only two and one-half hours' work out of twelve. He must eat, drink, and sleep at command. For satisfying the most imperative needs, he is vouchsafed the least possible time absolutely required by them. Whether his dwelling is a half-hour or a whole one removed from the factory does not concern his employer. The despotic bell calls him from his bed, his breakfast, his dinner.

What a time he has of it, too, inside the factory! Here the employer is absolute law-giver; he makes regulations at will, changes and adds to his codex at pleasure, and even, if he inserts the craziest stuff, the courts say to the working-man:

> "You were your own master, no one forced you to agree to such a contract if you did not wish to; but now, when you have freely entered into it, you must be bound by it."

And so the working-man only gets into the bargain the mockery of the Justice of the Peace who is a bourgeois himself, and of the law which is made by the bourgeoisie. Such decisions have been given often enough. In October, 1844, the operatives of Kennedy's mill, in Manchester, struck. Kennedy prosecuted them on the strength of a regulation placarded in the mill, that at no time more than two operatives in one room may quit work at once. And the court decided in his favour, giving the working-men the explanation cited above. And such rules as these usually are! For instance: 1. The doors are closed ten minutes after work begins, and thereafter no one is admitted until the breakfast hour; whoever is absent during this time forfeits 3d. per loom. 2. Every power-loom weaver detected absenting himself at another time, while the machinery is in motion, forfeits for each hour and each loom, 3d. Every person who leaves the room during working-hours, without obtaining permission from the overlooker, forfeits 3d. 3. Weavers who fail to supply themselves with scissors forfeit, per day, 1d. 4. All broken shuttles, brushes, oil-cans, wheels, window-panes, etc., must be paid for by the weaver. 5. No weaver to stop work without giving a week's notice. The manufacturer may dismiss any employee without notice for bad work or improper behaviour. 6. Every operative detected speaking to another, singing or whistling, will be fined 6d.; for leaving his place during working-hours, 6d. Another copy of factory regulations lies before me, according to which every operative who comes three minutes too late, forfeits the wages for a quarter of an hour, and every one who comes twenty minutes too late, for a quarter of a day. Every one who remains absent until breakfast forfeits a shilling on Monday, and sixpence every other day of the week, etc., etc. This last is the regulation of the Phoenix Works in Jersey Street, Manchester. It may be said that such rules are necessary in a great, complicated factory, in order to insure the harmonious working of the different parts; it may be asserted that such a severe discipline is as necessary here as in an army. This may be so, but what sort of a social order is it which cannot be maintained without such shameful tyranny? Either the end sanctifies the means, or the inference of the badness of the end from the badness of the means is justified. Every one who has served as a soldier knows what it is to be subjected even for a short time to military discipline. But these operatives are condemned from their ninth year to their death to live under the sword, physically and mentally. They are worse slaves than the Negroes in America, for they are more sharply watched, and yet it is demanded of them that they shall live like human beings, shall think and feel like men! Verily, this they can do only under glowing hatred towards their oppressors, and towards that order of things which places them in such a position, which degrades them to machines. But it is far more shameful yet, that according to the universal testimony of the operatives, numbers of manufacturers collect the fines imposed upon the operatives with the most heartless severity, and for the purpose of piling up extra profits out of the farthings thus extorted from the impoverished proletarians. Leach asserts, too, that the operatives often find the factory clock moved forward a quarter of an hour and the doors shut, while the clerk moves about with the fines-book inside, noting the many names of the absentees. Leach claims to have counted ninety-five operatives thus shut out, standing before a factory, whose clock was a quarter of an hour slower than the town clocks at night, and a quarter of an hour faster in the morning. The Factory Report relates similar facts. In one factory the clock was set back during working-hours, so that the operatives worked overtime without extra pay; in another, a whole quarter of an hour overtime was worked; in a third, there were two clocks, an ordinary one and a machine clock, which registered the revolutions of the main shaft; if the machinery went slowly, working-hours were measured by the machine clock until the number of revolutions due in twelve hours was reached; if work went well, so that the number was reached before the usual working-hours were ended, the operatives were forced to toil on to the end of the twelfth hour. The witness adds that he had known girls who had good work, and who had worked overtime, who, nevertheless, betook themselves to a life of prostitution rather than submit to this tyranny. To return to the fines. Leach relates having repeatedly seen women in the last period of pregnancy fined 6d. for the offence of sitting down a moment to rest. Fines for bad work are wholly arbitrary; the goods are examined in the wareroom, and the supervisor charges the fines upon a list without even summoning the operative, who only learns that he has been fined when the overlooker pays his wages, and the goods have perhaps been sold, or certainly been placed beyond his reach. Leach has in his possession such a fines list, ten feet long, and amounting to £35 17s. 10d. He relates that in the factory where this list was made, a new supervisor was dismissed for fining too little, and so bringing in five pounds too little weekly. And I repeat that I know Leach to be a thoroughly trustworthy man incapable of a falsehood.

But the operative is his employer's slave in still other respects. If his wife or daughter finds favour in the eyes of the master, a command, a hint suffices, and she must place herself at his disposal. When the employers wishes to supply with signatures a petition in favour of bourgeois interests, he need only send it to his mill. If he wishes to decide a Parliamentary election, he sends his enfranchised operatives in rank and file to the polls, and they vote for the bourgeois candidate whether they will or no. If he desires a majority in a public meeting, he dismisses them half-an-hour earlier than usual, and secures them places close to the platform, where he can watch them to his satisfaction.

Two further arrangements contribute especially to force the operative under the dominion of the manufacturer: the Truck system and the Cottage system. The truck system, the payment of the operatives in goods, was formerly universal in England. The manufacturer opens a shop, "for the convenience of the operatives, and to protect them from the high prices of the petty dealers". Here goods of all sorts are sold to them on credit; and to keep the operatives from going to the shops where they could get their goods more cheaply—the "Tommy shops" usually charging twenty-five to thirty per cent more than others—wages are paid in requisitions on the shop instead of money. The general indignation against this infamous system led to the passage of the Truck Act in 1831, by which, for most employees, payment in truck orders was declared void and illegal, and was made punishable by fine; but, like most other English laws, this has been enforced only here and there. In the towns it is carried out comparatively efficiently: but in the country, the truck system, disguised or undisguised, flourishes. In the town of Leicester, too, it is very common. There lie before me nearly a dozen convictions for this offence, dating from the period between November, 1843, and June, 1844, and reported, in part, in the *Manchester Guardian* and, in part, in the *Northern Star*. The system is, of course, less openly carried on at present: wages are usually paid in cash, but the employer still has means enough at command to force him to purchase his wares in the truck shop and nowhere else. Hence it is difficult to combat the truck system, because it can now be carried on under cover of the law, provided only that the operative receives his wages in money.

See also ENGELS, *ibid.*, 487.

MARX, A Bourgeois Document, *Articles from NRZ*, 206–210.
In England, where the rule of the bourgeoisie has reached the highest stage of development, public charity too, as we know, has assumed the most noble and magnanimous forms. In England's workhouses—those public institutions where the redundant labour population is allowed to vegetate at the expense of bourgeois society—charity is cunningly combined with the *revenge* which the bourgeoisie wreaks on the wretches who are compelled to appeal to its charity. Not only do the poor devils receive the bare and most meagre means of subsistence, hardly sufficient for physical reproduction, their activity, too, is restricted to a form of revolting, unproductive, meaningless drudgery, such as work at the treadmill, which deadens both mind and body. These unfortunate people have committed the crime of having ceased to be an object of exploitation yielding a profit to the bourgeoisie—as is the case in ordinary life—and having become instead an object of expenditure for those born to derive benefit from them: like so many barrels of alcohol which, left

unsold in the warehouse, become an object of expenditure to the dealer. To bring home to them the full magnitude of their crime, they are deprived of everything that is granted to the lowest criminal—association with their wives and children, recreation, talk—everything. Even this *"cruel charity"* is due not to enthusiasm but to thoroughly practical and rational reasons. On the one hand, if all the paupers in Great Britain were suddenly thrown into the street, bourgeois order and commercial activity would suffer to an alarming extent. On the other hand, British industry has alternate periods of feverish over-production, when the demand for hands can hardly be satisfied, and the hands are nevertheless to be obtained as cheaply as possible, followed by periods of slack business, when production is far larger than consumption and it is difficult to find useful employment even at half pay for half the labour army. Is there a more ingenious device than the workhouse for maintaining a reserve army in readiness for the favourable periods while converting them in these pious institutions during unfavourable commercial periods into unresisting machines without will, without aspirations and requirements? . . .

But the Prussian bourgeoisie approaches its British ideal in one respect—in its *shameless maltreatment of the working class.* . . . .

We publish here without any alterations the *"Worker's Card"*, which proletarians engaged on municipal works have to sign in the good city of Cologne; this historical document shows the impudence with which our bourgeoisie treat the working class.

WORKER'S CARD

§ 1. Every worker must *strictly obey* the instructions and orders of *all municipal supervisors*, who have been sworn in as *police officers. Disobedience and insubordination will entail immediate dismissal.*

§ 2. No worker is allowed to move from one section to another or to leave the building-site *without the special permission of the supervisor.*

§ 3. Workers purloining wheelbarrows, carts or other equipment from another section in order to use them in their work will be dismissed.

§ 4. Drunkenness, disturbance of the peace, and the starting of squabbles, quarrels and fights entail immediate dismissal.—In *appropriate cases* moreover legal proceedings will be taken against the culprits.

§ 5. A worker arriving *ten minutes late* at his place of work will be given no work on that *particular half day*; if this should occur three times he *may* be debarred from work.

§ 6. If workers are dismissed at their own request or by way of punishment, they will receive their wages at the next regular pay-day in accordance with the work done.

§ 7. A worker's dismissal is noted in the Worker's Card.—Should the dismissal be by way of punishment, the worker, *according to the circumstances*, is barred from re-employment either at the same place of work or at all municipal works.

§ 8. The *police* are always to be informed when workers are dismissed by way of punishment and of the reasons for their dismissal.

§ 9. Should workers have any *complaints* to make *against the building-site supervisor*, these are to be lodged with the *town surveyor* through an elected delegation of three workers. This officer will examine the cause of the complaint on the spot and *give his decision*.

§ 10. The working hours are from six thirty in the morning to twelve noon and from one o'clock in the afternoon till evening darkness scts in. (Wonderful style!)

§ 11. The worker is employed on these conditions.

§ 12. Payment is made on the building-site on Saturday afternoon.

The sworn building-site supervisor, for the present [. . .] whose instructions have to be obeyed.

Cologne

| Signature or sign | } of the worker | { Assigned to section of . . . and has, etc. |

Signature of the building-site supervisor

. . . .

This model law shows *what sort of Charter our bourgeoisie*, if it stood at the helm of state, *would impose on the people*.

See also MARX, On the Question of Free Trade, *MECW* VI, 456.

MARX, *Capital* I, 400.

The factory code in which capital formulates, like a private legislator, and at his own good will, his autocracy over his workpeople, unaccompanied by that division of responsibility, in other matters so much approved of by the bourgeoisie, and unaccompanied by the still more approved representative system, this code is but the capitalistic caricature of that social regulation of the labour-process which becomes requisite in co-operation on a great scale, and in the employment in common, of instruments of labour and especially of machinery. The place of the slave-driver's lash is taken by the overlooker's book of penalties. All punishments naturally resolve themselves into fines and deductions from wages, and the law-giving talent of the factory Lycurgus so arranges matters, that a violation of his laws is, if possible, more profitable to him than the keeping of them.

MARX, *ibid.*, 538.

The Roman slave was held by fetters: the wage-labourer is bound to his owner by invisible threads. The appearance of independence is kept up by means of a constant change of employers, and by the fictio juris of a contract.

In former times, capital resorted to legislation, whenever necessary, to enforce its proprietary rights over the free labourer. For instance, down to 1815, the emigration of mechanics employed in machine making was, in England, forbidden, under grievous pains and penalties.

MARX, Wages, Price and Profit, *MESW (3)* II, 55.

What the working man sells is not directly his *Labour*, but his *Labouring Power*, the temporary disposal of which he makes over to the capitalist. This is so much the case that I do not know whether by the English laws, but certainly by some Continental Laws, the *maximum time* is fixed for which a man is allowed to sell his labouring power. If allowed to do so for any indefinite period whatever, slavery would be immediately restored. Such a sale, if it comprised his lifetime, for example, would make him at once the lifelong slave of his employer.

4 Ideology

The Form of Ideology

In the course of their polemic against the Young Hegelians in "The German Ideology," Marx and Engels develop a concept of ideology which is both materialist and humanist. Engels continued to work with this conception, which in his later works he reiterated and elaborated in response to charges of simple economic determinism. Marx, however, having chosen the economy as the object of his major theoretical investigations, developed a structural and non-humanist conception of ideology, although he does not consider its applicability at levels other than the economic. The complexity of these never-admitted divergences—Engels claimed he was merely giving a voice to Marx' unspoken real position—becomes apparent when the form of ideology is made the focus of interest, as it is in the first set of extracts organized here.

An additional trend in Marx' and Engels' developing conception of ideology is that away from a mechanical and unidirectional correspondence between ruling class and ruling ideas such as is argued for in "The German Ideology". This was indeed modified later in that same work, in the pages referred to but not cited (see. p. 116), but only to admit a crude cultural lag theory designed to make sense of empirical discrepancies. In this case it is Marx' position which remains closer to the earlier formulation, for, as the next extract, from the third volume of *Capital* shows, he considers that both the form and the content of ideology under capitalism are necessarily bourgeois. Although at other points in his argument[1] he admits a place for perception and interpretation, the emphasis has now shifted from the bourgeois classes as thinkers to the systematic necessities of capitalism itself. The circuit of capital (from money to commodity to more money) in its process of reproduction generates appearances whose seeming reality exists independently of the law, but is taken as the object of legislation and legal pronouncements, and hence reinforced. Thus he argues that law provides the greatcoat of a transaction already well swaddled in mystifications: legal transactions reinforce the false appearance of economic transactions.[2]

For Engels, the thinker continues to be the source of ideology: social relations are important because they create and locate thinkers. He argues that the human originators of ideas (ideologies) then treat their productions *as if* they had an independent existence. Whereas for Marx in *Capital*, ideological forms are by their nature apparently independent of their economic origin, but in reality necessary expressions of it, for Engels thinkers let go the kite strings of their ideas, but in the logic of his argument they need not do so. The class basis of ideology in Engels' conception is indirect, resulting from the argument that human thinkers who produce these ideas are products of the material conditions of their own historical period. For Marx, ideology is a material constituent of capitalism, which could not be conceived as such in the absence, say, of ideological appearances such as the commodity or the wage relation. For Engels, the materiality of ideology is dependent on the argument that ideas which are treated as real are therefore materially consequential.

As Marx acknowledges a human role, so Engels states that "the economic life conditions of society" are expressed *directly* in law—a formulation reminiscent of *Capital*. But throughout most of the famous passage from "Ludwig Feuerbach," in which he deals with law and ideology, Engels maintains his humanist or thinker-based interpretation. More important here, for our purposes, is that law is seen as emanating from the state, and thus as a second-order level of abstraction from any concrete and individual concern. Engels' other discussions of the state from the same work can usefully be read in conjunction with this.[3]

In whichever way they theorized the source of the appearance of the autonomy of ideas, Marx and Engels continued to be agreed that the potency of ideology results from this 'independent' form Lawyers, as they note, make a living out of the reification of concepts, and so too do politicians. Neither writer, however, managed adequately to theorize the problem. Marx in his notebooks (*Grundrisse*, p. 109) promised to struggle further with this issue but in fact never did. For Marx, if forms of ideology are the *necessary* forms in which capitalist economic and social organization is comprehended, then how can historical and situational variation in these forms at the legal level be accounted for? His concept is able adequately and fully to explain only economic phenomena. Engels, on the other hand, attempted in his letter to Mehring (pp. 118–119) to develop the concept of the relative autonomy of ideology, but failed theoretically to provide limits to the independence of thought. Theories and ideologies may develop in accordance with their 'inner logic', but at some unspecified point for some unspecified reason this process has to stop. Variability in conception, however, is relatively easily accounted for by the humanist perspective, in terms of the varying life situations of the thinkers.

Each approach therefore raises and resolves different problems. For Engels, the issue of the constraint of ideologists by their own productions was a greater problem than in the conception in *Capital*. In the humanist conception, not only are the limits of what may be thought by any particular thinker difficult to identify theoretically, but in *Anti-Dühring*, Engels also ponders the fact that ideologies can be adopted by classes which did not produce them, and be turned against their masters. In *Capital*, on the other hand, forms of ideology are necessary expressions of the economic structure, and that they constrain understanding is intrinsic to their concept.

The Effectivity of Ideology

Form, function and content are of course materially inextricable and theoretically interrelated. This must be emphasized because there is a danger that, by separating their exposition for editorial reasons, credence may be lent to an alternative view. This section deals with the effects and consequences—the effectivities—of ideology.

It is because of the autonomy of ideologies, whether apparent or real, that they in fact obscure real relationships. Marx expresses cogently how phenomenal forms of the employment relation and juridical forms superimposed on these in capitalist society doubly mystify both the existence and the character of that surplus labour which is found in all modes of production. In capitalism uniquely labour has the form of abstract labour power but the wage relationship and the contract relationship conceal this. They make wages appear as the price of labour itself, and moreover, as the price of the labour actually performed, without any surplus. Economic theory reinforces this delusion. In a similar way, the real relationships are obscured as surplus value is deformed and distorted before being experienced as profit, interest and rent. The first of these ideas is rehearsed again by Engels in the course of his argument that the legal form of bourgeois marriage mystifies the real inequality between men and women within that institution.

When ideology is conceived as deriving from structure, legitimation as an effectivity of it stems from the obviousness, the seeming necessity of the phenomenal forms. The function is integral to this concept. From the thinker-based perspective, on the other hand, legitimation is made possible but not necessary by the setting free of ideas and consequent mystification of their human source. The extracts chosen to represent the authors' arguments for a legitimating function are all from Marx, and the latest to be written, from the *Grundrisse*, is presented first. This makes the general point that a democratic republic is a form of government which legitimates but does not obliterate the right of the stronger'. Both the Prussian and the French struggles yield examples of the importance of constitutionality for precisely this purpose. Victors need law: it is of little use to the defeated. Finally, the more obvious point is made that law can be used, possibly consciously, to legitimate a real appropriation.

The Content of Ideology

The lack of clarity about the form of ideology already alluded to results in an uncertainty about how many of the substantive ideas of bourgeois ideolgy were considered by Marx and Engels to be either necessary for or constitutive of the capitalist mode of production. In Marx' formulation this unclarity exists only at levels above the economic, and in Engels' formulation at all levels. None the less, both authors discuss the specific content of bourgeois ideology in several texts, and readers are therefore particularly recommended to follow up the additional references in this section.

In the second half of the last century, liberty, equality and, to a rapidly diminishing extent, fraternity, were still paramount

categories propounded by bourgeois ideologists. It is, therefore, no
matter of chance that although both liberty and equality are considered by Marx and Engels, the former is discussed at greatest length.
'Freedom', as the key concept of a rhetoric producing individua-
tion, producing no less than the bourgeois concept of 'man',
making possible, explaining and legitimating the new form of
capitalist wage labour, emerged during the struggle of the
bourgeoisie against the feudal order (p. 70). Six extracts have been
chosen to show these related ideas. The first three are from Engels:
one, from "The State of Germany", offers a general statement of the
origins of liberalism; the second deals with the mythological character of equal rights in a materially unequal world. Although, as his
early paper "Juristen Socialismus" shows, Engels was aware of the
political origin and use of the notion of equality, and of how
important a component it was of "the juridical world outlook of the
bourgeoisie", in the other two extracts Engels engages in a critique
of bourgeois democracy on its own terms, for equal and unequal
material conditions are located in the economic mechanisms of
distribution and exchange rather than production.

Marx in "The Eighteenth Brumaire" picks up these themes,
showing the internal contradictions confronting bourgeois legal
ideology when the issue is faced of *realizing* freedom in the material
world. Futile attempts are made by bourgeois ideologists to resolve
this by distinguishing between the particular application and the
universal abstract principle which, being ethereal, can remain unsul-
lied and inviolate in despite of all political abuse.

The necessary gap between rhetoric and reality, the ideological
subtleties involved in bridging it, and—importantly—the possibility
of exploiting it for class struggle, are recurrent topics. Marx,
however, goes further, emphasizing that the constitution of the free
labourer and his necessary extension as the individuated choosing
human subject is intrinsic to the capitalist mode of production. In the
early extract cited from "The Jewish Question", using strongly
Hegelian concepts, he shows how the isolated person is made the
basis of political society, while paradoxically being constituted in
himself as essentially and in nature non-political. This position is
maintained and strengthened a few years later (1845) in "The Holy
Family"; it is implicit in many of Marx' discussions of alienation and
of private property (see pp. 93–96).

Legal Thought

Thus Marx and Engels develop a framework of concepts within which to consider legal theory and the language of specific laws. The form of ideology is conceived differently, and consequently its effectivities result, in Marx' case from an *apparent*, and in Engels' case from a *relative*, autonomy, but the constituent content (man) is implicitly agreed, together with his essential attributes in bourgeois society (freedom and equality). The status of the variable and additional content, its necessity, contingence or fortuitousness, remains unclear.

In discussing particular juristic positions, Engels elaborately dissects the work of Dühring, demonstrating that writer's ignorance even of that bourgeois law which he purported to explain—an ignorance born in this case of a nationalistic myopia, the acceptance of a bourgeois ideological and political construct (the nation) as the unit of scientific analysis. His criticisms of Dühring on the grounds of idealism are presented elsewhere in this collection (pp. 236–240).

Both Marx and Engels explain and ironicize the bourgeois concept of justice. The concept of capitalism which Marx constructs has the notion of the independent person as a constitutive component. This ideological construct (the person) is constitutive of both economic and political structures in the capitalist mode of production. The bourgeois concept of justice is constituted in terms of these same notions of the person. Thus it must be regarded as fundamental in a hierarchy of determinations of legal thought. Reference to this conception must constantly be made, particular rules and decisions must be shown to emanate from it, changes must be assessed in terms of it, legal theories and legal concepts must demonstrably be congruent with it. Justice must be conceived in terms of and accorded to individuated, separate and isolated men, 'free and equal', who may subsequently and as part of this process be relocated in a social setting from which they are conceived independently to exist.

We have chosen a section from *Capital* III to exemplify this because it shows how certain forms of relationship are indeed 'natural' in capitalist society, and that justice as an approximate expression of these natural forms is not an intended duplicity by either maleficent or well-meaning bourgeois. There is a contingency and even an inevitability about that which will be conceived as just.

Marx in a more polemical mood in *Capital* I, p. 660, demonstrates a fundamental contradiction in 'capitalistic' ideology by parodying the discourse in which incompatibilities are reconciled between key concepts such as justice and equality. Together and separately Marx and Engels criticize idealist analyses of law based on the reification of such concepts. Engels, in particular, in a passage which we have been unable to include, cogently castigates Proudhon for this (see note on p. 138 and also pp. 141 and 235–236).

That social and productive relations are antecedent to juridical expressions is argued by Marx in the *Grundrisse*: the juridical category 'family' is antecedent to the category 'possession' as the latter is antecedent to 'property'. The priority of the most concrete category holds as a tenet of theory as well as historically. In the second of these two extracts Marx argues that the appropriate legal forms although contingent are not necessary for the emergence of capitalism. The point is not here developed. Engels in the final extract in the section ("Housing Question", pp. 308–309) implies the complete independence of the economic and legal levels, but this is done in polemic with Proudhon, who had conflated them. So the debate remains unresolved as to whether in Marxism a certain form or a particular content of law is constitutive of the capitalist mode of production, or whether such forms and contents are simply contingent upon it. We have argued that, on the whole, the former position is closer to the arguments presented in *Capital*, while the latter position is closer to Engels' subsequent interpretations.

Lawyers

Lawyers as an occupational group of professional ideologists are considered last in this section. The ideologically constituted occupation is presented first in "The German Ideology", where its ability to develop and reinforce ideology independently is argued. Judges as "irremovable inquisitors of legality" appear in "The Class Struggles in France", and lawyers appear in both *Capital* I and *Capital* II as part of a group who enrich themselves at the expense of others. Lawyers, as dupes of their own tortuous and reified thought processes,[4] are also discussed, as are lawyers as dangerous allies together with other disaffected "bourgeois doctrinaires", whose assistance is useful only if directly associated with the struggles of the working class. The last extract included is the subtle argument from *Theories of Surplus Value* I, in which Marx shows the shifting conceptions and evaluations of lawyers *within* bourgeois ideology, and relates these ideological constructions to the stage of development of the bourgeois class and of capitalism.

Notes

1. See, for example, *Capital* II, 229, for importance of professional thinkers, and *Capital* II, 270, for the important, but not *necessary*, thought processes going on in "the hollow skulls of the capitalists".
2. This interpretation of Marx can also be found in Rancière, J. (1976) The concept of "critique" and the "critique of political economy", *Economy and Society* **5,** No. 3. Rancière, however, treats Marx' discussions of consciousness as 'lapses' into an earlier mode of discourse, rather than as integral to Marx' later position.
3. Engels, F. Ludwig Feuerbach and the end of classical German philosophy, *MESW (3)* III, 369–370.
4. Engels, F. *Anti-Dühring*, 404, cited here on p. 122.

Extracts

The Form of Ideology

MARX/ENGELS, The German Ideology, *MECW* V, 59.

[III]

[I. THE RULING CLASS AND THE RULING IDEAS.
HOW THE HEGELIAN CONCEPTION OF THE DOMINATION
OF THE SPIRIT IN HISTORY AROSE]

[30] The ideas of the ruling class are in every epoch the ruling ideas: i.e., the class which is the ruling *material* force of society is at the same time its ruling *intellectual force*. The class which has the means of material production at its disposal, consequently also controls the means of mental production, so that the ideas of those who lack the means of mental production are on the whole subject to it. The ruling ideas are nothing more than the ideal expression of the dominant material relations, the dominant material relations grasped as ideas; hence of the relations which make the one class the ruling one, therefore, the ideas of its dominance. The individuals composing the ruling class possess among other things consciousness, and therefore think. Insofar, therefore, as they rule as a class and determine the extent and compass of an historical epoch, it is self-evident that they do this in its whole range, hence among other things rule also as thinkers, as producers of ideas, and regulate the production and distribution of the ideas of their age: thus their ideas are the ruling ideas of the epoch. For instance, in an age and in a country where royal power, aristocracy and bourgeoisie are contending for domination and where, therefore, domination is shared, the doctrine of the separation of powers proves to be the dominant idea and is expressed as an "eternal law".

See also MARX/ENGELS *ibid.*, 82–83.

MARX, *Capital* III, 347–349.

The return of capital to its point of departure is generally the characteristic movement of capital in its total circuit. This is by no means a feature of interest-bearing capital alone. What singles it out is rather the external form of its return without the intervention of any circuit. The loaning capitalist gives away his capital, transfers it to the industrial capitalist, without receiving any equivalent. His transfer is not an act belonging to the real circulation process of capital at all. It serves merely to introduce this circuit, which is effected by the industrial capitalist. This first change of position of money does not express any act of the metamorphosis—neither buying nor selling. Ownership is not relinquished, because there is no exchange and no equivalent is received. The return of the money from the hands of the industrial capitalist to those of the loaning capitalist merely supplements the first act of giving away the capital. Advanced in the form of money, the capital again returns to the industrial capitalist through the circular process in the form of money. But since it did not belong to him when he invested it, it cannot belong to him on its return. Passing through the process of reproduction cannot by any means turn the capital into his property. He must therefore restore it to the lender. The first expenditure, which transfers the capital from the lender to the borrower, is a legal transaction which has nothing to do with the actual process of reproduction. It is merely a prelude to this process. The return payment, which again transfers the capital that has flowed back from the borrower to the lender is another legal transaction, a supplement of the first. One introduces the actual process, the other is an act supplementary to this process. Point of departure and point of return, the giving away and the recovery of the loaned capital, thus appear as arbitrary movements promoted by legal transactions, which take place before and after the actual movement of capital and have nothing to do with it as such. It would have been all the same as concerns this actual movement if the capital had from the first belonged to the industrial capitalist and had returned to him, therefore, as his own.

In the first introductory act the lender gives his capital to the borrower. In the supplemental and closing act the borrower returns the capital to the lender. As concerns the transaction between these two—and aside from the interest for the present—as concerns the movement of the loaned capital between lender and borrower, therefore, the two acts (separated by a longer or shorter time interval, during which the actual reproduction process of the capital takes place) embrace the entire movement. And this movement, disposing on condition of returning, constitutes *per se* the movement of lending and borrowing, that specific form of conditionally alienating money or commodities.

The characteristic movement of capital in general, the return of the money to the capitalist, i.e., the return of capital to its point of departure, assumes in the case of interest-bearing capital a wholly external appearance, separated from the actual movement, of which it is a form. A gives away his money not as money, but as capital. No transformation occurs in the capital. It merely changes hands. Its real transformation into capital does not take place until it is in the hands of B. But for A it becomes capital as soon as he gives it to B. The actual reflux of capital from the processes of production and circulation takes place only for B. But for A the reflux assumes the same form as the alienation. The capital returns from B to A. Giving away, i.e., loaning money for a certain time and receiving it back with interest (surplus–value) is the complete form of the movement peculiar to interest-bearing capital as such. . . . A special sort of commodity, capital has its own peculiar mode of alienation. Neither does its return, therefore, express itself as the consequence and result of some definite series of economic processes, but as the effect of a specific legal agreement between buyer and seller. The time of return depends on the progress of the process of reproduction; in the case of interest-bearing capital, its return as capital *seems* to depend on the mere agreement between lender and borrower. So that in regard to this transaction the return of capital no longer appears as a result arising out of the process of reproduction; it appears as if the loaned capital never lost the form of money.

.   .   .   .

But since money advanced as capital has the property of returning to the person who advanced it, to the one who expended it as capital, and since M—C—M′ is the immanent form of the movement of capital, the owner of the money can, for this very reason, loan it out as capital, as something that has the property of returning to its point of departure, of preserving, and increasing, its value in the course of its movement. He gives it away as capital, because it returns to its point of departure after having been employed as capital, hence can be restored by the borrower after a certain period precisely because it has come back to him.

Loaning money as capital—its alienation on the condition of it being returned after a certain time—presupposes, therefore, that it will be actually employed as capital, and that it actually flows back to its starting-point. The real cycle made by money as capital is, therefore, the premise for the legal transaction by which the borrower must return the money to the lender. If the borrower does not use the money as capital, that is his own business. The lender loans it as capital, and as such it is supposed to perform the functions of capital, which include the circuit of money-capital until it returns to its starting-point in the form of money.

ENGELS, Letter to Mehring, 14.7.1895, *MESC*, 434–435.

Ideology is a process accomplished by the so-called thinker consciously, indeed, but with a false consciousness. The real motives impelling him remain unknown to him, otherwise it would not be an ideological process at all. Hence he imagines false or apparent motives. Because it is a process of thought he derives both its form and its content from pure thought, either his own or that of his predecessors. He works with mere thought material which he accepts without examination as the product of thought, he does not investigate further for a more remote process independent of thought; indeed its origin seems obvious to him, because as all action is produced through the medium of thought it also appears to him to be ultimately based upon thought. The ideologist who deals with history (history is here simply meant to comprise all the spheres—political, juridical, philosophical, theological—belonging to society and not only to nature), the ideologist dealing with history then, possesses in every sphere of science material which has formed itself independently out of the thought of previous generations and has gone through an independent series of developments in the brains of these successive generations. True, external facts belonging to its own or other spheres may have exercised a co-determining influence on this development, but the tacit pre-supposition is that these facts themselves are also only the fruits of a process of thought, and so we still remain within that realm of pure thought which has successfully digested the hardest facts.

It is above all this appearance of an independent history of state constitutions, of systems of law, of ideological conceptions in every separate domain, which dazzles most people. If Luther and Calvin "overcome" the official Catholic religion, or Hegel "overcomes" Fichte and Kant, or if the constitutional Montesquieu is indirectly "overcome" by Rousseau with his "Social Contract," each of these events remains within the sphere of theology, philosophy or political science, represents a stage in the history of these particular spheres of thought and never passes outside the sphere of thought. And since the bourgeois illusion of the eternity and the finality of capitalist production has been added as well, even the victory of the physiocrats and Adam Smith over the mercantilists is accounted as a sheer victory of thought; not as the reflection in thought of changed economic facts but as the finally achieved correct understanding of actual conditions subsisting always and everywhere—in fact if Richard Coeur-de-Lion and Philip Augustus had introduced free trade instead of getting mixed up in the crusades we should have been spared five hundred years of misery and stupidity.

This side of the matter, which I can only indicate here, we have all, I think, neglected more than it deserves. It is the old story: form is always neglected at first for content. As I say, I have done that too, and the mistake has always only struck me later. So I am not only far from reproaching you with this in any way, but as the older of the guilty parties I have no right to do so, on the contrary; but I would like all the same to draw your attention to this point for the future. Hanging together with this too is the fatuous notion of the ideologists that because we deny an independent historical development to the various ideological spheres which play a part in history we also deny them any effect upon history. The basis of this is the common undialectical conception of cause and effect as rigidly opposite poles, the total disregarding of interaction; these gentlemen often almost deliberately forget that once an historic element has been brought into the world by other elements, ultimately by economic facts, it also reacts in its turn and may react on its environment and even on its own causes.

ENGELS, Ludwig Feuerbach and the End of Classical German Philosophy, *MESW (3)* III, 370–372.

But if even in our modern era, with its gigantic means of production and communication, the state is not an independent domain with an independent development, but one whose existence as well as development is to be explained in the last resort by the economic conditions of life of society, then this must be still more true of all earlier times when the production of the material life of man was not yet carried on with these abundant auxiliary means, and when, therefore, the necessity of such production must have exercised a still greater mastery over men. If the state even today, in the era of big industry and of railways, is on the whole only a reflection, in concentrated form, of the economic needs of the class controlling production, then this must have been much more so in an epoch when each generation of men was forced to spend a far greater part of its aggregate lifetime in satisfying material needs, and was therefore much more dependent on them than we are today. An examination of the history of earlier periods, as soon as it is seriously undertaken from this angle, most abundantly confirms this. But, of course, this cannot be gone into here.

If the state and public law are determined by economic relations, so, too, of course is private law, which indeed in essence only sanctions the existing economic relations between individuals which are normal in the given circumstances. The form in which this happens can, however, vary considerably. It is possible, as happened in England, in harmony with the whole national development, to retain in the main the forms of the old feudal laws while giving them a bourgeois content; in fact, directly reading a bourgeois meaning into the feudal name. But, also, as happened in western continental Europe, Roman Law, the first world law of a commodity-producing society, with its unsurpassably fine elaboration of all the essential legal relations of simple commodity owners (of buyers and sellers, debtors and creditors, contracts, obligations, etc.), can be taken as the foundation. In which case, for the benefit of a still petty-bourgeois and semi-feudal society, it can either be reduced to the level of such a society simply through judicial practice (common law) or, with the help of allegedly enlightened, moralising jurists; it can be worked into a special code of law to correspond with such social level—a code which in these circumstances will be a bad one also from the legal standpoint (for instance, Prussian *Landrecht*). In which case, however, after a great bourgeois revolution, it is also possible for such a classic law code of bourgeois society as the French *Code Civil* to be worked out upon the basis of this same Roman Law. If, therefore, bourgeois legal rules merely express the economic life conditions of society in legal form, then they can do so well or ill according to circumstances.

The state presents itself to us as the first ideological power over man. Society creates for itself an organ for the safeguarding of its common interests against internal and external attacks. This organ is the state power. Hardly come into being, this organ makes itself independent *vis-à-vis* society; and, indeed, the more so, the more it becomes the organ of a particular class, the more it directly enforces the supremacy of that class. The fight of the oppressed class against the ruling class becomes necessarily a political fight, a fight first of all against the political dominance of this class. The consciousness of the interconnection between this political struggle and its economic basis becomes dulled and can be lost altogether. While this is not wholly the case with the participants, it almost always happens with the historians. Of the ancient sources on the struggles within the Roman Republic only Appian tells us clearly and distinctly what was at issue in the last resort—namely, landed property.

But once the state has become an independent power *vis-à-vis* society, it produces forthwith a further ideology. It is indeed among professional politicians, theorists of public law and jurists of private law that the connection with economic facts gets lost for fair. Since in each particular case the economic facts must assume the form of juristic motives in order to receive legal sanction; and since, in so doing, consideration of course has to be given to the whole legal system already in operation, the juristic form is, in consequence, made everything and the economic content nothing. Public law and private law are treated as independent spheres, each having its own independent historical development, each being capable of and needing a systematic presentation by the consistent elimination of all inner contradictions.

Still higher ideologies, that is, such as are still further removed from the material, economic basis, take the form of philosophy and religion. Here the interconnection between conceptions and their material conditions of existence becomes more and more complicated, more and more obscured by intermediate links. But the interconnection exists. Just as the whole Renaissance period, from the middle of the fifteenth century, was an essential product of the towns and, therefore, of the burghers, so also was the subsequently newly-awakened philosophy. Its content was in essence only the philosophical expression of the thoughts corresponding to the development of the small and middle burghers into a big bourgeoisie. Among last century's Englishmen and Frenchmen who in many cases were just as much political economists as philosophers, this is clearly evident; and we have proved it above in regard to the Hegelian school.

We will now in addition deal only briefly with religion, since the latter stands furthest away from material life and seems to be most alien to it. Religion arose in very primitive times from erroneous, primitive conceptions of men about their own nature and external nature surrounding them. Every ideology, however, once it has arisen, develops in connection with the given concept-material, and develops this material further; otherwise it would not be an ideology, that is, occupation with thoughts as with independent entities, developing independently and subject only to their own laws. That the material life conditions of the persons inside whose heads this thought process goes on in the last resort determine the course of this process remains of necessity unknown to these persons, for otherwise there would be an end to all ideology.

ENGELS, *ibid.*, 374–375.

We see, therefore: religion, once formed, always contains traditional material, just as in all ideological domains tradition forms a great conservative force. But the transformations which this material undergoes spring from class relations, that is to say, out of the economic relations of the people who execute these transformations. And here that is sufficient.

See also MARX/ENGELS, The Communist Manifesto, *MECW* VI, 494–495; ENGELS, *Anti-Dühring*, 130–131.

MARX, *Grundrisse*, 109.

(6) *The uneven development of material production relative to e.g. artistic development.* In general, the concept of progress not to be conceived in the usual abstractness. Modern art etc. This disproportion not as important or so difficult to grasp as within practical-social relations themselves. E.g. the relation of education. Relation of the *United States* to Europe. But the really difficult point to discuss here is how relations of production develop unevenly as legal relations. Thus e.g. the relation of Roman private law (this less the case with criminal and public law) to modern production.

ENGELS, *Anti-Dühring*, 404.

And not only the labourers, but also the classes directly or indirectly exploiting the labourers are made subject, through the division of labour, to the tool of their function: the empty-minded bourgeois to his own capital and his own insane craving for profits; the lawyer to his fossilized legal conceptions, which dominate him as an independent power; the "educated classes" in general to their manifold species of local narrow-mindedness and one-sidedness, to their own physical and mental short-sightedness, to their stunted growth due to their narrow specialized education and their being chained for life to this specialized activity—even when this specialized activity is merely to do nothing.

ENGELS, *Anti-Dühring*, 146–147.

As is well known, however, from the moment when the bourgeoisie emerged from feudal burgherdom, when this estate of the Middle Ages developed into a modern class, it was always and inevitably accompanied by its shadow, the proletariat. And in the same way bourgeois demands for equality were accompanied by proletarian demands for equality. From the moment when the bourgeois demand for the abolition of class *privileges* was put forward, alongside it appeared the proletarian demand for the abolition of the *classes themselves*—at first in religious form, leaning towards primitive Christianity, and later drawing support from the bourgeois equalitarian theories themselves. The proletarians took the bourgeoisie at its word: equality must not be merely apparent, must not apply merely to the sphere of the state, but must also be real, must also be extended to the social, economic sphere. And especially since the French bourgeoisie, from the great revolution on, brought civil equality to the forefront, the French proletariat has answered blow for blow with the demand for social, economic equality, and equality has become the battle-cry particularly of the French proletariat.

The demand for equality in the mouth of the proletariat has therefore a double meaning. It is either—as was the case especially at the very start, for example in the Peasant War—the spontaneous reaction against the crying social inequalities, against the contrast between rich and poor, the feudal lords and their serfs, the surfeiters and the starving, as such it is simply an expression of the revolutionary instinct, and finds its justification in that, and in that only. Or, on the other hand, this demand has arisen as a reaction against the bourgeois demand for equality, drawing more or less correct and more far-reaching demands from this bourgeois demand, and serving as an agitational means in order to stir up the workers against the capitalists with the aid of the capitalists' own assertions; and in this case it stands or falls with bourgeois equality itself.

See also, for discussions of ideologists as moral exemplars and of legal lag: ENGELS, Socialism, Utopian and Scientific, *MESW (3)* III, 107–108; MARX/ENGELS, The German Ideology, *MECW* V, 419–420; MARX, *Grundrisse,* 469–470; MARX, *Capital* III, 788.

MARX, *Capital* I, 505.
The wage-form thus extinguishes every trace of the division of the working-day into necessary labour and surplus-labour, into paid and unpaid labour. All labour appears as paid labour. In the corvée, the labour of the worker for himself, and his compulsory labour for his lord, differ in space and time in the clearest possible way. In slave-labour, even that part of the working-day in which the slave is only replacing the value of his own means of existence, in which, therefore, in fact, he works for himself alone, appears as labour for his master. All the slave's labour appears as unpaid labour. In wage-labour, on the contrary, even surplus-labour, or unpaid labour, appears as paid. There the property-relation conceals the labour of the slave for himself; here the money-relation conceals the unrequited labour of the wage-labourer.

Hence, we may understand the decisive importance of the transformation of value and price of labour-power into the form of wages, or into the value and price of labour itself. This phenomenal form, which makes the actual relation invisible, and, indeed, shows the direct opposite of that relation, forms the basis of all the juridical notions of both labourer and capitalist, of all the mystifications of the capitalistic mode of production, of all its illusions as to liberty, of all the apologetic shifts of the vulgar economists.

If history took a long time to get at the bottom of the mystery of wages, nothing, on the other hand, is more easy to understand than the necessity, the *raison d'être*, of this phenomenon.

The exchange between capital and labour at first presents itself to the mind in the same guise as the buying and selling of all other commodities. The buyer gives a certain sum of money, the seller an article of a nature diffcrent from money. The jurist's consciousness recognises in this, at most, a material difference, expressed in the juridically equivalent formulae: "Do ut des, do ut facias, facio ut des, facio ut facias."

See also MARX, *Grundrisse*, 464–465; MARX, *Grundrisse*, 514 (this adds the dimension of alienation); MARX, Wages, Prices, and Profit, *MESW (3)* II, 60.

The Effectivity of Ideology

MARX, *Theories of Surplus Value* III, *609*.

Thus it is *interest*, not *profit*, which appears to be the *creation of value* arising from capital as such and therefore from the mere ownership of capital; consequently it is regarded as the specific revenue created by capital. This is also the form in which it is conceived by the vulgar economists. In this form all intermediate links are obliterated, and the *fetishic feature* of capital, as also the concept of the *capital-fetish*, is complete. This form arises necessarily, because the juridical aspect of property is separated from its economic aspect and one part of the profit under name of interest accrues to *capital* which is completely separated from the production process, or to the *owner of this capital*.

MARX, *Capital* III, 476–477.

Secondly: To what extent does a scarcity of money, i.e., a shortage of loan capital, express a shortage of real capital (commodity-capital and productive capital)? To what extent does it coincide, on the other hand, with a shortage of money as such, a shortage of the medium of circulation?

In so far as we have hitherto considered the peculiar form of accumulation of money-capital and of money wealth in general, it has resolved itself into an accumulation of claims of ownership upon labour. The accumulation of the capital of the national debt has been revealed to mean merely an increase in a class of state creditors, who have the privilege of a firm claim upon a certain portion of the tax revenue. By means of these facts, whereby even an accumulation of debts may appear as an accumulation of capital, the height of distortion taking place in the credit system becomes apparent. These promissory notes, which are issued for the originally loaned capital long since spent, these paper duplicates of consumed capital, serve for their owners as capital to the extent that they are saleable commodities and may, therefore, be reconverted into capital.

Titles of ownership to public works, railways, mines, etc., are indeed, as we have also seen, titles to real capital. But they do not place this capital at one's disposal. It is not subject to withdrawal. They merely convey legal claims to a portion of the surplus-value to be produced by it. But these titles likewise become paper duplicates of the real capital; it is as though a bill of lading were to acquire a value separate from the cargo, both concomitantly and simultaneously with it. They come to nominally represent non-existent capital. For the real capital exists side by side with them and does not change hands as a result of the transfer of these duplicates from one person to another. They assume the form of interest-bearing capital, not only because they guarantee a certain income, but also because, through their sale, their repayment as capital-values can be obtained. To the extent that the accumulation of this paper expresses the accumulation of railways, mines, steamships, etc., to that extent does it express the extension of the actual reproduction pro-cess—just as the extension of, for example, a tax list on movable property indicates the expansion of this property. But as duplicates which are themselves objects of transactions as commodities, and thus able to circulate as capital-values, they are illusory, and their value may fall or rise quite independently of the movement of value of the real capital for which they are titles.

MARX, *ibid.*, 634.

Whatever the specific form of rent may be, all types have this in common: the appropriation of rent is that economic form in which landed property is realised, and ground-rent, in turn, presupposes the existence of landed property, the ownership of certain portions of our planet by certain individuals. The owner may be an individual represent-ing the community, as in Asia, Egypt, etc.; or this landed property may be merely incidental to the ownership of the immediate producers themselves by some individual as under slavery or serfdom; or it may be a purely private ownership of Nature by non-producers, a mere title to land; or, finally, it may be a relationship to the land which, as in the case of colonists and small peasants owning land, seems to be directly included—in the isolated and not socially developed labour—in the appropriation and production of the products of particular plots of land by the direct producers.

This *common element* in the various forms of rent, namely that of being the economic realisation of landed property, of legal fiction by grace of which certain individuals have an exclusive right to certain parts of our planet—makes it possible for the differences to escape detection.

ENGELS, Origin of the Family, Private Property and the State, *MESW (3)* III, 244–246.

Sex love in the relation of husband and wife is and can become the rule only among the oppressed classes, that is, at the present day, among the proletariat, no matter whether this relationship is officially sanctioned or not. But here all the foundations of classical monogamy are removed. Here, there is a complete absence of all property, for the safeguarding and inheritance of which monogamy and male domination were established. Therefore, there is no stimulus whatever here to assert male domination. What is more, the means, too, are absent; bourgeois law, which protects this domination, exists only for the propertied classes and their dealings with the proletarians. It costs money, and therefore, owing to the worker's poverty, has no validity in his attitude towards his wife. Personal and social relations of quite a different sort are the decisive factors here. Moreover, since large-scale industry has transferred the woman from the house to the labour market and the factory, and makes her, often enough, the bread-winner of the family, the last remnants of male domination in the proletarian home have lost all founda-tion—except, perhaps, for some of that brutality towards women which became firmly rooted with the establishment of monogamy. Thus, the proletarian family is no longer monogamian in the strict sense, even in cases of the most passionate love and strictest faithfulness of the two parties, and despite all spiritual and worldly benedictions which may have been received. The two eternal adjuncts of monogamy—hetaerism and adultery—therefore, play an almost negligible role here; the woman has regained, in fact, the right of separation, and when the man and woman cannot get along they prefer to part. In short, proletarian marriage is monogamian in the etymological sense of the word, but by no means in the historical sense.

Our jurists, to be sure, hold that the progress of legislation to an increasing degree removes all cause for complaint on the part of the woman. Modern civilised systems of law are recognising more and more, first, that, in order to be effective, marriage must be an agreement voluntarily entered into by both parties; and secondly, that during marriage, too, both parties must be on an equal footing in respect to rights and obligations. If, however, these two demands were consistently carried into effect, women would have all that they could ask for.

This typical lawyer's reasoning is exactly the same as that with which the radical republican bourgeois dismisses the proletarian. The labour contract is supposed to be voluntarily entered into by both parties. But it is taken to be voluntarily entered into as soon as the law has put both parties on an equal footing *on paper*. The power given to one party by its different class position, the pressure it exercises on the other—the real economic position of both—all this is no concern of the law. And both parties, again, are supposed to have equal rights for the duration of the labour contract, unless one or the other of the parties expressly waived them. That the concrete economic situation compels the worker to forego even the slightest semblance of equal rights—this again is something the law cannot help.

As far as marriage is concerned, even the most progressive law is fully satisfied as soon as the parties formally register their voluntary desire to get married. What happens behind the legal curtains, where real life is enacted, how this voluntary agreement is arrived at—is no concern of the law and the jurist. And yet the simplest comparison of laws should serve to show the jurist what this voluntary agreement really amounts to. In countries where the children are legally assured of an obligatory share of their parents' property and thus cannot be disinherited—in Germany, in the countries under French law, etc.—the children must obtain their parents' consent in the question of marriage. In countries under English law, where parental consent to marriage is not legally requisite, the parents have full testatory freedom over their property and can, if they so desire, cut their children off with a shilling. It is clear, therefore, that despite this, or rather just because of this, among those classes which have something to inherit, freedom to marry is not one whit greater in England and America than in France or Germany.

The position is no better with regard to the juridical equality of man and woman in marriage. The inequality of the two before the law, which is a legacy of previous social conditions, is not the cause but the effect of the economic oppression of women. In the old communistic household, which embraced numerous couples and their children, the administration of the household, entrusted to the women, was just as much a public, a socially necessary industry as the providing of food by the men. This situation changed with the patriarchal family, and even more with the monogamian individual family. The administration of the household lost its public character. It was no longer the concern of society. It became a *private service*. The wife became the first domestic servant, pushed out of participation in social production. Only modern large-scale industry again threw open to her—and only to the proletarian woman at that—the avenue to social production; but in such a way that, when she fulfils her duties in the private service of her family, she remains excluded from public production and cannot earn anything; and when she wishes to take part in public industry and earn her living independently, she is not in a position to fulfil her family duties. What applies to the woman in the factory applies to her in all the professions, right up to medicine and law. The modern individual family is based on the open or disguised domestic enslavement of the woman; and modern society is a mass composed solely of individual families as its molecules. Today, in the great majority of cases, the man has to be the earner, the bread-winner of the family, at least among the propertied classes, and this gives him a dominating position which requires no special legal privileges. In the family, he is the bourgeois; the wife represents the proletariat. In the industrial world, however, the specific character of the economic oppression that weighs down the proletariat stands out in all its sharpness only after all the special legal privileges of the capitalist class have been set aside and the complete juridical equality of both classes is established. The democratic republic does not abolish the antagonism between the two classes; on the contrary, it provides the field on which it is fought out. And, similarly, the peculiar character of man's domination over woman in the modern family, and the necessity, as well as the manner, of establishing real social equality between the two, will be brought out into full relief only when both are completely equal before the law. It will then become evident that the first premise for the emancipation of women is the reintroduction of the entire female sex into public industry; and that this again demands that the quality possessed by the individual family of being the economic unit of society be abolished.

MARX, *Grundrisse*, 88.

Protection of acquisitions etc. When these trivialities are reduced to their real content, they tell more than their preachers know. Namely that every form of production creates its own legal relations, form of government, etc. In bringing things which are organically related into an accidental relation, into a merely reflective connection, they display their crudity and lack of conceptual understanding. All the bourgeois economists are aware of is that production can be carried on better under the modern police than e.g. on the principle of might makes right. They forget only that this principle is also a legal relation, and that the right of the stronger prevails in their 'constitutional republics' as well, only in another form.

When the social conditions corresponding to a specific stage of production are only just arising, or when they are already dying out, there are, naturally, disturbances in production, although to different degrees and with different effects.

To summarize: There are characteristics which all stages of production have in common, and which are established as general ones by the mind; but the so-called *general preconditions* of all production are nothing more than these abstract moments with which no real historical stage of production can be grasped.

MARX, The Bourgeoisie and the Counter-revolution, *Articles from NRZ*, 181.

The main contingents for the new ministries were supplied by the *Rhineland* and *Silesia*, the provinces with the most advanced bourgeoisie. They were followed by a whole train of Rhenish lawyers. As the bourgeoisie was pushed into the background by the feudal aristocracy, the Rhineland and Silesia were replaced in the cabinets by the old Prussian provinces. The only link of the Brandenburg cabinet with the

Rhineland is through a single Elberfeld Tory. *Hansemann* and *von der Heydt!* These two names exemplify the whole difference between March and December 1848 for the Prussian bourgeoisie.

The Prussian bourgeoisie reached the political summit not by means of a *peaceful deal with the Crown*, as it had desired, but as the result of a *revolution*. It was to defend, not its own interests, but *those of the people*—for a *popular movement* had prepared the way for the bourgeoisie—against the Crown, in other words, against *itself*. For the bourgeoisie regarded the Crown simply as a cloak provided by the grace of God, a cloak that was to conceal its own profane interests. The inviolability of *its* own interests and of the political forms appropriate to these interests, expressed in constitutional language, is *inviolability of the Crown*. Hence the enthusiasm of the German bourgeoisie and in particular of the Prussian bourgeoisie for the *constitutional monarchy*.

MARX, The Civil War in France: Address of the General Council, *MESW (3)* II, 231.

Meanwhile, his relations with the provinces become more and more difficult. Not one single address of approval came in to gladden Thiers and his Rurals. Quite the contrary. Deputations and addresses demanding, in a tone anything but respectful, conciliation with Paris on the basis of the unequivocal recognition of the republic, the acknowledgement of communal liberties, and the dissolution of the National Assembly, whose mandate was extinct, poured in from all sides, and in such numbers that Dufaure, Thiers's Minister of Justice, in his circular of 23 April to the public prosecutors, commanded them to treat 'the cry of conciliation' as a crime! In regard, however, of the hopeless prospect held out by his campaign, Thiers resolved to shift his tactics by ordering, all over the country, municipal elections to take place on 30 April, on the basis of the new municipal law dictated by himself to the National Assembly. What with the intrigues of his prefects, what with police intimidation, he felt quite sanguine of imparting, by the verdict of the provinces, to the National Assembly that moral power it had never possessed, and of getting at last from the provinces the physical force required for the conquest of Paris.

MARX, *ibid.*, 232.

Dufaure, this old Orleanist lawyer, had always been the justiciary of the state of siege, as now in 1871, under Thiers, so in 1839 under Louis Philippe, and in 1849 under Louis Bonaparte's presidency. While out of office he made a fortune by pleading for the Paris capitalists, and made political capital by pleading against the laws he had himself originated. He now hurried through the National Assembly not only a set of repressive laws which were, after the fall of Paris, to extirpate the last remnants of republican liberty in France; he foreshadowed the fate of Paris by abridging the, for him, too slow procedure of courts-martial, and by a new-fangled, Draconic code of deportation. The revolution of 1848, abolishing the penalty of death for political crimes, had replaced it by deportation. Louis Bonaparte did not dare, at least not in theory, to re-establish the regime of the guillotine. The Rural Assembly, not yet bold enough even to hint that the Parisians were not rebels, but assassins, had therefore to confine its prospective vengeance against Paris to Dufaure's new code of deportation.

MARX, *ibid*., 234.

As soon as MacMahon was able to assure him that he could shortly enter Paris, Thiers declared to the Assembly that

> "he would enter Paris with the *laws* in his hands, and demand a full expiation from the wretches who had sacrificed the lives of soldiers and destroyed public monuments."

As the moment of decision drew near he said—to the Assembly, "I shall be pitiless!"—to Paris, that it was doomed; and to his Bonapartist banditti, that they had State licence to wreak vengeance upon Paris to their hearts' content. At last, when treachery had opened the gates of Paris to General Douay, on the 21st of May, Thiers, on the 22nd, revealed to the Rurals the "goal" of his conciliation comedy, which they had so obstinately persisted in not understanding.

> "I told you a few days ago that we were approaching *our goal;* today I come to tell you *the goal* is reached. The victory of order, justice and civilisation is at last won!"

So it was. The civilisation and justice of bourgeois order comes out in its lurid light whenever the slaves and drudges of that order rise against their masters. Then this civilisation and justice stand forth as undisguised savagery and lawless revenge. Each new crisis in the class struggle between the appropriator and the producer brings out this fact more glaringly. Even the atrocities of the bourgeois in June, 1848, vanish before the ineffable infamy of 1871. The self-sacrificing heroism with which the population of Paris—men, women and children—fought for eight days after the entrance of the Versaillese, reflects as much the grandeur of their cause, as the infernal deeds of the soldiery reflect the innate spirit of that civilisation of which they are the mercenary vindicators. A glorious civilisation, indeed, the great problem of which is how to get rid of the heaps of corpses it made after the battle was over!

MARX, *ibid*., 236–237.

In all its bloody triumphs over the self-sacrificing champions of a new and better society, that nefarious civilisation, based upon the enslavement of labour, drowns the moans of its victims in a hue-and-cry of calumny, reverberated by a world-wide echo. The serene working men's Paris of the Commune is suddenly changed into a pandemonium by the bloodhounds of "order." And what does this tremendous change prove to the bourgeois mind of all countries? Why, that the Commune has conspired against civilisation! The Paris people die enthusiastically for the Commune in numbers unequalled in any battle known to history. What does that prove? Why, that the Commune was not the people's own government but the usurpation of a handful of criminals! The women of Paris joyfully give up their lives at the barricades and on the place of execution. What does this prove? Why, that the demon of the Commune has changed them into Megaeras and Hecates! The moderation of the Commune during two months of undisputed sway is equalled only by the heroism of its defence. What does that prove? Why, that for months the Commune carefully hid, under a mask of moderation and humanity, the blood-thirstiness of its fiendish instincts, to be let loose in the hour of its agony!

See also **MARX**, *ibid.*, 204 and 205.

MARX, *Capital* III, 770.

Thirdly. In all ancient civilisations, old historical and traditional relations, for instance, in the form of state-owned lands, communal lands, etc., have purely arbitrarily withheld from cultivation large tracts of land, which only return to it little by little. The succession in which they are brought under cultivation depends neither upon their good quality nor siting, but upon wholly external circumstances. In tracing the history of English communal lands turned successively into private property through the Enclosure Bills and brought under the plough, nothing would be more ridiculous than the fantastic idea that a modern agricultural chemist, such as Liebig, had indicated the selection of land in this succession, designating certain fields for cultivation owing to chemical properties and excluding others. What was more decisive in this case was the opportunity which makes the thief, the more or less plausible legalistic subterfuges of the big landlords to justify their appropriation.

See also **MARX**, *ibid.*, 619.

The Content of Ideology

ENGELS, The State of Germany, *MECW* VI, 28–29.

After the downfall of Napoleon, which I must repeat again, by the kings and aristocrats of the time, was totally identified with the putting down of the French Revolution, or, as they called it, the revolution, after 1815, in all countries, the anti-revolutionary party held the reins of government. The feudalist aristocrats ruled in all cabinets from London to

Naples, from Lisbon to St. Petersburg. However, the middle classes, who had paid for the job and assisted in doing it, wanted to have their share of the power. It was by no means their interest which was placed in the ascendant by the restored governments. On the contrary, middle-class interests were neglected everywhere, and even openly set at nought. The passing of the English Corn Law of 1815 is the most striking example of a fact which was common to all Europe; and yet the middle classes were more powerful then than ever they had been. Commerce and manufactures had been extending everywhere, and had swelled the fortunes of the fat bourgeois; their increased well-being was manifested in their increased spirit of speculation, their growing demand for comforts and luxuries. It was impossible, then, that they should quietly submit to be governed by a class whose decay had been going on for centuries—whose interests were opposed to those of the middle clas-ses—whose momentary return to power was the very work of the bourgeois. The struggle between the middle classes and the aristocracy was inevitable; it commenced almost immediately after the peace.

The middle classes being powerful by money only, cannot acquire political power but by making money the only qualification for the legislative capacity of an individual. They must merge all feudalistic privileges, all political monopolies of past ages, in the one great privilege and monopoly of *money*. The political dominion of the middle classes is, therefore, of an essentially *liberal* appearance. They destroy all the old differences of several estates co-existing in a country, all arbitrary privileges and exemptions; they are obliged to make the elective principle the foundation of government—to recognise equality in principle, to free the press from the shackles of monarchical censorship, to introduce the jury, in order to get rid of a separate class of judges, forming a state in the state. So far they appear thorough democrats. But they introduce all the improvements so far only, as thereby all former individual and heredit-ary privileges are replaced by the privilege of *money*. Thus the principle of election is, by property qualifications for the right of electing and being elected, retained for their own class. Equality is set aside again by restraining it to a mere "equality before the law", which means equality in spite of the inequality of rich and poor—equality within the limits of the chief inequality existing—which means, in short, nothing else but giving *inequality* the name of equality. Thus the liberty of the press is, of itself, a middle-class privilege, because printing requires *money*, and buyers for the printed productions, which buyers must have money again. Thus the jury is a middle-class privilege, as proper care is taken to bring none but "respectables" into the jury-box.

ENGELS, Ludwig Feuerbach and the End of Classical German Philoso-phy, *MESW (3)* III, 356 and 358–359.

The latter's ethics, or doctrine of moral conduct, is the philosophy of right and embraces: 1) abstract right; 2) morality; 3) social ethics [*Sittlichkeit*], under which again are comprised: the family, civil society and the state. Here the content is as realistic as the form is idealistic. Besides morality the whole sphere of law, economy, politics is here included. With Feuerbach it is just the reverse. In form he is realistic since he takes his start from man; but there is absolutely no mention of the world in which this man lives; hence, this man remains always the same abstract man who occupied the field in the philosophy of religion. For this man is not born of woman; he issues, as from a chrysalis, from the god of the monotheistic religions. He therefore does not live in a real world historically come into being and historically determined. True, he has intercourse with other men; however, each one of them is just as much an abstraction as he himself.

.   .   .   .

Do matters fare any better in regard to the equal right of others to satisfy their urge towards happiness? Feuerbach posed this claim as absolute, as holding good for all times and circumstances. But since when has it been valid? Was there ever in antiquity between slaves and masters, or in the Middle Ages between serfs and barons, any talk about an equal right to the urge towards happiness? Was not the urge towards happiness of the oppressed class sacrificed ruthlessly and "by right of law" to that of the ruling class? Yes, that was indeed immoral; nowadays, however, equality of rights is recognised. Recognised in words ever since and inasmuch as the bourgeoisie, in its flight against feudalism and in the development of capitalist production, was compelled to abolish all privileges of estate, that is, personal privileges, and to introduce the equality of all individuals before the law, first in the sphere of private law, then gradually also in the sphere of public law. But the urge towards happiness thrives only to a trivial extent on ideal rights. To the greatest extent of all it thrives on material means; and capitalist production takes care to ensure that the great majority of those with equal rights shall get only what is essential for bare existence. Capitalist production has, therefore, little more respect, if indeed any more, for the equal right to the urge towards happiness of the majority than had slavery or serfdom.

See also ENGELS, Preface to MARX, *The Poverty of Philosophy*, 14; ENGELS, *Anti-Dühring*, 28–29; ENGELS, Ludwig Feuerbach and the End of Classical German Philosophy, *MESW (3)* III, 355.

ENGELS, Juristen-Socialismus, quoted in TUMANOV, *Contemporary Bourgeois Legal Thought*, 40.

This was the theological outlook which had acquired a secular character. The place of dogma and of divine law had been taken by the law of man, the place of the Church by the State. Economic and social relationships, which earlier, having had the sanction of the church and regarded as creations of the church and dogma, were now seen as being founded on law and created by the state. Since commodity exchange on the scale of society and in its more developed form . . . necessitates complex contractual relations, the generally acceptable rules established by society as a whole—legal norms sanctioned by the state—the idea took shape that these laws originated not in the economic facts but were formally established by the state and introduced by it. And since competition—the basic form of the contacts between commodity producers—is the great equaliser, equality before the law became the grand rallying cry of the bourgeoisie. The fact that the struggle waged by this new, rising class against the feudal overlords and the absolute monarchy, which came to their defence at the time, could not but be, as with any class struggle, a political struggle, a struggle for state power and for legal demands—this fact helped in consolidating the juridical world outlook.

MARX, The Eighteenth Brumaire of Louis Bonaparte, *MESW (3)* I, 408–409.

The inevitable general staff of the liberties of 1848, personal liberty, liberty of the press, of speech, of association, of assembly, of education and religion, etc., received a constitutional uniform, which made them invulnerable. For each of these liberties is proclaimed as the *absolute* right of the French *citoyen* but always with the marginal note that it is unlimited so far as it is not limited by the "*equal rights of others* and the *public safety*" or by "laws" which are intended to mediate just this harmony of the individual liberties with one another and with the public safety. For example: "The citizens have the right of association, of peaceful and unarmed assembly, of petition and of expressing their opinions, whether in the press or in any other way. *The enjoyment of these rights has no limit save the equal rights of others and the public safety*." (Chapter II of the French Constitution. §8.)—"Education is free. Freedom of education shall be *enjoyed* under the conditions fixed by law and under the supreme control of the state." (*Ibidem*, §9.)—"The home of every citizen is inviolable *except* in the forms prescribed by law," (Chapter II, §3.) Etc., etc.—The Constitution, therefore, constantly refers to future *organic* laws which are to put into effect those marginal notes and regulate the enjoyment of these unrestricted liberties in such manner that they will collide neither with one another nor with the public safety. And later, these organic laws were brought into being by the friends of order and all those liberties regulated in such manner that the bourgeoisie in its enjoyment of them finds itself unhindered by the equal rights of the other classes. Where it forbids these liberties entirely to "the others" or permits enjoyment of them under conditions that are just so many police traps, this always happens solely in the interest of "*public safety*," that is, the safety of the bourgeoisie, as the Constitution prescribes. In the sequel, both sides accordingly appeal with complete justice to the Constitution:

the friends of order, who abrogated all these liberties, as well as the democrats, who demanded all of them. For each paragraph of the Constitution contains its own antithesis, its own Upper and Lower House, namely, liberty in the general phrase, abrogation of liberty in the marginal note. Thus, so long as the *name* of freedom was respected and only its actual realisation prevented, of course in a legal way, the constitutional existence of liberty remained intact, inviolate, however mortal the blows dealt to its existence *in actual life*.

See also MARX, *Theories of Surplus Value* III, 431; ENGELS, Origin of the Family, Private Property and the State, *MESW (3)* III, 252.

MARX, *Capital* I, 172.

This sphere that we are deserting, within whose boundaries the sale and purchase of labour-power goes on, is in fact a very Eden of the innate rights of man. There alone rule Freedom, Equality, Property and Bentham. Freedom, because both buyer and seller of a commodity, say of labour-power, are constrained only by their own free will. They contract as free agents, and the agreement they come to, is but the form in which they give legal expression to their common will. Equality, because each enters into relation with the other, as with a simple owner of commodities, and they exchange equivalent for equivalent. Property, because each disposes only of what is his own. And Bentham, because each looks only to himself. The only force that brings them together and puts them in relation with each other, is the selfishness, the gain and the private interests of each. Each looks to himself only, and no one troubles himself about the rest, and just because they do so, do they all, in accordance with the pre-established harmony of things, or under the auspices of an all-shrewd providence, work together to their mutual advantage, for the common weal and in the interest of all.

On leaving this sphere of simple circulation or of exchange of commodities, which furnishes the "Free-trader Vulgaris" with his views and ideas, and with the standard by which he judges a society based on capital and wages, we think we can perceive a change in the physiognomy of our dramatis personæ. He, who before was the money-owner, now strides in front as capitalist; the possessor of labour-power follows as his labourer. The one with an air of importance, smirking, intent on business; the other, timid and holding back, like one who is bringing his own hide to market and has nothing to expect but—a hiding.

See also MARX, *Grundrisse* 243–246; MARX/ENGELS, The Communist Manifesto, *MECW*, VI, 501.

MARX, On the Jewish Question, *MECW* III, 166–167.

The political revolution which overthrew this sovereign power and raised state affairs to become affairs of the people, which constituted the political state as a matter of *general* concern, that is, as a real state, necessarily smashed all estates, corporations, guilds, and privileges, since they were all manifestations of the separation of the people from the community. The political revolution thereby *abolished* the *political character of civil society*. It broke up civil society into its simple component parts; on the one hand, the *individuals*; on the other hand, the *material* and *spiritual elements* constituting the content of the life and social position of these individuals. It set free the political spirit, which had been, as it were, split up, partitioned and dispersed in the various blind alleys of feudal society. It gathered the dispersed parts of the political spirit, freed it from its intermixture with civil life, and established it as the sphere of the community, the *general* concern of the nation, ideally independent of those *particular* elements of civil life. A person's *distinct* activity and distinct situation in life were reduced to a merely individual significance. They no longer constituted the general relation of the individual to the state as a whole. Public affairs as such, on the other hand, became the general affair of each individual, and the political functions became the individual's general function.

But the completion of the idealism of the state was at the same time the completion of the materialism of civil society. Throwing off the political yoke meant at the same time throwing off the bonds which restrained the egoistic spirit of civil society. Political emancipation was at the same time the emancipation of civil society from politics, from having even the *semblance* of a universal content.

Feudal society was resolved into its basic element—*man*, but man as he really formed its basis—*egoistic* man.

This *man*, the member of civil society, is thus the basis, the precondition, of the *political* state. He is recognised as such by this state in the rights of man.

The liberty of egoistic man and the recognition of this liberty, however, is rather the recognition of the *unrestrained* movement of the spiritual and material elements which form the content of his life.

Hence man was not freed from religion, he received religious freedom. He was not freed from property, he received freedom to own property. He was not freed from the egoism of business, he received freedom to engage in business.

The *establishment of the political state* and the dissolution of civil society into independent *individuals*—whose relations with one another depend on *law*, just as the relations of men in the system of estates and guilds depended on *privilege*—is accomplished by *one and the same act*. Man as a member of civil society, *unpolitical* man, inevitably appears, however, as the *natural* man. The *droits de l'homme* appear as *droits naturels*, because *conscious activity* is concentrated on the *political act*. *Egoistic* man is the *passive* result of the dissolved society, a result that is simply *found in existence*, an object of *immediate certainty*, therefore a *natural* object. The *political revolution* resolves civil life into its component parts, without *revolutionising* these components themselves or subjecting them to criticism. It regards civil society, the world of needs, labour, private interests, civil law, as the *basis of its existence*, as a *precondition* not requiring further substantiation and therefore as its *natural basis*. Finally, man as a member of civil society is held to be man *in the proper sense, homme* as distinct from the *citoyen*, because he is man in his sensuous, individual, *immediate* existence, whereas *political* man is only abstract, artificial man, man as an *allegorical, juridical* person. The real man is recognised only in the shape of the *egoistic* individual, the *true* man is recognised only in the shape of the *abstract citoyen*.

See also MARX/ENGELS, The Holy Family, *MECW* IV, 116–117.

Legal Thought

ENGELS, *Anti-Dühring*, 152–153 and 155.

We can accordingly come to no other final conclusion than that Herr Dühring's most exhaustive specialized study consisted in his absorption for three years in the theoretical study of the *Corpus Juris*, and for a further three years in the practical study of the noble Prussian *Landrecht*. That is certainly quite meritorious, and would be ample for a really respectable district judge or lawyer in old Prussia. But when a person undertakes to compose a legal philosophy for all worlds and all ages, he should at least have some degree of acquaintance with legal systems like those of the French, English and Americans, nations which have played quite a different role in history from that played by the little corner of Germany in which the Prussian *Landrecht* flourishes. But let us follow him further.

. . . .

Enough of this. The grandiloquent boasts of legal erudition have as their basis—at best—only the most commonplace professional knowledge of quite an ordinary jurist of old Prussia. The sphere of legal and political science, the attainments in which Herr Dühring consistently expounds, "coincides" with the area where the Prussian *Landrecht* holds sway. Apart from the Roman law, with which every jurist is fairly familiar, now even in England, his knowledge of law is confined wholly and entirely to the Prussian *Landrecht*—that legal code of an enlightened patriarchal despotism which is written in a German such as Herr Dühring appears to have been trained in, and which, with its moral glosses, its juristic vagueness and inconsistency, its caning as a means of torture and punishment, belongs entirely to the pre-revolutionary epoch. Whatever exists beyond this Herr Dühring regards as evil—both modern civil French law, and English law with its quite peculiar development and its safeguarding of personal liberty, unknown anywhere on the Continent. The philosophy which "does not allow the validity of any merely *apparent* horizon, but in its powerfully revolutionizing movement unfolds all earths and heavens of outer and inner nature"—has as its *real* horizon: the boundaries of the six eastern provinces of old Prussia, and in addition perhaps the few other patches of land where the noble *Landrecht* holds sway; and beyond this horizon it unfolds neither earths nor heavens, neither outer nor inner nature, but only a picture of the crassest ignorance of what is happening in the rest of the world.

MARX, *Capital* III, 339–340.

Suppose the annual average rate of profit is 20%. In that case a machine valued at £100, employed as capital under average conditions and an average amount of intelligence and purposive effort, would yield a profit of £20. A man in possession of £100, therefore, possesses the power to make £120 out of £100, or to produce a profit of £20. He possesses a potential capital of £100. If he gives these £100 to another for one year, so the latter may use them as real capital, he gives him the power to produce a profit of £20—a surplus-value which costs this other nothing, and for which he pays no equivalent. If this other should pay, say, £5 at the close of the year to the owner of the £100 out of the profit produced, he would thereby pay the use-value of the £100—the use-value of its function as capital, the function of producing a profit of £20. The part of the profit paid to the owner is called interest, which is just another name, or special term, for a part of the profit given up by capital in the process of functioning to the owner of the capital, instead of putting it into its own pocket.

It is plain that the possession of £100 gives their owner the power to pocket the interest—that certain portion of profit produced by means of his capital. If he had not given the £100 to the other person, the latter could not have produced any profit, and could not at all have acted as a capitalist with reference to these £100.

To speak here of natural justice, as Gilbart does (see note)*, is nonsense. The justice of the transactions between agents of production rests on the fact that these arise as natural consequences out of the production relationships. The juristic forms in which these economic transactions appear as wilful acts of the parties concerned, as expressions of their common will and as contracts that may be enforced by law against some individual party, cannot, being mere forms, determine this content. They merely express it. This content is just whenever it corresponds, is appropriate, to the mode of production. It is unjust whenever it contradicts that mode. Slavery on the basis of capitalist production is unjust; likewise fraud in the quality of commodities.

See also MARX, *Capital* I, 660; ENGELS, The Housing Question, *MESW (3)* II, 362–363.

* "That a man who borrows money with a view of making a profit by it, should give some portion of his profit to the lender, is a self-evident principle of natural justice." (Gilbart, *The History and Principles of Banking*, London, 1834, p. 163.) [*original note—eds*].

MARX, *Grundrisse*, 102–103.

But do not these simpler categories also have an independent historical or natural existence predating the more concrete ones? That depends. Hegel, for example, correctly begins the Philosophy of Right with possession, this being the subject's simplest juridical relation. But there is no possession preceding the family or master-servant relations, which are far more concrete relations. However, it would be correct to say that there are families or clan groups which still merely *possess*, but have no *property*. The simple category therefore appears in relation to property as a relation of simple families or clan groups. In the higher society it appears as the simpler relation of a developed organization. But the concrete substratum of which possession is a relation is always presupposed. One can imagine an individual savage as possessing something. But in that case possession is not a juridical relation. It is incorrect that possession develops historically into the family. Possession, rather, always presupposes this 'more concrete juridical category'. There would still always remain this much, however, namely that the simple categories are the expressions of relations within which the less developed concrete may have already realized itself before having posited the more many-sided connection or relation which is mentally expressed in the more concrete category; while the more developed concrete preserves the same category as a subordinate relation. Money may exist, and did exist historically, before capital existed, before banks existed, before wage labour existed, etc. Thus in this respect it may be said that the simpler category can express the dominant relations of a less developed whole, or else those subordinate relations of a more developed whole which already had a historic existence before this whole developed in the direction expressed by a more concrete category. To that extent the path of abstract thought, rising from the simple to the combined, would correspond to the real historical process.

It may be said on the other hand that there are very developed but nevertheless historically less mature forms of society, in which the highest forms of economy, e.g. cooperation, a developed division of labour, etc., are found, even though there is no kind of money, e.g. Peru. Among the Slav communities also, money and the exchange which determines it play little or no role within the individual communities, but only on their boundaries, in traffic with others; it is simply wrong to place exchange at the centre of communal society as the original, constituent element. It originally appears, rather, in the connection of the different communities with one another, not in the relations between the different members of a single community. Further, although money everywhere plays a role from very early on, it is nevertheless a predominant element, in antiquity, only within the confines of certain one-sidedly developed nations, trading nations. And even in the most advanced parts of the ancient world, among the Greeks and Romans, the full development of money, which is presupposed in modern bourgeois society, appears only in the period of their dissolution. This very simple category, then, makes a historic appearance in its full intensity only in the most developed conditions of society. By no means does it wade its way through all economic relations. For example, in the Roman Empire, at its highest point of development, the foundation remained taxes and payments in kind. The money system actually completely developed there only in the army. And it never took over the whole of labour. Thus, although the simpler category may have existed historically before the more concrete, it can achieve its full (intensive and extensive) development precisely in a combined form of society, while the more concrete category was more fully developed in a less developed form of society.

MARX, *ibid.*, 651.

The predominance of capital is the presupposition of free competition, just as the despotism of the Roman Caesars was the presupposition of the free Roman 'private law'. As long as capital is weak, it still itself relies on the crutches of past modes of production, or of those which will pass with its rise. As soon as it feels strong, it throws away the crutches, and moves in accordance with its own laws. As soon as it begins to sense itself and become conscious of itself as a barrier to development, it seeks refuge in forms which, by restricting free competition, seem to make the rule of capital more perfect, but are at the same time the heralds of its dissolution and of the dissolution of the mode of production resting on it.

See also MARX, *Capital* II, 325.

ENGELS, The Housing Question, *MESW* II, 308–309.

Here we have at once Proudhon in his entirety. First, it is forgotten that the rent must not only pay the interest on the building costs, but must also cover repairs and the average amount of bad debts and unpaid rents as well as the occasional periods when the house is untenanted, and finally must pay off in annual instalments the building capital which has been invested in a house, which is perishable and which in time becomes uninhabitable and worthless. Secondly, it is forgotten that the rent must also pay interest on the increased value of the land upon which the building is erected and that, therefore, a part of it consists of ground rent. Our Proudhonist immediately declares, it is true, that since this increment is brought about without the landowner having contributed anything, it does not equitably belong to him but to society as a whole. However, he overlooks the fact that he is thereby in reality demanding the abolition of landed property, a point which would lead us too far if we went into it here. And finally he overlooks the fact that the whole transaction is not at all one of buying the house from its owner, but of buying only its use for a certain time. Proudhon, who never bothered himself about the real, the actual conditions under which any economic phenomenon occurs, is naturally also unable to explain how the original cost price of a house is under certain circumstances paid back ten times over in the course of fifty years in the form of rent. Instead of examining this not at all difficult question economically and establishing whether it is really in contradiction to economic laws, and if so how, Proudhon resorts to a bold leap from economics into jurisprudence: "The house, once it has been built, serves as a *perpetual legal title*" to a certain annual payment. How this comes about, *how* the house *becomes* a legal title, on this Proudhon is silent. And yet that is just what he should have explained. Had he examined this question he would have found that not all the legal titles in the world, no matter how perpetual, could give a house the power of obtaining its cost price back ten times, over the course of fifty years, in the form of rent, but that only economic conditions (which may have obtained social recognition in the form of legal titles) can accomplish this. And with this he would again be where he started from.

The whole Proudhonist teaching rests on this saving leap from economic reality into legal phraseology. Every time our good Proudhon loses the economic hang of things—and this happens to him with every serious problem—he takes refuge in the sphere of law and appeals to *eternal justice*.

"Proudhon begins by taking his ideal of justice, of '*justice éternelle*,' from the juridical relations that correspond to the production of commodities; thereby, it may be noted, he proves, to the consolation of all good citizens, that the production of commodities is a form of production as everlasting as justice. Then he turns round and seeks to reform the actual production of commodities, and the actual legal system corresponding thereto, in accordance with this ideal. What opinion should we have of a chemist, who, instead of studying the actual laws of the molecular changes in the composition and decomposition of matter, and on that foundation solving definite problems, claimed to regulate the composition and decomposition of matter by means of the 'eternal ideas,' '*naturalité and affinité*'? Do we really know any more about 'usury,' when we say it contradicts '*justice éternelle*,' '*équité éternelle*,' '*mutualité éternelle*,' and other '*vérités éternelles*,' than the fathers of the church did when they said it was incompatible with '*grâce éternelle*,' '*foi éternelle*,' and '*la volonté éternelle de Dien*'?" (Marx, *Capital*, Vol. I, p. 45.)

Our Proudhonist does not fare any better than his lord and master:

> "The rent agreement is one of the thousand exchanges which are as necessary in the life of modern society as the circulation of the blood in the bodies of animals. Naturally, it would be in the interest of this society if all these exchanges were pervaded by a *conception of right*, that is to say, if they were carried out everywhere according to the strict demands of justice. In a word, the economic life of society must, as Proudhon says, raise itself to the heights of *economic right*. In reality, as we know, exactly the opposite takes place."

It is credible that five years after Marx had characterised Proudhonism so summarily and convincingly precisely from this decisive angle, one can still print such confused stuff in the German language? What does this rigmarole mean? Nothing more than that the practical effects of the economic laws which govern present-day society run contrary to the author's sense of justice and that he cherishes the pious wish that the matter might be so arranged as to remedy this situation. Yes, if toads had tails they would no longer be toads! And is then the capitalist mode of production not "pervaded by a conception of right," namely, that of its own right to exploit the workers? And if the author tells us that is not *his* conception of right, are we one step further?

Lawyers

MARX/ENGELS, The German Ideology, *MECW* V, 92–93.

[12. FORMS OF SOCIAL CONSCIOUSNESS]

The influence of the division of labour on science.

The role of *repression* with regard to the state, law, morality, etc.

It is precisely because the bourgeoisie rules as a class that in the law it must give itself a general expression.

Natural science and history.

There is no history of politics, law, science, etc., of art, religion, etc.*

Why the ideologists turn everything upside-down.

Clerics, jurists, politicians.

Jurists, politicians (statesmen in general), moralists, clerics.

For this ideological subdivision within a class: 1) *The occupation assumes an independent existence owing to division of labour.* Everyone believes his craft to be the true one. Illusions regarding the connection between their craft and reality are the more likely to be cherished by them because of the very nature of the craft. In consciousness—in jurisprudence, politics, etc.—relations become concepts; since they do not go beyond these relations, the concepts of the relations also become fixed concepts in their mind. The judge, for example, applies the code, he therefore regards legislation as the real, active driving force. Respect for their goods, because their craft deals with general matters.

Idea of law. Idea of state. The matter is turned upside-down in *ordinary* consciousness.

Religion is from the outset *consciousness of the transcendental* arising from *actually existing* forces.

This more popularly.

Tradition, with regard to law, religion, etc.

See also MARX/ENGELS, *ibid.*, 203–210.

---

* To the "community" as it appears in the ancient state, in feudalism, and in the absolute monarchy, to this bond correspond especially the religious conceptions. [*Original note—eds*].

MARX/ENGELS, Fictitious Splits in the International, *MESW (3)* II, 256.

It goes without saying that none of the conditions accepted by the Alliance have ever been fulfilled. Its sham sections have remained a mystery to the General Council. Bakunin sought to retain under his personal direction the few groups scattered in Spain and Italy and the Naples section which he had detached from the International. In the other Italian towns he corresponded with small cliques composed not of workers but of lawyers, journalists and other bourgeois doctrinaires. At Barcelona some of his friends maintained his influence. In some towns in the South of France the Alliance made an effort to found separatist sections under the direction of Albert Richard and Gaspard Blanc, of Lyons, about whom we shall have more to say later. In a word, the international society within the International continued to operate.

See also MARX, The Class Struggles in France, *MESW (3)* I, 235; MARX, *Capital* I, 446; MARX, *Capital* II, 319; ENGELS, Letter to Marx, 15.12.1882, *MESC*, 334–335; ENGELS, *Anti-Dühring*, 35; ENGELS, The Origin of the Family, *MESW (3)* III, 317.

MARX, *Theories of Surplus Value* I, 300–301.
And once more the following passage—*

> "The labour of some of the most respectable orders in the society is, like that of *menial servants, unproductive of any value*," <it has value, and therefore costs an equivalent, but it produces no value> "and does not fix or realise itself in any permanent subject, or vendible commodity. . . . The sovereign, for example, with all the officers both of justice and war who serve under him, the whole army and navy, are *unproductive labourers*. They are the *servants* of the public, and are maintained by a part of the annual produce of the *industry of other people*. . . . In the *same class* must be ranked . . . churchmen, lawyers, physicians, men of letters of all kinds; players, buffoons, musicians, opera-singers, opera-dancers, etc." (l.c., pp. 94–95).

This is the language of the still revolutionary bourgeoisie, which has not yet subjected to itself the whole of society, the State, etc. All these illustrious and time-honoured occupations—sovereign, judge, officer, priest, etc.,—with all the old ideological professions to which they give rise, their men of letters, their teachers and priests, are *from an economic standpoint* put on the same level as the swarm of their own lackeys and jesters maintained by the bourgeoisie and by idle wealth—the landed nobility and idle capitalists. They are mere *servants* of the public, just as the others are their servants. They live on the produce of *other* people's

---

* From Adam Smith.

industry, therefore they must be reduced to the smallest possible number. State, church, etc., are only justified in so far as they are committees to superintended or administer the common interests of the productive bourgeoisie; and their costs—since by their nature these costs belong to the overhead costs of production—must be reduced to the unavoidable minimum. This view is of historical interest in sharp contrast partly to the standpoint of antiquity, when material productive labour bore the stigma of slavery and was regarded merely as a pedestal for the idle citizen, and partly to the standpoint of the absolute or aristocratic-constitutional monarchy which arose from the disintegration of the Middle Ages—as Montesquieu, still captive to these ideas, so naïvely expressed them in the following passage (*Esprit des lois*, 1. VII, ch. IV): "If the rich do not spend much, the poor will perish of hunger".

When on the other hand the bourgeoisie has won the battle, and has partly itself taken over the State, partly made a compromise with its former possessors; and has likewise given recognition to the ideological professions as flesh of its flesh and everywhere transformed them into its functionaries, of like nature to itself; when it itself no longer confronts these as the representative of productive labour, but when the real productive labourers rise against it and moreover tell it that it lives on other people's industry; when it is enlightened enough not to be entirely absorbed in production, but to want also to consume "in an enlightened way"; when the spiritual labours themselves are more and more per-formed in its *service* and enter into the service of capitalist produc-tion—then things take a new turn, and the bourgeoisie tries to justify "economically", from its own standpoint, what at an earlier stage it had criticised and fought against. Its spokesmen and conscience-salvers in this line are the Garniers, etc. In addition to this, these economists, who themselves are priests, professors, etc., are eager to prove their "produc-tive" usefulness, to justify their wages "economically".

See also **MARX**, *ibid.*, 287; **MARX**, *Capital* II, 133.

5   The State, Law and Crime

Introduction

This chapter is concerned with a number of related but distinct facets of the treatment of law by Marx and Engels. We have made the following subdivisions: (1) law and the state, (2) law and repression, (3) crime, and (4) punishment.

A central feature of their discussion of law is the emphasis on its intimate relation with the state. In contrast to conventional juristic notions of the separation of powers, they emphasize the relationship between law and the state apparatus of class society. To have included all Marx' and Engels' writings on the state would have filled another volume. Our selection is necessarily limited, but in it we have sought to achieve two objectives. First we aim to give a general presentation of their more central and persistent concerns in the analysis of the state. Hence a number of passages appear which make no direct reference to law. These concern three features of their treatment of the state: first, the general evolution of state; second, the 'dictatorship of the proletariat'; and third, the 'withering away of the state'. We have not dealt at length with these topics which are discussed in many works on Marxist theory and politics.[1]

Our second objective has been to reproduce more exhaustively those passages which specifically locate law within its relationship to the state.

The writings of Marx and Engels on the state must be approached with a certain caution. The state never figured as a specific object of inquiry, with the possible exception of Engels' "Origin of the Family, Private Property and the State". Hence we cannot find in a developed form a 'Marxist theory of the state'. Just as it is not possible to assemble a Marxist theory of law by bringing together the comments of Marx and Engels, the same problem is encountered with respect to the state. Much of the Marxist discussion on the state has however proceeded on this basis, including Lenin's very important and influential text, *The State and Revolution*,[2] which takes a limited selection of 'key' quotations from Marx and Engels and treats them as the building blocks for 'the Marxist theory of the state'.

In "Origin of the Family", Engels forms his object of inquiry with the primary focus on familial and property relations, and additionally his focus is upon precapitalist societies. His treatment is very heavily influenced by an evolutionist conception of 'stages', through which family, property and the state pass. This work poses the important question of whether the state and law should be regarded as concepts which transcend particular modes of production; Engels' position is that they relate to all forms of *class* society, whereas Pashukanis argues that law is to be found only within the capitalist mode of production.[3]

The absence in both Marx and Engels of a systematic analysis of the state has the result that they advance manifestly different positions in the course of their writings. There are both differences between Marx and Engels, and also the coexistence of positions that can be seen to have divergent theoretical characteristics.

The themes which are present in the extracts concerning the state presented in this chapter are presented in a developmental sequence. These themes rarely appear in a pure form and are often found together in the same passage. The early discussions of the state were characterized either by specific political polemics, for example the attack upon the censorship policy of the Prussian state, or an equally specific theoretical polemic against the Hegelian idealist theory of the state. As against a conception of the state as a realization of an ideal of the unity of society, Marx worked towards a conception of the state as a product of social relations at specific stages of development. Here the state, whilst a product of society, appears in form which seems to stand above society. We see in Marx the development which starts from a heavy reliance on the distinction between 'state' and 'civil society'; this conceptualization disappears after "The German Ideology".

The formulations of Engels tend to be marked by either instrumentalism in which the state is presented as an instrument or tool of a dominant class, or by a functionalist position, in which certain general functions attributed to the state are to be found in all forms of class society. More generally, and particularly in his later writings, Engels is strongly influenced by an evolutionary perspective.

One further theme should be noted. Whilst in general Engels' writing emphasizes the class character of the state, there is another strand which is present, for example in both "Origin of the Family" and in *Anti-Dühring,* which lays emphasis on the fact that the state carries out certain functions that correspond to the general interests of the community. Related to this is his contention, that is also present in Marx, that the state functions in such a way as to prevent the conflicting classes consuming each other in their mutual struggle. Marx gives this more concrete form in his analysis of Bonapartism as a political form which comes into existence because neither the bourgeoisie nor the working class are capable of exercising power on their own account.

The most developed analyses of the state are provided by Marx in his historico-political texts, in particular "The Eighteenth Brumaire", but not in a theoretical form. We encounter Marx retaining the essential simplification (the state is the class state of the dominant class), but applying it in a complex form to the specific historical conjuncture in which the immediate holders of political power cannot be reduced simply to a dominant economic class. He also gives effect to a notion of 'the relative autonomy' of the state, but in a 'practical' and untheorized form. The analysis is 'practical' in the sense that it relates to the specific historical period of the French state and politics between 1848 and 1852. He argues that during this period the French state, as it became personified in the regime of Louis Bonaparte, derived its autonomy from the inability of the contending classes to impose their own solution, and while appearing in the clothing of the peasantry, directed its power against this class as it did against the working class.

This question of 'relative autonomy' needs to be borne in mind also with respect to the relationship between law, as an apparatus within the state, and the state as a whole. The most persistent theme that emerges is that the state, as an apparatus under the general domination of the economically dominant class, gives the class interests which it protects and advances the form of the 'general' or 'universal will'. Law is central to this process; its mode of operation is specifically characterized by its universal form. Legal rights and duties are not attached to classes or statuses, rather they pertain to 'the citizen', devoid of rank and title, all formally equal. The law protects the property of all, and in so doing, as has been seen in more detail in the previous chapter, obliterates or obscures the real relations between social classes. Both Marx and Engels emphasize that the universalism of law in capitalist society gives law a special significance at this stage of historical development.

The next section deals with the repressive character and application of law. The extracts we cite, in general, do not go much beyond being illustrative of the repressive character of law. These examples in the main refer to the repressive use of law against the working class and the workers' movement. Readers should note that the most extensive illustrations of the repressive application of law have been placed in Chapter 3 in the section dealing with the role of law in the transition from feudalism to capitalism, in which law played an important part in coercing the expropriation of the rural poor and in their transformation into an industrial labour force. It should be noted that other classes also experience legal repression.

There is often a strongly propagandist flavour in these passages; they point to the hypocrisy of the ruling classes in making claim to civilized rule when the reality is the repression of the Irish, the poor and of the democratic and working class movement.

We find Marx, when charged with instigating revolt by agitating for a tax strike, using a strictly moral and humanitarian argument. In his speech to the jury, he attacks the hypocrisy of the government in seeking to invoke laws which the counter-revolution it has just effected has itself overthrown. There is a general assertion of the social character of law which allows him to argue that once the law fails to reflect current social relations, it becomes mere paper and ceases to require obedience; here he draws heavily on his very earliest writings. The jury acquitted Marx and his fellow defendants; the jury foreman is reported to have thanked Marx for his "instructive explanation".[4]

The passages on the repressive application of law reveal little about the specific mechanisms or conditions of legal repression. One finds merely hints, because the writings are in the main of a journalistic and propagandist nature.

The third section brings together passages on crime. There has been controversy about the extent to which it is possible to find a 'theory of crime' in the writings of Marx and Engels.[5] Without entering into that debate it is important to state that there is no ready-made 'Marxist theory of crime' to be found in the texts. This is true despite the fact that the majority of the extracts advance some 'explanation' of the phenomenon of crime. With few exceptions the passages are taken from the earlier works. The numerous passages from Engels' "The Condition of the Working Class in England" are framed in the context of the critique of the social conditions created by the advance of industrial capitalism; there is a strong strand of moral condemnation of these social consequences. The most persistent feature is a notion of 'demoralization' lying at the root of crime. The conditions of labour, recreation and family life spawned by industrial capitalism lead to the brutalization and degradation of life; the advance of crime is a direct index of this process. It expresses itself in Engels' very moralistic and Victorian attitudes towards the employment of women.

However, the emphasis on demoralization cannot simply be seen as an early ethical critique of capitalism. Engels in *Anti-Dühring* (p. 352) repeats a very direct association between capitalism, social misery and the increase in crime. The focus on demoralization is closely linked in a number of passages to the relationship between crime and competition. The competition endemic within capitalism results in a competition between people for their conditions of existence, which are closely tied to property relations, to which theft is a natural and, in Engels' view, legitimate response. It is the existence of private property which brings forth competition within the working class both in the sphere of employment and around the means of survival.

Throughout their writings both Marx and Engels take crime to be a self-evident social phenomenon. It is assumed that there are certain forms of behaviour and action which are intrinsically 'criminal', which violate an unstated but nevertheless real set of criteria. This unproblematic conception of crime Marx and Engels shared with the majority of nineteenth, and indeed twentieth, century writers on crime and criminality. It is the great merit of the deviancy theory that emerged in the 1960s, whatever its other defects, to have made the concept of 'crime itself problematic, thereby requiring us to move beyond a commonsense and taken-for-granted approach to its analysis.

The emphasis on demoralization and competition highlights the persistent assertion of the social character of crime against classical criminology with its emphasis upon individual responsibility founded upon the moral individualism of the Enlightenment. Thus we find in "The Holy Family" the demand that it is not the individual who should be punished but the social conditions which breed crime that should be treated. The creation of a human and humane environment is the key to the unquestioned goal of crime reduction. Similarly, Marx, in the passage on capital punishment, quotes approvingly from the sociological positivist Quetelet, for whom the demonstration of statistical correlations between crime rates and specific social conditions constitutes proof of the social, as against individual, causation of crime.

There is a related but distinct emphasis which emerges in the passages on crime which may be characterized as the 'primitive rebellion' thesis. It is expressed most directly in "The German Ideology" with the definition of crime as the struggle of the isolated individual against the existing social conditions. More generally, and particularly in "The Condition of the Working Class", crime is presented as both the individual (e.g. theft) and the collective (e.g. incendiarism) nascent revolt in the social war between labour and capital.

The emphasis on the relation between crime and class society is underlined by their view that in the classless society of the future, crime will disappear with the creation of fully social conditions. The seeds of this possibility were seen by Marx in the experience of the Paris Commune with the startling decline in robberies and burglaries and the increase in general safety of the streets.

Finally, with respect to crime, a comment should be made about the widely quoted passage from *Theories of Surplus Value* concerning the 'productivity of crime', and the similar comment from *Grundrisse*. The context of these passages makes it clear that their intention is deeply ironic; they are parodies of simple functionalist accounts.

We end the chapter with a small section on punishment and penology which exhibits a substantial continuity with the treatment of crime in the previous section. The classical penology of the Enlightenment is criticized because of its moral individualism; in its place they advance what remains a moral critique, but one of the social conditions which underlie criminality. They therefore reject an individualist calculus of deterrence and reform. Again they attack the hypocrisy of bourgeois humanism as revealed in the brutalizing treatment of the offender. Again they point to the class bias in the enforcement of criminal law; but neither Marx nor Engels are fatalistic. Limited working class resistance in the courts is possible and provides a starting point for a wider resistance. They argue that the bourgeois ideology of equality and legalism can itself provide a basis for this resistance.

While many of the topics dealt with in this chapter remain largely untheorized and appear in a very immediate and practical context, we would wish to argue for the possibility of developing specific regional Marxist theories, both of crime and of punishment. These theories, however, cannot be put together through a simple compilation of their utterances on these questions. Nor, on the other hand, is there a direct method whereby regional theories can be arrived at by a purely logical elaboration from a limited range of concepts; it is not possible, for example, to deduce a Marxist theory of law from the concept of 'mode of production'. Any regional theory requires the development of concepts that are appropriate to its specific object. The development of a Marxist theory of crime is important theoretically and politically for the light it is able to throw on the wider process of the reproduction of capitalist social relations. Such an undertaking is also important at a more immediate political level; 'socialist policy' in the area of crime, crime control and penology has largely remained moulded within a limited liberal and anti-authoritarian tradition. In this sense it has been reactive rather than constituting a concrete base for an intervention in the politics of crime and crime control.

Notes

1. See for important recent discussions, Balibar, E. (1977) *On the Dictatorship of the Proletariat*, New Left Books, London; Miliband, R. (1977) *Marxism and Politics*, Oxford University Press, London.
2. Lenin, V. I. *Collected Works*, Vol. 25, pp. 381–481. The same method characterizes Kautsky, K. (1971) *The Dictatorship of the Proletariat*, Ann Arbor, and Lenin's reply: The Proletarian Revolution and the Renegade Kautsky, *Collected Works*, Vol. 28, pp. 227–325.
3. Pashukanis, E. B. (1951) The General Theory of Law and Marxism, in *Soviet Legal Philosophy* (H. Babbs and J. Hazard, eds), Harvard University Press, Cambridge, Mass.

4. Mehring, K. (1948) *Karl Marx: The Story of his Life,* p. 183, Allen and Unwin, London.

5. See the polemic between Hirst, P. Q. and Taylor, Walton and Young, which originally appeared in *Economy and Society*, now reprinted in Taylor, I., Walton, P. and Young, J. (1975) *Critical Criminology*, pp. 203–244, Routledge and Kegan Paul, London.

Extracts

The State and Law

MARX/ENGELS, The German Ideology, *MECW* V, 329–330.

In actual history, those theoreticians who regard *might* as the basis of right were in direct contradiction to those who looked on *will* as the basis of right—a contradiction which Saint Sancho could have regarded also as that between realism (the child, the ancient, the Negro, etc.) and idealism (the youth, the modern, the Mongol, etc.). If power is taken as the basis of right, as Hobbes, etc., do, then right, law, etc., are merely the symptom, the expression of *other* relations upon which state power rests. The material life of individuals, which by no means depends merely on their "will", their mode of production and form of intercourse, which mutually determine each other—this is the real basis of the state and remains so at all the stages at which division of labour and private property are still necessary, quite independently of the *will* of individuals. These actual relations are in no way created by the state power; on the contrary they are the power creating it. The individuals who rule in these conditions—leaving aside the fact that their power must assume the form of the *state*—have to give their will, which is determined by these definite conditions, a universal expression as the will of the state, as law, an expression whose content is always determined by the relations of this class, as the civil and criminal law demonstrates in the clearest possible way. Just as the weight of their bodies does not depend on their idealistic will or on their arbitrary decision, so also the fact that they enforce their own will in the form of law, and at the same time make it independent of the personal arbitrariness of each individual among them, does not depend on their idealistic will. Their personal rule must at the same time assume the form of average rule. Their personal power is based on conditions of life which as they develop are common to many individuals, and the continuance of which they, as ruling individuals, have to maintain against others and, at the same time, to maintain that they hold good for everybody. The expression of this will, which is determined by their common interests, is the law. . . . .

The same applies to the classes which are ruled, whose will plays just as small a part in determining the existence of law and the state. For example, so long as the productive forces are still insufficiently developed to make competition superfluous, and therefore would give rise to competition over and over again, for so long the classes which are ruled would be wanting the impossible if they had the "will" to abolish competition and with it the state and the law. Incidentally, too, it is only in the imagination of the ideologist that this "will" arises before relations have developed far enough to make the emergence of such a will possible. After relations have developed sufficiently to produce it, the ideologist is able to imagine this will as being purely arbitrary and therefore as conceivable at all times and under all circumstances.

MARX/ENGELS, *ibid.,* 330–331.

The same visionaries who see in right and law the domination of some independently existing general will can see in crime the mere violation of right and law. Hence the state does not exist owing to the dominant will, but the state, which arises from the material mode of life of individuals, has also the form of a dominant will. If the latter loses its domination, it means that not only the will has changed but also the material existence and life of the individuals, and only for that reason has their will changed. It is possible for rights and law to be "inherited", but in that case they are no longer dominant, but nominal, of which striking examples are furnished by the history of ancient Roman law and English law. We saw earlier how a theory and history of pure thought could arise among philosophers owing to the separation of ideas from the individuals and their empirical relations which serve as the basis of these ideas. In the same way, here too one can separate right from its real basis, whereby one obtains a "dominant will" which in different eras undergoes various modifications and has its own, independent history in its creations, the laws. On this account, political and civil history becomes ideologically merged in a history of the domination of successive laws. This is the specific illusion of lawyers and politicians, which Jacques le bonhomme adopts *sans façon.* . . . .

The most superficial examination of legislation, e.g., poor laws in all countries, shows how far the rulers got when they imagined that they could achieve something by means of their "dominant will" alone, i.e., simply by exercising their will.

MARX/ENGELS, *ibid.,* 342–343.

The history of right shows that in the earliest, most primitive epochs these individual, factual relations in their crudest form directly constituted right. With the development of civil society, hence with the development of private interests into class interests, the relations of right underwent changes and acquired a civilised form. They were no longer regarded as individual, but as universal relations. At the same time, division of labour placed the protection of the conflicting interests of separate individuals into the hands of a few persons, whereby the barbaric enforcement of right also disappeared. Saint Sancho's entire criticism of right in the above-mentioned antitheses is limited to declaring the *civilised* form of legal relations and the civilised division of labour to be the fruit of the "fixed idea", of the holy, and, on the other hand, to claiming for *himself* the barbaric expression of relations of right and the barbaric method of settling conflicts. For him it is all *only* a matter of *names*; he does not touch on the content itself, since he does not know the real relations on which these different forms of right are based, and in the juridical expression of class relations perceives only the idealised names of those barbaric relations. Thus, in Stirner's declaration of will, we rediscover the feud; in hostility, self-defence, etc.—a copy of club-law and practice of the old feudal mode of life; in satisfaction, vengeance, etc.—the *jus talionis*, the old German *Gewere, compensatio, satisfactio*—in short, the chief elements of the *leges barbarorum* and *consuetudines feudorum*, which Sancho has appropriated for himself and taken to his heart not from libraries, but from the tales of his former master about Amadis of Gaul. In the final analysis, therefore, Saint Sancho again arrives merely at an impotent moral injunction that everybody should himself obtain satisfaction and carry out punishment. He believes Don Quixote's assurance that by a mere moral injunction he can without more ado convert the material forces arising from the division of labour into personal forces. How closely juridical relations are linked with the development of these material forces due to the division of labour is already clear from the historical development of the power of the law courts and the complaints of the feudal lords about the legal development. It was just in the epoch between the rule of the aristocracy and the rule of the bourgeoisie, when the interests of two classes came into conflict, when trade between the European nations began to be important, and hence international relations themselves assumed a *bourgeois* character, it was just at that time that the power of the courts of law began to be important, and under the rule of the bourgeoisie, when this broadly developed division of labour becomes absolutely essential, the power of these courts reaches its highest point. What the servants of the division of labour, the judges and still more the *professores juris*, imagine in this connection is a matter of the greatest indifference.

MARX/ENGELS, *ibid.,* 348.

From the fact that in any state there are people who attach importance to it, i.e., who, in the state and thanks to the state, *themselves* acquire importance, Sancho concludes that the state is a power standing above these people. Here again it is only a matter of getting the fixed idea about the state out of one's mind. Jacques le bonhomme continues to imagine that the state is a mere idea and he believes in the independent power of this idea of the state. He is the true "politician who believes in the state, is possessed by the state" (p. 309). Hegel idealises the conception of the state held by the political ideologists who still took separate individuals as their point of departure, even if it was merely the *will* of these individuals; Hegel transforms the common will of these individuals into the absolute will, and Jacques le bonhomme *bona fide* accepts this idealisation of ideology as the correct view of the state and, in this belief, criticises it by declaring the Absolute to be the Absolute.

ENGELS, Origin of the Family, Private Property and the State, *MESW(3)*, III, 326–330.

The state is, therefore, by no means a power forced on society from without; just as little is it "the reality of the ethical idea", "the image and reality of reason", as Hegel maintains. Rather, it is a product of society at a certain stage of development; it is the admission that this society has become entangled in an insoluble contradiction with itself, that it has split into irreconcilable antagonisms which it is powerless to dispel. But in order that these antagonisms, classes with conflicting economic interests, might not consume themselves and society in fruitless struggle, it became necessary to have a power seemingly standing above society that would alleviate the conflict and keep it within the bounds of "order"; and this power, arisen out of society but placing itself above it, and alienating itself more and more from it, is the state.

As distinct from the old gentile order, the state, first, divides its subjects *according to territory*. As we have seen, the old gentile associations, built upon and held together by ties of blood, became inadequate, largely because they presupposed that the members were bound to a given territory, a bond which had long ceased to exist. The territory remained, but the people had become mobile. Hence, division according to territory was taken as the point of departure, and citizens were allowed to exercise their public rights and duties wherever they settled, irrespective of gens and tribe. This organisation of citizens according to locality is a feature common to all states. That is why it seems natural to us; but we have seen what long and arduous struggles were needed before it could replace, in Athens and Rome, the old organisation according to gentes.

The second distinguishing feature is the establishment of a *public power* which no longer directly coincides with the population organising itself as an armed force. This special public power is necessary because a self-acting armed organisation of the population has become impossible since the split into classes. The slaves also belonged to the population; the 90,000 citizens of Athens formed only a privileged class as against the 365,000 slaves. The people's army of the Athenian democracy was an aristocratic public power against the slaves, whom it kept in check; however, a gendarmerie also became necessary to keep the citizens in check, as we related above. This public power exists in every state; it consists not merely of armed men but also of material adjuncts, prisons and institutions of coercion of all kinds, of which gentile [clan] society knew nothing. It may be very insignificant, almost infinitesimal, in societies where class antagonisms are still undeveloped and in out-of-the-way places as was the case at certain times and in certain regions in the United States of America. It [the public power] grows stronger, however, in proportion as class antagonisms within the state become more acute, and as adjacent states become larger and more populous. We have only to look at our present-day Europe, where class struggle and rivalry in conquest have tuned up the public power to such a pitch that it threatens to swallow the whole of society and even the state.

In order to maintain this public power, contributions from the citizens become necessary—*taxes*. These were absolutely unknown in gentile society; but we know enough about them today. As civilisation advances, these taxes become inadequate; the state makes drafts on the future, contracts loans, *public debts*. Old Europe can tell a tale about these, too.

Having public power and the right to levy taxes, the officials now stand, as organs of society, *above* society. The free, voluntary respect that was accorded to the organs of the gentile [clan] constitution does not satisfy them, even if they could gain it; being the vehicles of a power that is becoming alien to society, respect for them must be enforced by means of exceptional laws by virtue of which they enjoy special sanctity and inviolability. The shabbiest police servant in the civilised state has more "authority" than all the organs of gentile society put together; but the most powerful prince and the greatest statesman, or general, of civilisation may well envy the humblest gentile chief for the unstrained and undisputed respect that is paid to him. The one stands in the midst of society, the other is forced to attempt to represent something outside and above it.

Because the state arose from the need to hold class antagonisms in check, but because it arose, at the same time, in the midst of the conflict of these classes, it is, as a rule, the state of the most powerful, economically dominant class, which, through the medium of the state, becomes also the politically dominant class, and thus acquires new means of holding down and exploiting the oppressed class. Thus, the state of antiquity was above all the state of the slave owners for the purpose of holding down the slaves, as the feudal state was the organ of the nobility for holding down the peasant serfs and bondsmen, and the modern representative state is an instrument of exploitation of wage labour by capital. By way of exception, however, periods occur in which the warring classes balance each other so nearly that the state power, as ostensible mediator, acquires, for the moment, a certain degree of independence of both. Such was the absolute monarchy of the seventeenth and eighteenth centuries, which held the balance between the nobility and the class of burghers; such was the Bonapartism of the First, and still more of the Second French Empire, which played off the proletariat against the bourgeoisie and the bourgeoisie against the proletariat. The latest performance of this kind, in which ruler and ruled appear equally ridiculous, is the new German Empire of the Bismarck nation: here capitalists and workers are balanced against each other and equally cheated for the benefit of the impoverished Prussian cabbage junkers.

In most of the historical states, the rights of citizens are, besides, apportioned according to their wealth, thus directly expressing the fact that the state is an organisation of the possessing class for its protection against the non-possessing class. It was so already in the Athenian and Roman classification according to property. It was so in the mediaeval feudal state, in which the alignment of political power was in conformity with the amount of land owned. It is seen in the electoral qualifications of the modern representative states. Yet this political recognition of property distinctions is by no means essential. On the contrary, it marks a low stage of state development. The highest form of the state, the democratic republic, which under our modern conditions of society is more and more becoming an inevitable necessity, and is the form of state in which alone the last decisive struggle between proletariat and bourgeoisie can be fought out—the democratic republic officially knows nothing any more of property distinctions. In it wealth exercises its power indirectly, but all the more surely. On the one hand, in the form of the direct corruption of officials, of which America provides the classical example; on the other hand, in the form of an alliance between government and Stock Exchange, which becomes the easier to achieve the more the public debt increases and the more joint-stock companies concentrate in their hands not only transport but also production itself, using the Stock Exchange as their centre. The latest French republic as well as the United States is a striking example of this; and good old Switzerland has contributed its share in this field. But that a democratic republic is not essential for this fraternal alliance between government and Stock Exchange is proved by England and also by the new German Empire, where one cannot tell who was elevated more by universal suffrage, Bismarck or Bleichröder. And lastly, the possessing class rules directly through the medium of universal suffrage. As long as the oppressed class, in our case, therefore, the proletariat, is not yet ripe to emancipate itself, it will in its majority regard the existing order of society as the only one possible and, politically, will form the tail of the capitalist class, its extreme Left wing. To the extent, however, that this class matures for its self-emancipation, it constitutes itself as its own party and elects its own representatives, and not those of the capitalists. Thus, universal suffrage is the gauge of the maturity of the working class. It cannot and never will be anything more in the present-day state; but that is sufficient. On the day the thermometer of universal suffrage registers boiling point among the workers, both they and the capitalists will know what to do.

The state, then, has not existed from all eternity. There have been societies that did without it, that had no idea of the state and state power. At a certain stage of economic development, which was necessarily bound up with the split of society into classes, the state became a necessity owing to this split. We are now rapidly approaching a stage in the development of production at which the existence of these classes not only will have ceased to be a necessity, but will become a positive hindrance to production. They will fall as inevitably as they arose at an earlier stage. Along with them the state will inevitably fall. Society, which will reorganise production on the basis of a free and equal association of the producers, will put the whole machinery of state where it will then belong: into the museum of antiquities, by the side of the spinning-wheel and the bronze axe.

ENGELS, *Anti-Dühring*, 246–251.
The relationships based on domination and subjection have therefore still to be explained.

They arose in two ways.

As men originally made their exit from the animal world—in the narrower sense of the term—so they made their entry into history: still half animal, brutal, still helpless in face of the forces of nature, still ignorant of their own strength; and consequently as poor as the animals and hardly more productive than they. There prevailed a certain equality in the conditions of existence, and for the heads of families also a kind of equality of social position—at least an absence of social classes—which continued among the primitive agricultural communities of the civilized peoples of a later period. In each such community there were from the beginning certain common interests the safeguarding of which had to be handed over to individuals, true, under the control of the community as a whole: adjudication of disputes; repression of abuse of authority by individuals; control of water supplies, especially in hot countries; and finally, when conditions were still absolutely primitive, religious functions. Such offices are found in aboriginal communities of every period—in the oldest German marks and even today in India. They are naturally endowed with a certain measure of authority and are the beginnings of state power. The productive forces gradually increase; the increasing density of the population creates at one point common interests, at another conflicting interests, between the separate communities, whose grouping into larger units brings about in turn a new division of labour, the setting up of organs to safeguard common interests and combat conflicting interests. These organs which, if only because they represent the common interests of the whole group, hold a special position in relation to each individual community—in certain circumstances even one of opposition—soon make themselves still more independent, partly through heredity of functions, which comes about almost as a matter of course in a world where everything occurs spontaneously, and partly because they become increasingly indispensable owing to the growing number of conflicts with other groups. It is not necessary for us to examine here how this independence of social functions in relation to society increased with time until it developed into domination over society; how he who was originally the servant, where conditions were favourable, changed gradually into the lord; how this lord, depending on the conditions, emerged as an Oriental despot or satrap, the dynast of a Greek tribe, chieftain of a Celtic clan, and so on; to what extent he subsequently had recourse to force in the course of this transformation; and how finally the individual rulers united into a ruling class. Here we are only concerned with establishing the fact that the exercise of a social function was everywhere the basis of political supremacy; and further that political supremacy has existed for any length of time only when it discharged its social functions.

. . . .

We may add at this point that all historical antagonisms between exploiting and exploited, ruling and oppressed classes to this very day find their explanation in this same relatively undeveloped productivity of human labour. So long as the really working population were so much occupied with their necessary labour that they had no time left for looking after the common affairs of society—the direction of labour, affairs of state, legal matters, art, science, etc.—so long was it necessary that there should constantly exist a special class, freed from actual labour, to manage these affairs: and this class never failed, for its own advantage, to impose a greater and greater burden of labour on the working masses. Only the immense increase of the productive forces attained by modern industry has made it possible to distribute labour among all members of society without exception, and thereby to limit the labour-time of each individual member to such an extent that all have enough free time left to take part in the general—both theoretical and practical—affairs of society. It is only now, therefore, that every ruling and exploiting class has become superfluous and indeed a hindrance to social development, and it is only now, too, that it will be inexorably abolished, however much it may be in possession of "direct force."

ENGELS, Letter to Bernstein, 24.3.1884, *MESC*, 350.
In my opinion what should have been said is the following: The proletariat too needs democratic *forms* for the seizure of political power but they are for it, like all political forms, mere means. But if today democracy is wanted as an *end* it is necessary to rely on the peasantry and petty bourgeoisie, i.e., on classes that are in process of dissolution and *reactionary* in relation to the proletariat when they try to maintain themselves artificially. Furthermore it must not be forgotten that it is precisely the democratic republic which is the *logical* form of bourgeois rule: a form however that has become too dangerous only because of the level of development the proletariat has already reached: but France and America show that it is still possible as purely bourgeois rule. . . . .
And yet the democratic republic always remains the *last* form of bourgeois rule, that in which it goes to pieces.

MARX, The Eighteenth Brumaire, *MESW(3)* I, 476.

But if the overthrow of the parliamentary republic contains within itself the germ of the triumph of the proletarian revolution, its immediate and palpable result was *the victory of Bonaparte over parliament, of the executive power over the legislative power, of force without phrases over the force of phrases.* In parliament the nation made its general will the law, that is, it made the law of the ruling class its general will. Before the executive power it renounces all will of its own and submits to the superior command of an alien will, to authority. The executive power, in contrast to the legislative power, expresses the heteronomy of a nation, in contrast to its autonomy. France, therefore, seems to have escaped the despotism of a class only to fall back beneath the despotism of an individual, and, what is more, beneath the authority of an individual without authority. The struggle seems to be settled in such a way that all classes, equally impotent and equally mute, fall on their knees before the rifle butt.

MARX, The Civil War in France, *MESW(3)* II, 217–221.

But the working class cannot simply lay hold of the ready-made state machinery, and wield it for its own purposes.

The centralised State power, with its ubiquitous organs of standing army, police, bureaucracy, clergy, and judicature—organs wrought after the plan of a systematic and hierarchic division of labour—originates from the days of absolute monarchy, serving nascent middle class society as a mighty weapon in its struggles against feudalism. Still, its development remained clogged by all manner of mediaeval rubbish, seignorial rights, local privileges, municipal and guild monopolies and provincial constitutions. The gigantic broom of the French Revolution of the eighteenth century swept away all these relics of bygone times, thus clearing simultaneously the social soil of its last hindrances to the superstructure of the modern State. . . . .

At the same pace at which the progress of modern industry developed, widened, intensified the class antagonism between capital and labour, the State power assumed more and more the character of the national power of capital over labour, of a public force organised for social enslavement, of an engine of class despotism. After every revolution marking a progressive phase in the class struggle, the purely repressive character of the State power stands out in bolder and bolder relief. The Revolution of 1830, resulting in the transfer of Government from the landlords to the capitalists, transferred it from the more remote to the more direct antagonists of the working men. . . . .

If the Parliamentary Republic, as Mr. Thiers said, "divided them (the different fractions of the ruling class) least", it opened an abyss between that class and the whole body of society outside their spare ranks. The restraints by which their own divisions had under former *regimes* still checked the State power, were removed by the union; and in view of the threatening upheaval of the proletariat, they now used that State power mercilessly and ostentatiously as the national war-engine of capital against labour. In their uninterrupted crusade against the producing masses they were, however, bound not only to invest the executive with continually increased powers of repression, but at the same time to divest their own parliamentary stronghold—the National Assembly—one by one, of all its own means of defence against the Executive. . . . .

The empire, with the *coup d'état* for its certificate of birth, universal suffrage for its sanction, and the sword for its sceptre, professed to rest upon the peasantry, the large mass of producers not directly involved in the struggle of capital and labour. It professed to save the working class by breaking down Parliamentarism, and, with it, the undisguised subserviency of Government to the propertied classes. It professed to save the propertied classes by upholding their economic supremacy over the working class; and, finally, it professed to unite all classes by reviving for all the chimera of national glory. In reality, it was the only form of government possible at a time when the bourgeoisie had already lost, and the working class had not yet acquired, the faculty of ruling the nation. . . . .

The cry of "social republic", with which the revolution of February was ushered in by the Paris proletariat, did but express a vague aspiration after a Republic that was not only to supersede the monarchical form of class-rule, but class-rule itself. The Commune was the positive form of that Republic. . . . .

Having once got rid of the standing army and the police, the physical force elements of the old Government, the Commune was anxious to break the spiritual force of repression, the "parson-power," by the disestablishment and disendowment of all churches as proprietary bodies. The priests were sent back to the recesses of private life, there to feed upon the alms of the faithful in imitation of their predecessors, the Apostles. The whole of the educational institutions were opened to the people gratuitously, and at the same time cleared of all interference of Church and State. Thus, not only was education made accessible to all, but science itself freed from the letters which class prejudice and governmental force had imposed upon it.

The judicial functionaries were to be divested of that sham independence which had but served to mask their abject subserviency to all succeeding governments to which, in turn, they had taken, and broken, the oaths of allegiance. Like the rest of public servants, magistrates and judges were to be elective, responsible, and revocable. . . . .

While the merely repressive organs of the old governmental power were to be amputated, its legitimate functions were to be wrested from an authority usurping pre-eminence over society itself, and restored to the responsible agents of society. Instead of deciding once in three or six years which member of the ruling class was to misrepresent the people in

Parliament, universal suffrage was to serve the people, constituted in Communes.

See also MARX, First Draft of "The Civil War in France", *First International and After*, 246–253.

MARX, Critique of the Gotha Programme, *MESW(3)* III, 25–26.

I come now to the democratic section.

A. *"The free basis of the State."*

First of all, according to H, the German workers' party strives for "the free state."

Free state—what is this?

It is by no means the aim of the workers, who have got rid of the narrow mentality of humble subjects, to set the state free. In the German Empire the "state" is almost as "free" as in Russia. Freedom consists in converting the state from an organ superimposed upon society into one completely subordinate to it, and today, too, the forms of state are more free or less free to the extent that they restrict the "freedom of the state."

The German workers' party—at least if it adopts the programme—shows that its socialist ideas are not even skin-deep; in that, instead of treating existing society (and this holds good for any future one) as the basis of the existing state (or of the future state in the case of future society); it treats the state rather as an independent entity that possesses its own *intellectual, ethical and libertarian bases*.

. . . .

The question then arises: what transformation will the state undergo in communist society? In other words, what social functions will remain in existence there that are analogous to present state functions? This question can only be answered scientifically, and one does not get a flea-hop nearer to the problem by a thousandfold combination of the word people with the word state.

Between capitalist and communist society lies the period of the revolutionary transformation of the one into the other. Corresponding to this is also a political transition period in which the state can be nothing but *the revolutionary dictatorship of the proletariat*.

Now the programme does not deal with this nor with the future state of communist society.

Its political demands contain nothing beyond the old democratic litany familiar to all: universal suffrage, direct legislation, popular rights, a people's militia, etc.

ENGELS, *Anti-Dühring*, 386–387.

Whilst the capitalist mode of production more and more completely transforms the great majority of the population into proletarians, it creates the power which, under penalty of its own destruction, is forced to accomplish this revolution. Whilst it forces on more and more the transformation of the vast means of production, already socialized, into state property, it shows itself the way to accomplishing this revolution. *The proletariat seizes political power and turns the means of production in the first instance into state property.*

But, in doing this, it abolishes itself as proletariat, abolishes all class distinctions and class antagonisms, abolishes also the state as state. Society thus far, based upon class antagonisms, had need of the state, that is, of an organization of the particular class, which was *pro tempore* the exploiting class, for the maintenance of its external conditions of production, and, therefore, especially, for the purpose of forcibly keeping the exploited classes in the condition of oppression corresponding with the given mode of production (slavery, serfdom, wage-labour). The state was the official representative of society as a whole; the gathering of it together into a visible embodiment. But it was this only in so far as it was the state of that class which itself represented, for the time being, society as a whole: in ancient times, the state of slave-owning citizens; in the Middle Ages, the feudal lords; in our own time, the bourgeoisie. When at last it becomes the real representative of the whole of society, it renders itself unnecessary. As soon as there is no longer any social class to be held in subjection; as soon as class rule, and the individual struggle for existence based upon our present anarchy in production, with the collisions and excesses arising from these, are removed, nothing more remains to be repressed, and a special repressive force, a state, is no longer necessary. The first act by virtue of which the state really constitutes itself the representative of the whole of society—the taking possession of the means of production in the name of society—this is, at the same time, its last independent act as a state. State interference in social relations becomes, in one domain after another, superfluous, and then withers away of itself; the government of persons is replaced by the administration of things, and by the conduct of processes of production. The state is not "abolished." *It withers away.*

ENGELS, Letter to Van Patten, 18.4.1883, *MESC*, 340–341.

Marx and I, ever since 1845, have held the view that *one* of the final results of the future proletarian revolution will be the gradual dissolution and ultimate disappearance of that political organisation called *the state*; an organisation the main object of which has ever been to secure, by armed force, the economical subjection of the working majority to the wealthy minority. With the disappearance of wealthy minority the necessity for an armed repressive state-force disappears also. At the same time we have always held that in order to arrive at this and the other, far more important ends of the social revolution of the future, the proletarian class will first have to possess itself of the organised political force of the state and with this aid stamp out the resistance of the capitalist class and re-organise society. This is stated already in the *Communist Manifesto* of 1847, end of Chapter II.

The Anarchists reverse the matter. They say, that the proletarian revolution has to *begin* by abolishing the political organisation of the state. But after the victory of the proletariat, the only organisation the victorious working class finds ready-made for use is that of the state. It may require adaptation to the new functions. But to destroy that at such a moment, would be to destroy the only organism by means of which the victorious working class can exert its newly conquered power, keep down its capitalist enemies and carry out that economic revolution of society without which the whole victory must end in a defeat and in a massacre of the working class like that after the Paris Commune.

See also ENGELS, Letter to Cuno, 24.1.1872, *MESC*, 257–258.

Law and Repression

ENGELS, The Condition of the Working Class in England, *MECW* IV, 514–517.

A word or two as to the respect for the law in England. True, the law is sacred to the bourgeois, for it is his own composition, enacted with his consent, and for his benefit and protection. He knows that, even if an individual law should injure him, the whole fabric protects his interests; and more than all, the sanctity of the law, the sacredness of order as established by the active will of one part of society, and the passive acceptance of the other, is the strongest support of his social position. Because the English bourgeois finds himself reproduced in his law, as he does in his God, the policeman's truncheon which, in a certain measure, is his own club, has for him a wonderfully soothing power. But for the working-man quite otherwise! The working-man knows too well, has learned from too oft-repeated experience, that the law is a rod which the bourgeois has prepared for him; and when he is not compelled to do so he never appeals to the law. It is ridiculous to assert that the English working-man fears the police, when every week in Manchester police-men are beaten, and last year an attempt was made to storm a station-house secured by iron doors and shutters. The power of the police in the turnout of 1842 lay, as I have already said, in the want of a clearly defined object on the part of the working-men themselves.

MARX, The Bourgeoisie and the Counter-revolution, *Articles from NRZ*, 193–194.

Hansemann's words: *"restoration of the shaken trust"*, expressed the fixed idea of the Prussian bourgeoisie.

Credit depends on the confidence that the exploitation of wage labour by capital, of the proletariat by the bourgeoisie, of the petty bourgeois by the big bourgeois, will continue in the traditional manner. Hence any political move of the proletariat, whatever its nature, unless it takes place under the direct command of the bourgeoisie, shakes this trust, impairs credit. "Restoration of the shaken trust" when uttered by Hansemann signifies:

Suppression of every political move of the proletariat and of all social strata whose interests do not completely coincide with the interests of the class which believes itself to be standing at the helm of state.

Hansemann accordingly placed the *"strengthening of the state"* side by side with the "restoration of the shaken trust". But he mistook the character of this "state". He sought to strengthen the state which served credit and bourgeois trust, but he strengthened the state which demands trust and if necessary extorts this trust with the help of grape-shot, because it has no credit. He wanted to economise on the costs of bourgeois rule but has instead burdened the bourgeoisie with the exorbitant millions which the restoration of Prussian feudal rule costs.

He told the workers quite laconically that he had an excellent remedy for them. But before he could produce it the "shaken trust" must first of all be restored. To restore this trust the working class had to give up all political activity and interference in the business of state and revert to its former habits. If it followed his advice and trust were restored, this mysterious potent remedy would prove effective if only because it would no longer be required or applicable, since in this case the malady itself—the upset of bourgeois law and order—would have been elimi- nated. And what need is there of a medicine when there is no malady? But if the people obstinately stuck to their purpose, very well, then he would *"strengthen* the state", the police, the army, the courts, the bureaucracy, and would set his bears on them, for "trust" had become a "business question", and:

> *"Gentlemen, business is business!"*

MARX, Economic and Philosophic Manuscripts, *MECW* III, 241.

When society is in a state of decline, the worker suffers most severely. The specific severity of his burden he owes to his position as a worker, but the burden as such to the position of society.

But when society is in a state of progress, the ruin and impoverishment of the worker is the product of his labour and of the wealth produced by him. The misery results, therefore, from the *essence* of present-day labour itself.

Society in a state of maximum wealth—an ideal, but one which is approximately attained, and which at least is the aim of political economy as a civil society—means for the workers *static misery*.

It goes without saying that the *proletarian*, i.e., the man who, being without capital and rent, lives purely by labour, and by a one-sided, abstract labour, is considered by political economy only as a *worker*. Political economy can therefore advance the proposition that the proletarian, the same as any horse, must get as much as will enable him to work. It does not consider him when he is not working, as a human being; but leaves such consideration to criminal law, to doctors, to religion, to the statistical tables, to politics and to the poor-house overseer.

MARX, The Civil War in France, *MESW(3)* II, 226.

The French peasant had elected Louis Bonaparte president of the Republic; but the Party of Order created the Empire. What the French peasant really wants he commenced to show in 1849 and 1850, by opposing his *maire* to the Government's prefect, his schoolmaster to the Government's priest, and himself to the Government's gendarme. All the laws made by the Party of Order in January and February, 1850, were avowed measures of repression against the peasant. The peasant was a Bonapartist, because the great Revolution with all its benefits to him, was, in his eyes, personified in Napoleon.

See also MARX, English Government and Fenian Prisoners, *On Ireland*, 166–167; MARX, The Civil War in France, *MESW (3)* II, 214–215.

MARX, Letter to Engels, 30.1.1865, *MESC*, 148–149

What kind of people our Progressives are is shown once more by their conduct in the combination question. (*By the way*, the Prussian Anti-Combination Law, like all continental laws of this description, takes its origin from the decree of the *Constituent Assembly of June 14, 1791*, in which the French bourgeois strictly punish anything of the sort, and indeed any kind of workers' associations—condemning violators to, for instance, a year's loss of civil rights—on the pretext that this is a *restoration of the guilds* and a contravention of constitutional liberty and the "rights of man". It is very characteristic of Robespierre that at a time when it was a crime punishable by guillotining to be "constitutional" in the sense of the Assembly of 1789 all its laws *against* the workers remained in force.)

MARX, Letter to Weydemeyer, 13.2.1852, *Letters to Americans*, 36–37.

I enclose a note on the situation of our friends in jail in Cologne. Make an article out of this note.

They have been imprisoned for ten months by now.

In November the case came before the court of inquiry, which decided to hold them for jury trial. After this the case was transferred to the criminal court. The latter handed down its decision just before Christmas; it reads: "In view of the absence of facts constituting a crime, there is no basis for sustaining the indictment" (but in view of the importance that the government attaches to this case, we are afraid we might lose our jobs if the judicial prosecution of the defendants were dismissed), "we therefore return the case to the examining magistrate for the elucidation of various matters." The principal reason for the delay is the government's conviction that it would be disgracefully defeated in a jury trial. In the interim it hopes to set up a supreme court to try cases of treason or, at the very least, to abolish trial by jury for all political offenses—a bill to that effect has already been introduced into the Prussian Upper House. Our friends are held in solitary confinement, isolated from one another and from the world outside; they are not allowed mail or visitors, and they don't even get books, which have never been denied to common criminals in Prussia.

MARX, The Class Struggles in France, *MESW(3)* I, 262–263.

A new *press law*, a new *law of association*, a new *law on the state of siege*, the prisons of Paris overflowing, the political refugees driven out, all the journals that go beyond the limits of the *National* suspended. Lyons and the five departments surrounding it abandoned to the brutal persecution of military despotism, the courts ubiquitous and the army of officials, so often purged, purged once more—these were the inevitable, the constantly recurring *commonplaces* of victorious reaction, worth mentioning after the massacres and the deportations of June only because this time they were directed not only against Paris, but also against the departments, not only against the proletariat, but, above all, against the middle classes.

MARX, *ibid.*, 292.

The election law still needs one thing to complete it, a new *press law*. This was not long in coming. A proposal of the government, made many times more drastic by amendments of the party of Order, increased the caution money, put an extra stamp on feuilleton novels (answer to the election of Eugène Sue), taxed all publications appearing weekly or monthly up to a certain number of sheets and finally provided that every article of a journal must bear the signature of the author. The provisions concerning the caution money killed the so-called revolutionary press; the people regarded its extinction as satisfaction for the abolition of universal suffrage. However, neither the tendency nor the effect of the new law extended only to this section of the press. As long as the newspaper press was anonymous, it appeared as the organ of a numberless and nameless public opinion; it was the third power in the state. Through the signaure of every article, a newspaper became a mere collection of literary contributions from more or less known individuals.

Every article sank to the level of an advertisement. Hitherto the newspapers had circulated as the paper money of public opinion; now they were resolved into more or less bad *solo* bills, whose worth and circulation depended on the credit not only of the drawer but also of the endorser. The press of the party of Order had incited not only for the repeal of universal suffrage but also for the most extreme measures against the bad press. However, in its sinister anonymity even the good press was irksome to the party of Order and still more to its individual provincial representatives. As for itself, it demanded only the paid writer, with name, address and description. In vain the good press bemoaned the ingratitude with which its services were rewarded. The law went through; the provision concerning the giving of names hit it hardest of all. The names of republican journalists were pretty well known; but the respectable firms of the *Journal des Débats*, the *Assemblée Nationale*, the *Constitutionnel*, etc., etc., cut a sorry figure in their high protestations of state wisdom, when the mysterious company all at once disintegrated into purchasable penny-a-liners of long practice, who had defended all possible causes for cash, like Granier de Cassagnac, or into old milksops who called themselves statesmen, like Capefigue, or into coquettish fops, like M. Lemoinne of the *Débats*.

In the debate on the press law the *Montagne* had already sunk to such a level of moral degeneracy that it had to confine itself to applauding the brilliant tirades of an old notability of Louis Philippe's time, M. Victor Hugo.

With the election law and the press law the revolutionary and democratic party exits from the official stage.

MARX, Anti-church Movement, *Articles on Britain*, 238–239.

London, June 25. It is an old and historically established maxim that obsolete social forces, nominally still in possession of all the attributes of power and continuing to vegetate long after the basis of their existence has rotted away, inasmuch as the heirs are quarrelling among themselves over the inheritance even before the obituary notice has been printed and the testament read—that these forces once more summon all their strength before their agony of death, pass from the defensive to the offensive, challenge instead of giving way, and seek to draw the most extreme conclusions from premises which have not only been put in question but already condemned. Such is today the English oligarchy. Such is the *Church*, its twin sister. Countless attempts at reorganisation have been made within the Established Church, both the High and the Low, attempts to come to an understanding with the Dissenters and thus to set up a compact force to oppose the profane mass of the nation. There has been a rapid succession of measures of religious coercion. The pious Earl of Shaftesbury, formerly known as Lord Ashley, bewailed the fact in the House of Lords that in England alone five million had become wholly alienated not only from the Church but from Christianity altogether. *"Compelle intrare"*,* replies the Established Church. It leaves it to Lord Ashley and similar dissenting, sectarian and hysterical pietists to pull the chestnuts out of the fire for it.

The first measure of religious coercion was the Beer Bill, which shut down all places of public entertainment on Sundays, except between 6 and 10 p.m. This bill was smuggled through the House at the end of a sparsely attended sitting, after the pietists had bought the support of the big public-house owners of London by guaranteeing them that the license system would continue, that is, that big capital would retain its monopoly. Then came the Sunday Trading Bill, which has now passed on its third reading in the Commons and separate clauses of which have just been debated in the Committee of the whole House. This new coercive measure too was ensured the vote of big capital, because only small shopkeepers keep open on Sunday and the proprietors of the big shops are quite willing to do away with the Sunday competition of the small fry by parliamentary means. In both cases there is a conspiracy of the Church with monopoly capital, but in both cases there are religious penal laws against the lower classes to set the conscience of the privileged classes at rest. The *Beer Bill* was as far from hitting the aristocratic clubs as the *Sunday Trading Bill* is from hitting the Sunday occupations of genteel society. The workers get their wages late on Saturday; they are the only ones for whom shops open on Sundays. They are the only ones compelled to make their purchases, small as they are, on Sundays. The new bill is therefore directed against them alone. In the eighteenth century the French aristocracy said: For us, Voltaire; for the people, the mass and the tithes. In the nineteenth century the English aristocracy says: For us, pious phrases; for the people, Christian practice. The classical saint of Christianity mortified *his* body for the salvation of the souls of the masses; the modern, educated saint mortifies *the bodies of the masses* for the salvation of his own soul.

MARX, Report to the Basle Congress, *The First International and After*, 110–111.

England also had this year to boast a workmen's massacre of its own. The Welsh coal-miners, at Leeswood Great Pit, near Mold, in Denbighshire, had received sudden notice of a reduction of wages by the manager of those works, whom, long since, they had reason to consider a most incorrigible petty oppressor. Consequently, they collected aid from the neighbouring collieries, and, besides assaulting him, attacked his house, and carried all his furniture to the railway station, these wretched men

---

* Initial Latin words of the biblical phrase: ". . . compel *them* to come in, that my house may be filled."

fancying in their childish ignorance thus to get rid of him for good and all. Proceedings were of course taken against the rioters; but one of them was rescued by a mob of 1,000 men, and conveyed out of the town. On 28 May, two of the ringleaders were to be taken before the magistrates of Mold by policemen under the escort of a detachment of the 4th Regiment of the line, 'The King's Own'. A crowd of miners, trying to rescue the prisoners, and, on the resistance of the police and the soldiers, showering stones at them, the soldiers—without any previous warning—returned the shower of stones by a shower of bullets from their breachloaders (Snider fusils). Five persons, two of them females, were killed, and a great many wounded. So far there is much analogy between the Mold and the Ricamarie massacres, but here it ceases. In France, the soldiers were only responsible to their commander. In England, they had to pass through a coroner's jury inquest; but this coroner was a deaf and daft old fool, who had to receive the witnesses' evidence through an ear trumpet, and the Welsh jury, who backed him, were a narrowly prejudiced class jury. They declared the massacre 'justifiable homicide'.

In France, the rioters were sentenced to from three to eighteen months' imprisonment, and soon after, amnestied. In England, they were condemned to ten years' penal servitude! In France, the whole press resounded with cries of indignation against the troops. In England, the press was all smiles for the soldiers, and all frowns for their victims! Still, the English workmen have gained much by losing a great and dangerous illusion. Till now they fancied to have their lives protected by the formality of the Riot Act, and the subordination of the military to the civil authorities. They know now, from the official declaration of Mr Bruce, the Liberal Home Secretary, in the House of Commons—firstly, that without going through the premonitory process of reading the Riot Act, any country magistrate, some fox-hunter or parson, has the right to order the troops to fire on what he may please to consider a riotous mob; and, secondly, that the soldier may give fire on his own book, on the plea of self-defence. The Liberal minister forgot to add that, under these circumstances, every man ought to be armed, at public expense, with a breachloader, in self-defence against the soldier.

ENGELS, The Antwerp Death Sentences, *Articles from NRZ*, 110–111.

Cologne, September 2. Belgium, the model constitutional state, has produced further brilliant proof of the excellence of her institutions. *Seventeen death sentences* resulting from the ridiculous Risquons-Tout affair! Seventeen death sentences to avenge the humiliation inflicted upon the prudish Belgian nation by a few imprudent men, a few hopeful fools, who attempted to raise a small corner of the constitutional cloak! Seventeen death sentences—what savagery!

The Risquons-Tout incident is well known. Belgian workers in Paris joined forces to attempt a republican invasion of their country. Belgian democrats came from Brussels to support the venture. Ledru-Rollin assisted as much as he could. Lamartine, the "noble-minded" traitor, who was not sparing of fine words and ignoble deeds as far as both the foreign and French democrats were concerned—Lamartine, who prides himself on having conspired with the anarchists, like a lightning conductor with the lightning—Lamartine at first supported the Belgian Legion the better to be able later to betray it. The Legion set out. Delescluze, Prefect of the Department du Nord, *sold* the first column to Belgian railway officials; the train which carried them was treacherously hauled into Belgian territory right into the midst of the Belgian bayonets. The second column was led by *three Belgian spies* (we were told this by a member of the Paris Provisional Government, and the course of events confirms it), and these treacherous leaders brought it into a forest on Belgian territory, where an ambush of loaded guns was waiting for it. The column was shot down and most of its members were captured.

This tiny episode of the 1848 revolution—an episode which assumed a farcical aspect as a result of the many betrayals and the magnitude ascribed to it in Belgium—served the Brussels prosecutor as a canvas on which to embroider the most colossal plot that was ever devised. Old General Mellinet, the liberator of Antwerp, Tedesco and Ballin, in short the most resolute and most active democrats of Brussels, Liége and Ghent were implicated. Mr. Bavay would even have Mr. Jottrand of Brussels dragged into it, had not the latter known things and possessed documents whose publication would greatly compromise the entire Belgian government, the wise Leopold included.

Why were these democrats arrested, why were these monstrous proceedings started against men who knew as much about the whole thing as the jurymen who faced them? It was meant to scare the Belgian bourgeoisie and, under cover of this scare, to collect the excessive taxes and forced loans, which are the cement of the glorious Belgian political edifice, and the payments on which were rather behindhand.

In short, the accused were arraigned before the Antwerp jury, the élite of the Flemish faro-playing fraternity, who lack both the élan of French political dedication and the cool assurance of grandiose English materialism, i.e., before those dried-cod merchants who spend their whole life vegetating in philistine utilitarianism, in the most short-sighted and timid profiteering. The great Bavay knew his men and appealed to the their fear.

Indeed, had anyone ever seen a republican in Antwerp? Now thirty-two of the monsters faced the terrified men of Antwerp, and the trembling jury in concert with the wise bench consigned seventeen of the accused to the tender mercies of Article 86 and others of the Code pénal, i.e., the death sentence.

MARX, The Trial of the Rhenish District Committee of Democrats, *Articles from NRZ*, 227–247.

Gentlemen of the jury, if this action had been brought *before* December 5, I could have understood the charge made by the public prosecutor. Now, *after* the 5th of December, I do not understand how he dares to invoke against us laws which the Crown itself has trampled in the dirt.

. . . .

And so, gentlemen, the fact cannot be denied, and no future historian will deny it—the Crown has made a revolution, it has overthrown the existing legal system, it cannot appeal to the laws it has itself so scandalously annulled. After successfully carrying out a revolution one can hang one's opponents, but one cannot convict them. Defeated enemies can be put out of the way, but they cannot be arraigned as criminals. After a revolution or counter-revolution has been consummated the invalidated laws cannot be used against the *defenders* of these laws. This would be a cowardly pretence of legality which you, gentlemen, will not sanctify by your verdict.

. . . .

But quite irrespective of this most authoritative judgment, you will agree with me, gentlemen, that in the present case no crime in the ordinary sense of the word has been committed, in this case no infringement of the law falling within your jurisdiction has occurred at all. Under ordinary conditions the existing laws are enforced by the public authorities; whoever infringes these laws or prevents the public authorities from enforcing them is a criminal. In the present case one public authority has infringed the law, another public authority, it makes no difference which, has upheld it. The struggle between these two political powers lies neither within the sphere of civil law, nor within the sphere of criminal law. The question of who was in the right, the Crown or the National Assembly, is a matter for history. All the juries, all the courts of Prussia cannot decide it. Only one power can supply the answer—history. I do not understand, therefore, how, on the basis of the Code pénal, we could be placed in the dock.

. . . .

How then was the idea conceived to allow the United Provincial Diet, the representative of the old society, to dictate laws to the new society which asserted its rights through the revolution?

Allegedly in order to maintain the *legal basis*. But what do you understand by maintaining the legal basis? To maintain laws belonging to a bygone social era and framed by representatives of vanished or vanishing social interests, who consequently give the force of law only to these interests, which run counter to the public needs. Society is not founded upon the law; this is a legal fiction. On the contrary, the law must be founded upon society, it must express the common interests and needs of society—as distinct from the caprice of the individuals—which arise from the material mode of production prevailing at the given time.

This Code Napoléon, which I am holding in my hand, has not created modern bourgeois society. On the contrary, bourgeois society, which emerged in the eighteenth century and developed further in the nineteenth, merely finds its legal expression in this Code. As soon as it ceases to fit the social conditions, it becomes simply a bundle of paper. You cannot make the old laws the foundation of the new social development, any more than these old laws created the old social conditions.

.   .   .   .

What took place here was not a political conflict between two parties within the framework of *one* society, but a *conflict between two societies*, a *social* conflict, which assumed a political form; *it was the struggle of the old feudal bureaucratic society with modern bourgeois society*, a struggle between the society of *free competition* and the *society of the guilds*, between the society of landownership and the industrial society, between a religious society and a scientific society. The *political* expression corresponding to the old society was the Crown by the grace of God, the bullying bureaucracy and the independent army. The *social* foundation corresponding to this old political power consisted of privileged aristocratic landownership with its enthralled or partially enthralled peasants, the small patriarchal or guild industries, the strictly separated estates, the sharp contradiction between town and country and, above all, the domination of the countryside over the town.

.   .   .   .

Just as modern industry is indeed a leveller, so modern society must break down all legal and political barriers between town and country. Modern society still has *classes*, but no longer *estates*. Its development lies in the struggle between these classes, but the latter stand united against the estates and their monarchy by the grace of God.

.   .   .   .

Gentlemen of the jury, to sum up briefly, the public prosecutor cannot charge us under the laws of April 6 and 8, 1848, when these laws have been torn up by the Crown. These laws by themselves are not decisive, as they were arbitrarily concocted by the United Provincial Diet. The resolution of the National Assembly regarding the refusal to pay taxes had the force of law both formally and materially. We went further than the National Assembly in our appeal. This was our right and our duty.

In conclusion, I repeat that we have seen only the first act of the drama. The struggle between the two societies, the medieval and the bourgeois society, will again be waged in political forms.

MARX, Persecution of Foreigners in Brussels, *MECW* VI, 567–568.
On Sunday, February 27 the Brussels Democratic Association held its first public meeting since the news of the proclamation of the French Republic. It was known in advance that an immense crowd of workers, determined to lend their active help to all measures that the Association

would judge it proper to undertake, would be present.

The government, for its part, had spread the rumour that king Leopold was ready to abdicate the moment the people wished it. This was a trap set for the Belgian democrats to make them undertake nothing decisive against such a good king, who asked nothing better than to shed the burden of royalty, provided that he was honourably left a reasonable pension.

At the same time the king's government had ready a list of people whom it considered proper to arrest that very night as disturbers of public order. It had agreed with M. Hody, the chief of public security, to have on this list the foreigners as chief instigators of an artificial riot, as much to cover the arrest of Belgians known as resolute republicans as to awake national susceptibilities. This explains why, later on, his excellency M. Rogier, who is no more Belgian than His Majesty King Leopold is French, had published an ordinance which commanded the authorities to watch carefully the French and the Germans, the former compatriots of M. Rogier, the latter compatriots of Leopold. This ordinance recalls, in its form of wording, the laws on suspects.

This clever plan was executed in a manner the more perfidious and brutal in that the people arrested on the evening of February 27 had abstained from any provocation.

It might be said that pleasure had been taken in arresting these persons in order to maltreat and abuse them at leisure.

Immediately after their arrest they were showered with punches, kicks and sabre-blows; they were spat in the face, these *republicans*. They were maltreated in the presence of the philanthropist Hody, who was delighted to give these foreigners proof of his powers.

As there were no charges against them it only remained to release them. But no! They were kept in the cells for six days! Then the foreign prisoners were separated from the rest and taken directly in Black Marias to the railway station. There they were again put into vans, each in a separate cell, and sent in this way to Quiévrain where Belgian police received them and dragged them to the French frontier.

When at last they were able to collect themselves on the soil of liberty, they found they had in their pockets nothing but expulsion papers, dated the eve of their arrests.

Crime and Criminality

ENGELS, Outlines of a Critique of Political Economy, *MECW* III, 442.

Competition has penetrated all the relationships of our life and completed the reciprocal bondage in which men now hold themselves. Competition is the great mainspring which again and again jerks into activity our aging and withering social order, or rather disorder; but with each new exertion it also saps a part of this order's waning strength.

Competition governs the numerical advance of mankind; it likewise governs its moral advance. Anyone who has any knowledge of the statistics of crime must have been struck by the peculiar regularity with which crime advances year by year, and with which certain causes produce certain crimes. The extension of the factory system is followed everywhere by an increase in crime. The number of arrests, of criminal cases—indeed, the number of murders, burglaries, petty thefts, etc., for a large town or for a district—can be predicted year by year with unfailing precision, as has been done often enough in England. This regularity proves that crime, too, is governed by competition; that society creates a *demand* for crime which is met by a corresponding *supply*; that the gap created by the arrest, transportation or execution of a certain number is at once filled by others, just as every gap in population is at once filled by new arrivals; in other words, that crime presses on the means of punishment just as the people press on the means of employment. How just it is to punish criminals under these circumstances, quite apart from any other considerations, I leave to the judgment of my readers. Here I am merely concerned in demonstrating the extension of competition into the moral sphere, and in showing to what deep degradation private property has brought man.

Engels., *ibid.*, 437.

Malthus, the originator of this doctrine, maintains that population is always pressing on the means of subsistence; that as soon as production increases, population increases in the same proportion; and that the inherent tendency of the population to multiply in excess of the available means of subsistence is the root of all misery and all vice. For, when there are too many people, they have to be disposed of in one way or another; either they must be killed by violence or they must starve. But when this has happened, there is once more a gap which other multipliers of the population immediately start to fill up once more: and so the old misery begins all over again. What is more, this is the case in all circumstances—not only in civilised, but also in primitive conditions. In New Holland,* with a population density of *one* per square mile, the savages suffer just as much from over-population as England. In short, if we want to be consistent, we must admit *that the earth was already overpopulated when only one man existed.* The implications of this line of thought are that since it is precisely the poor who are the surplus, nothing should be done for them except to make their dying of starvation as easy as possible, and to convince them that it cannot be helped and that there is no other salvation for their whole class than keeping propagation down to the absolute minimum. Or if this proves impossible, then it is after all better to establish a state institution for the painless killing of the

* The old name for Australia.

children of the poor, such as "Marcus"† has suggested, whereby each working-class family would be allowed to have two and a half children, any excess being painlessly killed. Charity is to be considered a crime, since it supports the augmentation of the surplus population. Indeed, it will be very advantageous to declare poverty a crime and to turn poor-houses into prisons, as has already happened in England as a result of the new "liberal" Poor Law. Admittedly it is true that this theory ill conforms with the Bible's doctrine of the perfection of God and His creation.

MARX/ENGELS, The Holy Family, *MECW* IV, 130–131.

There is no need for any great penetration to see from the teaching of materialism on the original goodness and equal intellectual endowment of men, the omnipotence of experience, habit and education, and the influence of environment on man, the great significance of industry, the justification of enjoyment, etc., how necessarily materialism is connected with communism and socialism. If man draws all his knowledge, sensation, etc., from the world of the senses and the experience gained in it, then what has to be done is to arrange the empirical world in such a way that man experiences and becomes accustomed to what is truly human in it and that he becomes aware of himself as man. If correctly understood interest is the principle of all morality, man's private interest must be made to coincide with the interest of humanity. If man is unfree in the materialistic sense, i.e., is free not through the negative power to avoid this or that, but through the positive power to assert his true individuality, crime must not be punished in the individual, but the anti-social sources of crime must be destroyed, and each man must be given social scope for the vital manifestation of his being. If man is shaped by environment, his environment must be made human. If man is social by nature, he will develop his true nature only in society, and the power of his nature must be measured not by the power of the separate individual but by the power of society.

ENGELS, The Condition of the Working Class in England, *MECW* IV, 411–412.

So short-sighted, so stupidly narrow-minded is the English bourgeoisie in its egotism, that it does not even take the trouble to impress upon the workers the morality of the day, which the bourgeoisie has patched together in its own interest for its own protection! Even this precautionary measure is too great an effort for the enfeebled and sluggish bourgeoisie. A time must come when it will repent its neglect, too late. But it has no right to complain that the workers know nothing of its system of morals, and do not act in accordance with it.

† Malthusian pamphleteer.

Thus are the workers cast out and ignored by the class in power, morally as well as physically and mentally. The only provision made for them is the law, which fastens upon them when they become obnoxious to the bourgeoisie. Like the dullest of the brutes, they are treated to but one form of education, the whip, in the shape of force, not convincing but intimidating. There is, therefore, no cause for surprise if the workers, treated as brutes, actually become such; or if they can maintain their consciousness of manhood only by cherishing the most glowing hatred, the most unbroken inward rebellion against the bourgeoisie in power. They are men so long only as they burn with wrath against the reigning class. They become brutes the moment they bend in patience under the yoke, and merely strive to make life endurable while abandoning the effort to break the yoke.

This, then, is all that the bourgeoisie has done for the education of the proletariat—and when we take into consideration all the circumstances in which this class lives, we shall not think the worse of it for the resentment which it cherishes against the ruling class. The moral training which is not given to the worker in school is not supplied by the other conditions of his life; that moral training, at least, which alone has worth in the eyes of the bourgeoisie; his whole position and environment involves the strongest temptation to immorality. He is poor, life offers him no charm, almost every enjoyment is denied him, the penalties of the law have no further terrors for him; why should he restrain his desires, why leave to the rich the enjoyment of his birthright, why not seize a part of it for himself? What inducement has the proletarian not to steal? It is all very pretty and very agreeable to the ear of the bourgeois to hear the "sacredness of property" asserted; but for him who has none, the sacredness of property dies out of itself. Money is the god of this world; the bourgeois takes the proletarian's money from him and so makes a practical atheist of him. No wonder, then, if the proletarian retains his atheism and no longer respects the sacredness and power of the earthly God. And when the poverty of the proletarian is intensified to the point of actual lack of the barest necessaries of life, to want and hunger, the temptation to disregard all social order does but gain power. This the bourgeoisie for the most part recognises. Symons observes that poverty exercises the same ruinous influence upon the mind which drunkenness exercises upon the body; and Dr. Alison explains to property-holding readers, with the greatest exactness, what the consequences of social oppression must be for the working-class. Want leaves the working-man the choice between starving slowly, killing himself speedily, or taking what he needs where he finds it—in plain English, stealing. And there is no cause for surprise that most of them prefer stealing to starvation and suicide.

True, there are, within the working-class, numbers too moral to steal even when reduced to the utmost extremity, and these starve or commit suicide. For suicide, formerly the enviable privilege of the upper classes, has become fashionable among the English workers, and numbers of the poor kill themselves to avoid the misery from which they see no other means of escape.

ENGELS, *ibid.*, 424–427.

Thus the social order makes family life almost impossible for the worker. In a comfortless, filthy house, hardly good enough for mere nightly shelter, ill-furnished, often neither rain-tight nor warm, a foul atmosphere filling rooms overcrowded with human beings, no domestic comfort is possible. The husband works the whole day through, perhaps the wife also and the elder children, all in different places; they meet night and morning only, all under perpetual temptation to drink; what family life is possible under such conditions? Yet the working-man cannot escape from the family, must live in the family, and the consequence is a perpetual succession of family troubles, domestic quarrels, most demoralising for parents and children alike. Neglect of all domestic duties, neglect of the children, especially, is only too common among the English working-people, and only too vigorously fostered by the existing institutions of society. And children growing up in this savage way, amidst these demoralising influences, are expected to turn out goody-goody and moral in the end! Verily the requirements are naïve, which the self-satisfied bourgeois makes upon the working-man!

The contempt for the existing social order is most conspicuous in its extreme form—that of offences against the law. If the influences demoralising to the working-man act more powerfully, more concentratedly than usual, he becomes an offender as certainly as water abandons the fluid for the vaporous state at 80 degrees, Réaumur. Under the brutal and brutalising treatment of the bourgeoisie, the working-man becomes precisely as much a thing without volition as water, and is subject to the laws of Nature with precisely the same necessity; at a certain point all freedom ceases. Hence with the extension of the proletariat, crime has increased in England, and the British nation has become the most criminal in the world. From the annual criminal tables of the Home Secretary, it is evident that the increase of crime in England has proceeded with incomprehensible rapidity. The numbers of arrests for *criminal* offences reached in the years: 1805, 4,605, 1810, 5,146; 1815, 7,818; 1820, 13,710; 1825, 14,437; 1830, 18,107; 1835, 20,731; 1840, 27,187; 1841, 27,760; 1842, 31,309 in England and Wales alone. That is to say, they increased sevenfold in thirty-seven years. Of these arrests, in 1842, 4,497 were made in Lancashire alone, or more than 14 per cent of the whole; and 4,094 in Middlesex, including London, or more than 13 per cent. So that two districts which include great cities with large proletarian populations, produced one-fourth of the total amount of crime, though their population is far from forming one-fourth of the whole. Moreover, the criminal tables prove directly that nearly all crime arises within the proletariat; for, in 1842, taking the average, out of 100 criminals, 32.35 could neither read nor write; 58.32 read and wrote imperfectly; 6.77 could read and write well; 0.22 had enjoyed a higher education, while the degree of education of 2.34 could not be ascertained. In Scotland, crime has increased yet more rapidly. There were but 89 arrests for criminal offences in 1819, and as early as 1837 the number had risen to 3,126, and in 1842 to 4,189. In Lanarkshire, where Sheriff Alison himself made out the official report, population has doubled once in thirty years, and crime once in five and a half, or six times more rapidly than the population. The offences, as in all civilised countries, are, in the great majority of cases, against property, and have, therefore, arisen from want in some form; for what a man has, he does not steal. The proportion of offences against property to the population, which in the Netherlands is as 1:7,140, and in France, as 1:1,804, was in England, when Gaskell wrote, as 1:799. The proportion of offences against persons to the population is, in the Netherlands, 1:28,904; in France, 1:17,573; in England, 1:23,395; that of crimes in general to the population in the agricultural districts, as 1:1,043; in the manufacturing districts as 1:840. In the whole of England today the proportion is 1:660; though it is scarcely ten years since Gaskell's book appeared!

These facts are certainly more than sufficient to bring any one, even a bourgeois, to pause and reflect upon the consequences of such a state of things. If demoralisation and crime multiply twenty years longer in this proportion (and if English manufacture in these twenty years should be less prosperous than heretofore, the progressive multiplication of crime can only continue the more rapidly), what will the result be? Society is already in a state of visible dissolution; it is impossible to pick up a newspaper without seeing the most striking evidence of the giving way of all social ties. I look at random into a heap of English journals lying before me; there is the *Manchester Guardian* for October 30, 1844, which reports for three days. It no longer takes the trouble to give exact details as to Manchester, and merely relates the most interesting cases: that the workers in a mill have struck for higher wages without giving notice, and been condemned by a Justice of the Peace to resume work; that in Salford a couple of boys had been caught stealing, and a bankrupt tradesman tried to cheat his creditors. From the neighbouring towns the reports are more detailed: in Ashton, two thefts, one burglary, one suicide; in Bury, one theft; in Bolton, two thefts, one revenue fraud; in Leigh, one theft; in Oldham, one strike for wages, one theft, one fight between Irish women, one non–Union hatter assaulted by Union men, one mother beaten by her son, one attack upon the police, one robbery of a church; in Stockport, discontent of working-men with wages, one theft, one fraud, one fight, one wife beaten by her husband; in Warring-ton, one theft, one fight; in Wigan, one theft, and one robbery of a church. The reports of the London papers are much worse; frauds, thefts, assaults, family quarrels crowd one another. A *Times* of September 12,

1844, falls into my hand, which gives a report of a single day, including a theft, an attack upon the police, a sentence upon a father requiring him to support his illegitimate son, the abandonment of a child by its parents, and the poisoning of a man by his wife. Similar reports are to be found in all the English papers. In this country, social war is under full headway, every one stands for himself, and fights for himself against all comers, and whether or not he shall injure all the others who are his declared foes, depends upon a cynical calculation as to what is most advantageous for himself. It no longer occurs to any one to come to a peaceful understanding with his fellow-man; all differences are settled by threats, violence, or in a law-court. In short, every one sees in his neighbour an enemy to be got out of the way, or, at best, a tool to be used for his own advantage. And this war grows from year to year, as the criminal tables show, more violent, passionate, irreconcilable. The enemies are dividing gradually into two great camps—the bourgeoisie on the one hand, the workers on the other. This war of each against all, of the bourgeoisie against the proletariat, need cause us no surprise, for it is only the logical sequel of the principle involved in free competition. But it may very well surprise us that the bourgeoisie remains so quiet and composed in the face of the rapidly gathering storm-clouds, that it can read all these things daily in the papers without, we will not say indignation at such a social condition, but fear of its consequences, of a universal outburst of that which manifests itself symptomatically from day to day in the form of crime. But then it is the bourgeoisie, and from its standpoint cannot even see the facts, much less perceive their consequences. One thing only is astounding, that class prejudice and preconceived opinions can hold a whole class of human beings in such perfect, I might almost say, such mad blindness. Meanwhile, the development of the nation goes its way whether the bourgeoisie has eyes for it or not, and will surprise the property-holding class one day with things not dreamed of in its philosophy.

ENGELS, *ibid.*, 441–442.

But that is the least of the evil. The moral consequences of the employment of women in factories are even worse. The collecting of persons of both sexes and all ages in a single work-room, the inevitable contact, the crowding into a small space of people, to whom neither mental nor moral education has been given, is not calculated for the favourable development of the female character. The manufacturer, if he pays any attention to the matter, can interfere only when something scandalous actually happens; the permanent, less conspicuous influence of persons of dissolute character upon the more moral, and especially upon the younger ones, he cannot ascertain, and consequently cannot prevent. But precisely this influence is the injurious. The language used in the mills is characterised by many witnesses in the report of 1833, as "indecent", "bad", "filthy", etc. It is the same process upon a small scale which we have already witnessed upon a large one in the great cities. The centralisation of population has the same influence upon the same persons, whether it affects them in a great city or a small factory. The smaller the mill the closer the packing, and the more unavoidable the contact; and the consequences are not wanting. A witness in Leicester said that he would rather let his daughter beg than go into a factory; that they are perfect gates of hell; that most of the prostitutes of the town had their employment in the mills to thank for their present situation. Another, in Manchester, "did not hesitate to assert that three-fourths of the young factory employees, from fourteen to twenty years of age, were unchaste". Commissioner Cowell expresses it as his opinion, that the morality of the factory operatives is somewhat below the average of that of the working class in general. And Dr. Hawkins says:

> "An estimate of sexual morality is scarcely possible to be reduced into figures; but if I may trust my own observations, and the general opinion of those with whom I have conversed, and the spirit of our evidence, then a most discouraging view of the influence of the factory life upon the morality of female youth obtrudes itself."

It is, besides, a matter of course that factory servitude, like any other, and to an even higher degree, confers the *jus primae noctis* upon the master. In this respect also the employer is sovereign over the persons and charms of his employees. The threat of discharge suffices to overcome all resistance in nine cases out of ten, if not in ninety-nine out of a hundred, in girls who, in any case, have no strong inducements to chastity. If the master is mean enough, and the official report mentions several such cases, his mill is also his harem; and the fact that not all manufacturers use their power, does not in the least change the position of the girls. In the beginning of manufacturing industry, when most of the employers were upstarts without education or consideration for the hypocrisy of society, they let nothing interfere with the exercise of their vested rights.

ENGELS, *ibid.*, 494.

Immorality among young people seems to be more prevalent in Sheffield than anywhere else. It is hard to tell which town ought to have the prize, and in reading the report one believes of each one that this certainly deserves it! The younger generation spend the whole of Sunday lying in the street tossing coins or fighting dogs, go regularly to the gin palace, where they sit with their sweethearts until late at night, when they take walks in solitary couples. In an ale-house which the commissioner visited, there sat forty to fifty young people of both sexes, nearly all under seventeen years of age, and each lad beside his lass. Here and there cards were played, at other places dancing was going on, and everywhere drinking. Among the company were openly avowed professional prostitutes. No wonder, then, that, as all the witnesses testify, early, unbridled sexual intercourse, youthful prostitution, beginning with persons of fourteen to fifteen years, is extraordinarily frequent in Sheffield. Crimes of a savage and desperate sort are of common occurrence; one year before the commissioner's visit, a band, consisting chiefly of young persons, was arrested when about to set fire to the town, being fully equipped with lances and inflammable substances.

ENGELS, *ibid,* 502–504.

The revolt of the workers began soon after the first industrial development, and has passed through several phases. The investigation of their importance in the history of the English people I must reserve for separate treatment, limiting myself meanwhile to such bare facts as serve to characterise the condition of the English proletariat.

The earliest, crudest, and least fruitful form of this rebellion was that of crime. The working-man lived in poverty and want, and saw that others were better off than he. It was not clear to his mind why he, who did more for society than the rich idler, should be the one to suffer under these conditions. Want conquered his inherited respect for the sacredness of property, and he stole. We have seen how crime increased with the extension of manufacture; how the yearly number of arrests bore a constant relation to the number of bales of cotton annually consumed.

The workers soon realised that crime did not help matters. The criminal could protest against the existing order of society only singly, as one individual; the whole might of society was brought to bear upon each criminal, and crushed him with its immense superiority. Besides, theft was the most primitive form of protest, and for this reason, if for no other, it never became the universal expression of the public opinion of the working-men, however much they might approve of it in silence. As a class, they first manifested opposition to the bourgeoisie when they resisted the introduction of machinery at the very beginning of the industrial period. The first inventors, Arkwright and others, were persecuted in this way and their machines destroyed. Later, there took place a number of revolts against machinery, in which the occurrences were almost precisely the same as those of the printers' disturbances in Bohemia in 1844; factories were demolished and machinery destroyed.

This form of opposition also was isolated, restricted to certain localities, and directed against one feature only of our present social arrangements. When the momentary end was attained, the whole weight of social power fell upon the unprotected evil-doers and punished them to its heart's content, while the machinery was introduced none the less. A new form of opposition had to be found.

At this point help came in the shape of a law enacted by the old, unreformed, oligarchic-Tory Parliament, a law which never could have passed the House of Commons later, when the Reform Bill had legally sanctioned the distinction between bourgeoisie and proletariat, and made the bourgeoisie the ruling class. This was enacted in 1824, and repealed all laws by which coalitions between working-men for labour purposes had hitherto been forbidden. The working-men obtained a right previously restricted to the aristocracy and bourgeoisie, the right of free association. Secret coalitions had, it is true, previously existed, but could never achieve great results. In Glasgow as Symons relates, a general strike of weavers had taken place in 1812, which was brought about by a secret association. It was repeated in 1822, and on this occasion vitriol was thrown into the faces of the two working-men who would not join the association, and were therefore regarded by the members as traitors to their class. Both the assaulted lost the use of their eyes in consequence of the injury. So, too, in 1818 the association of Scottish miners was powerful enough to carry on a general strike. These associations required their members to take an oath of fidelity and secrecy, had regular lists, treasurers, book-keepers, and local branches. But the secrecy with which everything was conducted crippled their growth. When, on the other hand, the working-men received in 1824 the right of free association, these combinations were very soon spread over all England and attained great power.

ENGELS, *ibid.*, 508–510.

The workers are coming to perceive more clearly with every day how competition affects them; they see far more clearly than the bourgeois that competition of the capitalists among themselves presses upon the workers too, by bringing on commercial crises, and that this kind of competition, too, must be abolished. They will soon learn *how* they have to go about it.

That these Unions contribute greatly to nourish the bitter hatred of the workers against the property-holding class need hardly be said. From them proceed, therefore, with or without the connivance of the leading members, in times of unusual excitement, individual actions which can be explained only by hatred wrought to the pitch of despair, by a wild passion overwhelming all restraints. Of this sort are the attacks with vitriol mentioned in the foregoing pages, and a series of others, of which I shall cite several. In 1831, during a violent labour movement, young Ashton, a manufacturer in Hyde, near Manchester, was shot one evening when crossing a field, and no trace of the assassin discovered. There is no doubt that this was a deed of vengeance of the working-men. Incendiarisms and attempted explosions are very common. On Friday, September 29th, 1843, an attempt was made to blow up the saw-works of Padgin, in Howard Street. Sheffield. A closed iron tube filled with powder was the means employed, and the damage was considerable. On the following day, a similar attempt was made in Ibbetson's knife and file works at Shales Moor, near Sheffield. Mr. Ibbetson had made himself obnoxious by an active participation in bourgeois movements, by low wages, the exclusive employment of knobsticks, and the exploitation of the Poor Law for his own benefit. He had reported, during the crisis of 1842, such operatives as refused to accept reduced wages, as persons who could find work but would not take it, and were, therefore, not deserving of relief, so compelling the acceptance of reduction. Considerable damage was inflicted by the explosion, and all the working-men who came to view it regretted only "that the whole concern was not blown into the air". On Friday, October 6th, 1843, an attempt to set fire to the factory of Ainsworth and Crompton, at Bolton, did no damage; it was the third or fourth attempt in the same factory within a very short time. In the meeting of the Town Council of Sheffield, on Wednesday, January 10th, 1844, the Commissioner of Police exhibited a cast-iron machine, made for the express purpose of producing an explosion, and found filled with four pounds of powder, and a fuse which had been lighted but had not taken effect, in the works of Mr. Kitchen, Earl Street, Sheffield. On Sunday, January 21st, 1844, an explosion caused by a package of powder took place in the sawmill of Bentley & White, at Bury, in Lancashire, and produced considerable damage. On Thursday, February 1st, 1844, the Soho Wheel Works, in Sheffield, were set on fire and burnt up.

Here are six such cases in four months, all of which have their sole origin in the embitterment of the working-men against the employers. What sort of a social state it must be in which such things are possible I need hardly say. These facts are proof enough that in England, even in good business years, such as 1843, the social war is avowed and openly carried on, and still the English bourgeoisie does not stop to reflect! But the case which speaks most loudly is that of the Glasgow Thugs, which came up before the Assizes from the 3rd to the 11th of January, 1838. It appears from the proceedings that the Cotton-Spinners' Union, which existed here from the year 1816, possessed rare organisation and power. The members were bound by an oath to adhere to the decision of the majority, and had during every turnout a secret committee which was unknown to the mass of the members, and controlled the funds of the Union absolutely. This committee fixed a price upon the heads of knobsticks and obnoxious manufacturers and upon incendiarisms in mills. A mill was thus set on fire in which female knobsticks were employed in spinning in the place of men; a Mrs. M'Pherson, mother of one of these girls, was murdered, and both murderers sent to America at the expense of the association. As early as 1820, a knobstick named M'Quarry was shot at and wounded, for which deed the doer received twenty pounds from the Union, but was discovered and transported for life. Finally, in 1837, in May, disturbances occurred in consequence of a turnout in the Oatbank and Mile End factories, in which perhaps a dozen knobsticks were maltreated. In July, of the same year, the disturbances still continued, and a certain Smith, a knobstick, was so maltreated that he died. The committee was now arrested, an investigation begun, and the leading members found guilty of participation in conspiracies, maltreatment of knobsticks, and incendiarism in the mill of James and Francis Wood, and they were transported for seven years.

ENGELS, *Anti-Dühring*, 352.

The development of industry upon a capitalistic basis made poverty and misery of the working masses conditions of existence of society. Cash payment became more and more, in Carlyle's phrase, the sole nexus between man and man. The number of crimes increased from year to year. Formerly, the feudal vices had openly stalked about in broad daylight; though not eradicated, they were now at any rate thrust into the background. In their stead, the bourgeois vices, hitherto practised in secret, began to blossom all the more luxuriantly. Trade became to a greater and greater extent cheating. The "fraternity" of the revolutionary motto was realized in the chicanery and rivalries of the battle of competition. Oppression by force was replaced by corruption; the sword, as the first social lever, by gold. The right of the first night was transferred from the feudal lords to the bourgeois manufacturers. Prostitution increased to an extent never heard of. Marriage itself remained, as before, the legally recognized form, the official cloak of prostitution, and, moreover, was supplemented by rich crops of adultery.

MARX/ENGELS, The German Ideology, *MECW* V, 330.

Like right, so crime, i.e., the struggle of the isolated individual against the predominant relations, is not the result of pure arbitrariness. On the contrary, it depends on the same conditions as that domination.

MARX/ENGELS, *ibid.*, 339–340.

Having thus described for us political and juridical crime as an example of crime in general—namely his category of crime, sin, negation, enmity, insult, contempt for the holy, disreputable behaviour towards the holy—Saint Sancho can now confidently declare:

> "In crime, the egoist has hitherto asserted himself and mocked the holy" (p. 319).

In this passage all the crimes hitherto committed are assigned to the credit of the egoist in agreement with himself, although subsequently we shall have to transfer a few of them to the debit side. Sancho imagines that hitherto crimes have been committed only in order to mock at "the holy" and to assert oneself not against things, but against the holy *aspect* of things. Because the theft committed by a poor devil who appropriates someone else's taler can be put in the category of a crime against the law, *for that reason* the poor devil committed the theft just because of a desire to break the law. In exactly the same way as in an earlier passage Jacques le bonhomme imagined that laws are issued only for the sake of the holy, and that thieves are sent to prison only for the sake of the holy. . . .

Frederick William IV, who thinks he is able to promulgate laws in accordance with the holy, and therefore is always at loggerheads with the whole world, can comfort himself with the thought that in our Sancho he has found at least one man imbued with faith in the state. Let Saint Sancho just compare the Prussian marriage law, which exists only in the head of its author, with the provisions of the *Code civil*, which are operative in practice, and he will be able to discover the difference between holy and worldly marriage laws. In the Prussian phantasmagoria, for reasons of state, the sanctity of marriage is supposed to be enforced both upon husband and wife; in French practice, where the wife is regarded as the private property of her husband, only the wife can be punished for adultery, and then only on the demand of the husband, who exercises his property right.

MARX/ENGELS, *ibid.*, 341–342.

The very same ideologists who could imagine that right, law, state, etc., arose from a general concept, in the final analysis perhaps the concept of man, and that they were put into effect for the sake of this concept—these same ideologists can, of course, also imagine that crimes are committed purely because of a wanton attitude towards some concept, that crimes, in general, are nothing but making mockery of concepts and are only punished in order to do justice to the insulted concepts.

ENGELS, Speeches in Elberfeld, *MECW* IV, 248–249.

Present-day society, which breeds hostility between the individual man and everyone else, thus produces a social war of all against all which inevitably in individual cases, notably among uneducated people, assumes a brutal, barbarously violent form—that of crime. In order to protect itself against crime, against direct acts of violence, society requires an extensive, complicated system of administrative and judicial bodies which requires an immense labour force. In communist society this would likewise be vastly simplified, and precisely because—strange though it may sound—precisely because the administrative body in this society would have to manage not merely individual aspects of social life, but the whole of social life, in all its various activities, in all its aspects. We eliminate the contradiction between the individual man and all others, we counterpose social peace to social war, we put the axe to the *root* of crime—and thereby render the greatest, by far the greatest, part of the present activity of the administrative and judicial bodies superfluous. Even now crimes of passion are becoming fewer and fewer in comparison with calculated crimes, crimes of interest—crimes against *persons* are

declining, crimes against *property* are on the increase. Advancing civilisation moderates violent outbreaks of passion even in our present-day
society, which is on a war footing; how much more will this be the case
in communist, peaceful society! Crimes against property cease of their
own accord where everyone receives what he needs to satisfy his natural
and his spiritual urges, where social gradations and distinctions cease to
exist. Justice concerned with criminal cases ceases of itself, that dealing
with civil cases, which are almost all rooted in the property relations or at
least in such relations as arise from the situation of social war, likewise
disappears; conflicts can then be only rare exceptions, whereas they are
now the natural result of general hostility, and will be easily settled by
arbitrators. The activities of the administrative bodies at present have
likewise their source in the continual social war—the police and the entire
administration do nothing else but see to it that the war remains
concealed and indirect and does not erupt into open violence, into crimes.
But if it is infinitely easier to maintain peace than to keep war within
certain limits, so it is vastly more easy to administer a communist
community rather than a competitive one. And if civilisation has already
taught men to seek their interest in the maintenance of public order,
public security, and the public interest, and therefore to make the police,
administration and justice as superfluous as possible, how much more
will this be the case in a society in which community of interests has
become the basic principle, and in which the public interest is no longer
distinct from that of each individual! What already exists now, *in spite of*
the social organisation, how much more will it exist when it is no longer
hindered, but supported by the social institutions! We may thus also in
this regard count on a considerable increase in the labour force through
that part of the labour force of which society is deprived by the present
social condition.

MARX, The Civil War in France, *MESW(3)* II, 229.
    Wonderful, indeed, was the change the Commune had wrought in Paris!
No longer any trace of the meretricious Paris of the Second Empire. No
longer was Paris the rendezvous of British landlords, Irish absentees,
American ex-slaveholders and shoddy men, Russian ex-serfowners, and
Wallachian boyards. No more corpses at the morgue, no nocturnal
burglaries, scarcely any robberies; in fact, for the first time since the days
of February, 1848, the streets of Paris were safe, and that without any
police of any kind.

> "We," said a member of the Commune, "hear no longer of assassination,
> theft and personal assault; it seems indeed as if the police had dragged along
> with it to Versailles all its Conservative friends."

The *cocottes* had refound the scent of their protectors—the absconding
men of family, religion, and, above all, of property. In their stead, the real

women of Paris showed again at the surface—heroic, noble, and devoted, like the women of antiquity. Working, thinking, fighting, bleeding Paris—almost forgetful, in its incubation of a new society, of the cannibals at its gates—radiant in the enthusiasm of its historic initiative!

MARX, Population, Crime and Pauperism, *On Ireland*, 93–94.

There must be something rotten in the very core of a social system which increases its wealth without diminishing its misery, and increases in crimes even more rapidly than in numbers. It is true enough that, if we compare the year 1855 with the preceding years, there seems to have occurred a sensible decrease of crime from 1855 to 1858. The total number of people committed for trial, which in 1854 amounted to 29,359, had sunk down to 17,855 in 1858; and the number of convicted had also greatly fallen off, if not quite in the same ratio. This apparent decrease of crime, however, since 1854, is to be exclusively attributed to some technical changes in British jurisdiction; to the Juvenile Offenders' Act in the first instance, and, in the second instance, to the operation of the Criminal Justice Act of 1855, which authorises the Police Magistrates to pass sentences for short periods, with the consent of the prisoners. Violations of the law are generally the offspring of economical agencies beyond the control of the legislator, but, as the working of the Juvenile Offenders' Act testifies, it depends to some degree on official society to stamp certain violations of its rules as crimes or as transgressions only. This difference of nomenclature, so far from being indifferent, decides on the fate of thousands of men, and the moral tone of society. Law itself may not only punish crime, but improvise it, and the law of professional lawyers is very apt to work in this direction. Thus, it has been justly remarked by an eminent historian, that the Catholic clergy of the medieval times, with its dark views of human nature, introduced by its influence into criminal legislation, has created more crimes than forgiven sins.

Strange to say, the only part of the United Kingdom in which crime has seriously decreased, say by 50, and even by 75 per cent, is Ireland. How can we harmonise this fact with the public-opinion slang of England, according to which Irish nature, instead of British misrule, is responsible for Irish shortcomings? It is, again, no act on the part of the British ruler, but simply the consequence of a famine, an exodus, and a general combination of circumstances favourable to the demand for Irish labour, that has worked this happy change in Irish nature. However that may be, the significance of the following tabular statements cannot be misunderstood:

I.—Crimes in Ireland
—Committed for Trial—

Years	Males	Females	Total	Convicted
1844	14,799	4,649	19,448	8,042
1845	12,807	3,889	16,696	7,101
1846	14,204	4,288	18,192	8,639
1847	23,552	7,657	31,209	15,233
1848	28,765	9,757	38,522	18,206
1849	31,340	10,649	41,989	21,202
1850	22,682	3,644	31,326	17,108
1851	17,337	7,347	24,684	14,377
1852	12,444	5,234	17,678	10,454
1853	40,260	4,884	15,144	8,714
1854	7,937	3,851	11,788	7,051
1855	6,019	2,993	9,012	5,220
1856	5,097	2,002	7,099	4,024
1857	5,158	1,752	7,210	3,925
1858	4,708	1,600	6,308	3,350

II.—Paupers in Ireland

Years	No. of Parishes	Paupers	Years	No. of Parishes	Paupers
1849	880	82,357	1854	883	78,929
1850	880	79,031	1855	883	79,887
1851	881	76,906	1856	883	79,973
1852	882	75,111	1857	883	79,217
1853	882	75,437	1858	883	79,199

MARX, *Grundrisse*, 273.
   What the other economists advance against it is either horse-piss (for instance Storch, Senior even lousier etc.), namely that every action after all acts upon something, thus confusion of the product in its natural and in its economic sense; so that the pickpocket becomes a productive worker too, since he indirectly produces books on criminal law (this reasoning at least as correct as calling a judge a productive worker because he protects *from* theft).

MARX, *Theories of Surplus Value* I, 387–388.

[II. APOLOGIST CONCEPTION OF THE PRODUCTIVITY OF ALL PROFESSIONS]
[V—182] A philosopher produces ideas, a poet poems, a clergyman sermons, a professor compendia and so on. A criminal produces crimes. If we look a little closer at the connection between this latter branch of production and society as a whole, we shall rid ourselves of many prejudices. The criminal produces not only crimes but also criminal law, and with this also the professor who gives lectures on criminal law and in addition to this the inevitable compendium in which this same professor throws his lectures onto the general market as "commodities". This brings with it augmentation of national wealth, quite apart from the personal enjoyment which—as a competent witness, Herr Professor Roscher, [tells] us—the manuscript of the compendium brings to its originator himself.

The criminal moreover produces the whole of the police and of criminal justice, constables, judges, hangmen, juries, etc.; and all these different lines of business, which form equally many categories of the social division of labour, develop different capacities of the human spirit, create new needs and new ways of satisfying them. Torture alone has given rise to the most ingenious mechanical inventions, and employed many honourable craftsmen in the production of its instruments.

The criminal produces an impression, partly moral and partly tragic, as the case may be, and in this way renders a "service" by arousing the moral and aesthetic feelings of the public. He produces not only compendia on Criminal Law, not only penal codes and along with them legislators in this field, but also art, belles-lettres, novels, and even tragedies, as not only Müllner's *Schuld* and Schiller's *Räuber* show, but also [Sophocles'] *Oedipus* and [Shakespeare's] *Richard the Third*. The criminal breaks the monotony and everyday security of bourgeois life. In this way he keeps it from stagnation, and gives rise to that uneasy tension and agility without which even the spur of competition would get blunted. Thus he gives a stimulus to the productive forces. While crime takes a part of the superfluous population off the labour market and thus reduces competition among the labourers—up to a certain point preventing wages from falling below the minimum—the struggle against crime absorbs another part of this population. Thus the criminal comes in as one of those natural "counterweights" which bring about a correct balance and open up a whole perspective of "useful" occupations.

The effects of the criminal on the development of productive power can be shown in detail. Would locks ever have reached their present degree of excellence had there been no thieves? Would the making of bank-notes have reached its present perfection had there been no forgers? Would the microscope have found its way into the sphere of ordinary commerce (see Babbage) but for trading frauds? Doesn't practical chemistry owe just as much to adulteration of commodities and the efforts to show it up as to the honest zeal for production? Crime, through its constantly new methods of attack on property, constantly calls into being new methods of defence, and so is as productive as strikes for the invention of machines. And if one leaves the sphere of private crime: would the world-market ever have come into being but for national crime? Indeed, would even the nations have arisen? And hasn't the Tree of Sin been at the same time the Tree of Knowledge ever since the time of Adam?

Punishment

MARX/ENGELS, The Holy Family, *MECW* IV, 178–179.

What Rudolph, the man of pure Criticism, objects to in profane criminal justice is the too swift transition from the court to the scaffold. He, on the other hand, wants to link *vengeance* on the criminal with *penance* and *consciousness of sin* in the criminal, corporal punishment with spiritual punishment, sensuous torture with the non-sensuous torture of remorse. Profane punishment must at the same time be a means of Christian moral education.

This penal theory, which links *jurisprudence* with *theology*, this "revealed mystery of the mystery", is no other than the penal theory of the *Catholic* Church, as already expounded at length by *Bentham* in his work *Punishments and Rewards*. In that book Bentham also proved the moral futility of the punishments of today. He calls legal penalties "*legal parodies*".

The punishment that Rudolph imposed on the *maître d'école* is the same as that which *Origen* imposed on himself. He *emasculates* him, robs him of a *productive organ*, the eye. "The eye is the light of the body." It does great credit to Rudolph's religious instinct that he should hit, of all things, upon the idea of *blinding*. This punishment was current in the thoroughly Christian empire of Byzantium and came to full flower in the vigorous youthful period of the Christian-Germanic states of England and France. Cutting man off from the perceptile outer world, throwing him back into his abstract inner nature in order to correct him—blinding—is a necessary consequence of the Christian doctrine according to which the consummation of this cutting off, the pure isolation of man in his spiritualistic "ego", is *good itself*. If Rudolph does not shut the *maître d'école* up in a real monastery, as was the case in Byzantium and in Franconia, he at least shuts him up in an ideal monastery, in the cloister of an impenetrable night which the light of the outer world cannot pierce, the cloister of an idle conscience and consciousness of sin filled with nothing but the phantoms of memory.

A certain speculative bashfulness prevents Herr Szeliga from discussing openly the penal theory of his hero Rudolph that worldly punishment must be linked with Christian repentance and atonement. Instead he imputes to him—naturally as a mystery which is only just being revealed to the world—the theory that punishment must make the criminal the *"judge"* of his *"own"* crime.

The mystery of this revealed mystery is *Hegel's* penal theory. According to Hegel, the criminal in his punishment passes sentence on himself. *Gans* developed this theory at greater length. In Hegel this is the *speculative disguise* of the old *jus talionis*, which *Kant* expounded as the *only juridical* penal theory. For Hegel, self-judgment of the criminal remains a mere *"Idea"*, a mere speculative interpretation of the *current empirical punishments for criminals*. He thus leaves the mode of application to the respective stage of development of the state, i.e., he leaves punishments as it is. Precisely in that he shows himself more critical than his Critical echo. A *penal* theory which at the same time sees in the criminal the *man* can do so only in *abstraction*, in imagination, precisely because *punishment, coercion*, is contrary to *human* conduct. Moreover, this would be impossible to carry out. Purely subjective arbitrariness would take the place of the abstract law because it would always depend on the official, "honourable and decent" men to adapt the penalty to the individuality of the criminal. Plato long ago realised that the *law* must be one-sided and *take no account* of the individual. On the other hand, under *human* conditions punishment will *really* be nothing but the sentence passed by the culprit on himself. No one will want to convince him that *violence* from *without*, done to him by others, is violence which he had done to himself. On the contrary, he will see in *other* men his natural saviours from the punishment which he has imposed on himself; in other words, the relation will be reversed.

See also MARX/ENGELS, The Holy Family, *MECW* IV, 186–187.

MARX, Capital Punishment, *Articles on Britain*, 150–153.

The *Times* of Jan. 25 contains the following observations under the head of "Amateur Hanging":

> "It has often been remarked that in this country a public execution is generally followed closely by instances of death by hanging, either suicidal or accidental, in consequence of the powerful effect which the execution of a noted criminal produces upon a morbid and unmatured mind."

Of the several cases which are alleged by the *Times* in illustration of this remark, one is that of a lunatic of Sheffield, who, after talking with other lunatics respecting the execution of Barbour, put an end to his existence by hanging himself. Another case is that of a boy of 14 years, who also hung himself.

The doctrine to which the enumeration of these facts was intended to give its support, is one which no reasonable man would be likely to guess, it being no less than a direct apotheosis of the hangman, while capital punishment is extolled as the *ultima ratio* of society. This is done in a leading article of the "leading journal".

The Morning Advertiser, in some very bitter but just strictures on the hanging predilections and bloody logic of the *Times*, has the following interesting data on 43 days of the year 1849:

Executions of:		Murders and Suicides:	
Millan	March 20	Hannah Sandles	March 22
		M. G. Newton	March 22
Pulley	March 26	J. G. Gleeson—4 murders at Liverpool	March 27
Smith	March 27		
Howe	March 31	Murder and suicide at Leicester	April 2
		Poisoning at Bath	April 7
		W. Bailey	April 8
Landich	April 9	J. Ward murders his mother	April 13
Sarah Thomas	April 13	Yardley	April 14
		Doxy, parricide	April 14
		J. Bailey kills his two children and himself	April 17
J. Griffiths	April 18	Charles Overton	April 18
J. Rush	April 21	Daniel Holmston	May 2

This table, as the *Times* concedes, shows not only suicides, but also murders of the most atrocious kind, following closely upon the execution of criminals. It is astonishing that the article in question does not even produce a single argument or pretext for indulging in the savage theory therein propounded; and it would be very difficult, if not altogether impossible, to establish any principle upon which the justice or expediency of capital punishment could be founded in a society glorying in its civilisation. Punishment in general has been defended as a means either of ameliorating or of intimidating. Now what right have you to punish me for the amelioration or intimidation of others? And besides, there is history—there is such a thing as statistics—which prove with the most complete evidence that since Cain the world has neither been intimidated nor ameliorated by punishment. Quite the contrary. From the point of view of abstract right, there is only one theory of punishment which recognises human dignity in the abstract, and that is the theory of Kant especially in the more rigid formula given to it by Hegel. Hegel says:

> "Punishment is the *right* of the criminal. It is an act of his own will. The violation of right has been proclaimed by the criminal as his own right. His crime is the negation of right. Punishment is the negation of this negation,

and consequently an affirmation of right, solicited and forced upon the criminal by himself."

There is no doubt something specious in this formula, inasmuch as Hegel, instead of looking upon the criminal as the mere object, the slave of justice, elevates him to the position of a free and self-determined being. Looking, however, more closely into the matter, we discover that German idealism here, as in most other instances has but given a transcendental sanction to the rules of existing society. Is it not a delusion to substitute for the individual with his real motives, with multifarious social circumstances pressing upon him, the abstraction of "free-will"—one among the many qualities of man for man himself! This theory, considering punishment as the result of the criminal's own will, is only a metaphysical expression for the old "jus talionis"; eye against eye, tooth against tooth, blood against blood. Plainly speaking, and dispensing with all paraphrases, punishment is nothing but a means of society to defend itself against the infraction of its vital conditions, whatever may be their character. Now, what a state of society is that, which knows of no better instrument for its own defence than the hangman, and which proclaims through the "leading journal of the world" its own brutality as eternal law?

Mr. A. Quetelet, in his excellent and learned work, *l'Homme et ses Facultes*, says:

"There is a *budget* which we pay with frightful regularity—it is that of prisons, dungeons and scaffolds. . . . We might even predict how many individuals will stain their hands with the blood of their fellow men, how many will be forgers, how many will deal in poison, pretty nearly the same way as we may foretell the annual births and deaths."

And Mr. Quetelet, in a calculation of the probabilities of crime published in 1829, actually predicted with astonishing certainty, not only the amount but all the different kinds of crimes committed in France in 1830. That it is not so much the particular political institutions of a country as the fundamental conditions of modern bourgeois society in general, which produce an average amount of crime in a given national fraction of society, may be seen from the following table, communicated by Quetelet, for the years 1822–24. We find in a number of one hundred condemned criminals in America and France:

Age	Philadelphia	France
Under twenty-one years	19	19
Twenty-one to thirty	44	35
Thirty to forty	23	23
Above forty	14	23
Total	100	100

Now, if crimes observed on a great scale thus show, in their amount and their classification, the regularity of physical phenomena—if as Mr. Quetelet remarks, "it would be difficult to decide in respect to which of the two" (the physical world and the social system) "the acting causes produce their effect with the utmost regularity"—is there not a necessity for deeply reflecting upon an alteration of the system that breeds these crimes, instead of glorifying the hangman who executes a lot of criminals to make room only for the supply of new ones?

MARX, The Bourgeoisie and the Counter-revolution, *Articles from NRZ*, 195–196.

Numerous lawsuits against the press based on Prussian law, or, where it did not exist, on the Code pénal, numerous arrests on the same "sufficient grounds" (Auerswald's formula), introduction of a system of constables in Berlin at the rate of one constable per every two houses, police interference with the freedom of association, the use of soldiers against unruly citizens and of the Civil Guard against unruly workers, and the introduction, by way of deterrent, of martial law—all these events of Hansemann's Olympiad are still vividly remembered. No details need be mentioned.

This aspect of the efforts of the government of action was summarised by *Kühlwetter* in the following words:

> "A state that wants to be really free must have a really large police force as its executive arm",

to which Hansemann muttered one of his usual remarks:

> "This would also greatly help to *restore trust* and *revive the rather slack commercial activity*."

The government of action accordingly "*strengthened*" the old Prussian police force, the judiciary, the bureaucracy and the army, who, since they receive their *pay* from the bourgeoisie, also *serve* the bourgeoisie, as Hansemann thought. At any rate, they were "*strengthened*".

On the other hand, the temper of the proletariat and bourgeois democrats is expressed by *one* event. Because a few reactionaries maltreated a few democrats in Charlottenburg, the people stormed the residence of the Prime Minister in Berlin. So popular had the government of action become. The next day Hansemann tabled a law against riotous gatherings and public meetings. This shows how cunningly he intrigued against reaction.

Thus the actual, tangible, popular activity of the government of action was purely *policemanic* in character. In the eyes of the proletariat and the *urban* democrats this cabinet and the Assembly of conciliators, whose majority was represented in the cabinet, and the Prussian bourgeoisie, the majority of whom constituted the majority in the Assembly of conciliation, represented the *old*, refurbished *police and bureaucratic state*. To this was added resentment against the bourgeoisie, because it governed and had set up the *Civil Guard* as an integral part of the police.

The "achievement of the March events", as the people saw it, was that the liberal gentlemen of the bourgeoisie, too, took *police* duties upon themselves. There was thus a twin police force.

Not the actions of the government of action, but the drafts of its organic laws show clearly that it "*strengthened*" the "*police*"—the ultimate expression of the old state—and spurred it into action only in the interest of the bourgeoisie.

In the bills relating to *local government, jury,* and *Civil Guard,* introduced by the Hansemann cabinet, *property* in one form or another always forms the demarcation line between *lawful* and *unlawful* territory. All these bills contain the most servile concessions to royal power, for the bourgeois cabinet believed that the wings of royalty had been clipped and that it had become its ally; but as a consolation the ascendancy of capital over labour is all the more ruthlessly emphasised.

The Civil Guard Law approved by the assembly of conciliation was turned against the bourgeoisie and had to provide a legal pretext for disarming it. According to the fancy of its authors, however, it was to become valid only after the promulgation of the Law on Local Government and of the constitution, that is, after the consolidation of the rule of the bourgeoisie. The experience which the Prussian bourgeoisie gained in connection with the Civil Guard Law may contribute to its enlightenment and show it that for the time being all its actions that are meant to be directed against the people are only directed against itself.

ENGELS, The Condition of the Working Class in England, *MECW* IV, 567–568.

We have seen in the course of our report how the bourgeoisie exploits the proletariat in every conceivable way for its own benefit! We have, however, hitherto seen only how the single bourgeois maltreats the proletariat upon his own account. Let us turn now to the manner in which the bourgeoisie as a party, as the power of the State, conducts itself towards the proletariat. Laws are necessary only because there are persons in existence who own nothing; and although this is directly expressed in but few laws, as, for instance, those against vagabonds and tramps, in which the proletariat as such is outlawed, yet enmity to the proletariat is so emphatically the basis of the law that the judges, and especially the Justices of the Peace, who are bourgeois themselves, and with whom the proletariat comes most in contact, find this meaning in the laws without further consideration. If a rich man is brought up, or rather summoned, to appear before the court, the judge regrets that he is obliged to impose so much trouble, treats the matter as favourably as possible, and, if he is forced to condemn the accused, does so with extreme regret, etc., etc., and the end of it all is a miserable fine, which the bourgeois throws upon the table with contempt and then departs. But if a poor devil gets into such a position as involves appearing before the Justice of the Peace—he has almost always spent the night in the station-house with a crowd of his peers—he is regarded from the beginning as guilty; his defence is set aside with a contemptuous "Oh! we know the excuse", and a fine imposed which he cannot pay and must work out with several months on the treadmill. And if nothing can be proved against him, he is sent to the treadmill, none the less, "as a rogue and a vagabond". The partisanship of the Justices of the Peace, especially in the country, surpasses all description, and it is so much the order of the day that all cases which are not too utterly flagrant are quietly reported by the newspapers, without comment. Nor is anything else to be expected. For on the one hand, these Dogberries do merely construe the law according to the intent of the farmers, and, on the other, they are themselves bourgeois, who see the foundation of all true order in the interests of their class. And the conduct of the police corresponds to that of the Justices of the Peace. The bourgeois may do what he will and the police remain ever polite, adhering strictly to the law, but the proletarian is roughly, brutally treated; his poverty both casts the suspicion of every sort of crime upon him and cuts him off from legal redress against any caprice of the administrators of the law; for him, therefore, the protecting forms of the law do not exist, the police force their way into his house without further ceremony, arrest and abuse him; and only when a working-men's association, such as the miners, engages a Roberts, does it become evident how little the protective side of the law exists for the working-man, how frequently he has to bear all the burdens of the law without enjoying its benefits.

ENGELS, Postscript to "The Condition of the Working Class in England" *MECW* IV, 587–590.

Daniel Maude, Esq., is the "stipendiary magistrate" or paid Justice of the Peace in Manchester. The English magistrates are usually rich bourgeois or landowners, occasionally also clergymen, who are appointed by the Ministry. But since these Dogberries understand nothing about the law, they make the most flagrant blunders, bring the bourgeoisie into ridicule and do it harm, since, even when faced with a worker, they are frequently reduced to a state of confusion if he is defended by a skilful lawyer, and either neglect some legal form when sentencing him, which results in a successful appeal, or let themselves be misled into acquitting him. Besides, the rich manufacturers in the big towns and industrial areas have no time to spare for passing days of boredom in a court of law and prefer to instal a *remplaçant*. As a result in these towns, on the initiative of the towns themselves, paid magistrates are usually appointed, men versed in law, who are able to take advantage of all the twists and subtle distinctions of English law, and when necessary to supplement and improve it for the benefit of the bourgeoisie. Their efforts in this respect are illustrated by the following example.

Daniel Maude, Esq., is one of those liberal justices of the peace who were appointed in large numbers under the Whig Government. Among his heroic exploits, inside and outside the arena of the Manchester Borough Court, we will mention two. When in 1842 the manufacturers succeeded in forcing the workers of South Lancashire into an insurrection, which broke out in Stalybridge and Ashton at the beginning of August, some 10,000 workers, with *Richard Pilling*, the Chartist, at their head, marched on August 9 from there to Manchester

"to meet their masters on the Exchange and to see how the Manchester market was".

When they reached the outskirts of the town, they were met by Daniel Maude, Esq., with the whole estimable police force, a detachment of cavalry and a company of riflemen. But this was all only for the sake of appearances since it was in the interest of the manufacturers and liberals that the insurrection should spread and force the repeal of the Corn Laws. In this Daniel Maude, Esq., was in complete agreement with his worthy colleagues, and he began to come to terms with the workers and allowed them to enter the town on their promise to "keep the peace" and follow a prescribed route. He knew very well that the insurgents would not do this nor did he in the least wish them to—he could have nipped the whole contrived insurrection in the bud with a little energy but, had he done so, he would not have been acting in the interest of his Anti-Corn Law friends but in the interest of Sir Robert Peel. So he withdrew the soldiers and allowed the workers to enter the town, where they immediately brought all the factories to a standstill. But as soon as the insurrection proved to be definitely directed *against* the liberal bourgeoisie and completely ignored the "hellish Corn Laws", Daniel Maude, Esq., once more assumed his judicial office and had workers arrested by the dozen and marched off to prison without mercy for "breach of the peace"—so that he first caused the breaches and then punished them. Another characteristic feature in the career of this Manchester Solomon is revealed by the following. Since the Anti-Corn Law League was several times beaten up in public in Manchester, it holds private meetings, admission to which is by ticket only—but the decisions and petitions of which are presented to the public as those of public meetings, and as manifestations of Manchester "public opinion". In order to put a stop to this fraudulent boasting by the liberal manufacturers, three or four Chartists, among them my good friend *James Leach*, secured tickets for themselves and went to one of these meetings. When Mr. *Cobden* rose to speak, James Leach asked the Chairman whether this was a public meeting. Instead of answering, the Chairman called the police and had Leach arrested without more ado. A second Chartist asked the question again, then a third, and a fourth, all were set upon one after the other by the "bluebottles" (police) who stood massed at the door, and packed off to the Town Hall. They appeared the next morning before Daniel Maude, Esq., who was already fully informed about everything. They were charged with having caused a disturbance at a meeting, were hardly allowed to say a word, and then had to listen to a solemn speech by Daniel Maude, Esq., who told them that he knew them, that they were political vagabonds who did nothing but cause uproar at meetings and disturb decent, law-abiding *citizens* and a stop must be put to this kind of thing. Therefore—and Daniel Maude, Esq., knew very well that he could not impose any real punishment on them—therefore, he would sentence them to pay the costs this time.

It was before this same Daniel Maude, Esq., whose bourgeois virtues we have just described, that the recalcitrant workers from Pauling & Henfrey's were hauled. But they had brought a lawyer with them as a precaution. First to be heard was the worker newly arrived from Staffordshire who had refused to continue working at a place where others had stopped work in self-defence. Messrs. Pauling & Henfrey had a written contract signed by the workers from Staffordshire, and this was submitted to the magistrate*. The defending lawyer interjected that this agreement had been signed on a Sunday and was therefore invalid. With much dignity Daniel Maude, Esq., admitted that "business transactions" concluded on a Sunday were not valid, but said that he could not believe that Messrs. Pauling & Henfrey regarded this as a "business transaction"! So without spending very much time asking the worker whether he "regarded" the document as a "business transaction", he told the poor devil that he must either continue working or amuse himself on the treadmill for three months.—O'Solomon of Manchester!—After this case had been dealt with, Messrs. Pauling & Henfrey brought forward the second accused. His name was *Salmon*, and he was one of the firm's old workers who had stopped work. He was accused of having intimidated the new workers into taking part in the strike. The witness—one of these latter—stated that Salmon had taken him by the arm and spoken to him. Daniel Maude, Esq., asked whether the accused had perhaps used threats or beaten him?—No, said the witness. Daniel Maude, Esq., delighted at having found an opportunity to demonstrate his impartiality—after having just fulfilled his duty to the bourgeoisie—declared that there was nothing in the case incriminating the accused. He had every right to take a walk on the public highway and to talk to other people as

---

* This contract contained the following: the worker pledged himself to work for Pauling & Henfrey for *six months* and *to be satisfied with the wages which they would give him*; but Pauling & Henfrey were not bound to keep him for six months and could dismiss him *at any moment* with a week's notice, and although Pauling & Henfrey would pay his travelling expenses from Staffordshire to Manchester, they were to recover them by a weekly deduction of 2 shillings (20 silver groschen) from his wages. How do you like that really marvellous contract?—*Note by Engels.*

long as he did not indulge in intimidating words or actions—he was therefore acquitting him. But Messrs. Pauling & Henfrey had at least had the satisfaction, by paying the costs of the case, of having the said Salmon sent to the lock-up for a night—and that was something after all.

6   Law and Politics

Introduction

Marx and Engels were actively engaged in the political struggles of their time. But, although many of their writings involve acute political analyses, they did not elaborate fully a concept of political activity, nor of its place in the total social order. Marx developed a systematic concept only of what has come to be called the economic 'level' or 'instance'. None the less, he explicitly indicates, particularly in his letter to Bolte of 1871, the direction such an elaboration of the concept of the political might take. And just as in the case of ideology Marx and Engels made the major theoretical advance by first thinking the need for such a concept and then by formulating two possible ways of constituting and resolving the problem, so in the case of politics Marx and Engels exposed the need for and the possibility of a new way of thinking consistent with a materialist philosophy.

There is, however, a difference in the materials we have on politics from the materials available on ideology. While on the one hand the general statements about ideology can be characterized as insightful but pretheoretic speculation, and the few particular statements such as those about lawyers have been classified as 'ideology' by the present editors rather than by Marx, on the other hand the general statements about law and politics are relatively rare, while there are very many particular discussions which the authors themselves plainly regarded as treating politics. Most of the particular discussions of the later years are analyses of contemporary political situations, mainly in France and Germany. These were uncertain times of attempted revolutions and coups, and Marx and Engels interpreted their task as laying bare the social forces giving rise to these shifts at the level of the state, and accounting for the structures of the ensuing constitutions and for their successes and failures.

After the Marx family came to live in exile in Britain in 1849, both Engels and Marx prepared several detailed accounts of the struggles for the shorter working day which had been waged with increasing momentum throughout the nineteenth century, to the time of the production of *Capital* I. Indeed, Engels who was in England during 1843 and the latter part of 1842, had first shown an interest in this topic in 1843 when he attended a number of meetings in Manchester about the reduction of working hours and provision of education for factory children.[1] Altogether he produced some half dozen articles on the theme. His writings were political in that they were concerned with the details of the struggle. Marx' focus of concern in the culminating discussion of the issue in *Capital* I was the way in which the length of the working day affected the production of surplus value: his object of analysis was the economy, and not the political struggle as such. So despite the wealth of materials and the scope of his investigation, he here attempted to develop a concept of political activity even less than in the earlier discussions which took a particular political situation as their object.

In occasional writings—for example Marx in the letter to Bolte already cited, and Engels in a critique of Proudhon and the introduction to Marx' presentation of "The Class Struggles in France"—the authors almost fortuitously took the concept of political struggle as an object of their thought. Here, however, the concept is treated as if the elaborated theory was already well known. Between the two of them, it is safe to assume, the theory of politics was understood. For the rest of us it remains implicit, or even no more than a possibility to be extrapolated.

However, the primary argument for the importance of political struggle to Marx and Engels must be adduced from the way they led their lives. Political struggle takes as its object—that which is to be changed—not only social–economic relationships, but also ideological structures, the state itself, and the law. Such points are important to emphasize, for sophisticated arguments developed by Pashukanis are currently being debated.[2] By arguing that a given form of law is constitutive of the capitalist mode of production, and that mode only, and by restricting the theoretical category 'law' to this form, a limitation is placed on what could be achieved by taking law as an object of struggle. We argue that despite their subtlety these arguments render down to a strict economist position, claiming that the economy (albeit in the full Marxist sense of this term) gives rise to the shape and content of the rest of the social structure, rather than, as we would argue, setting limits to what is conceivable within the constitution of a particular mode. The corollaries of Pashukanis' and other economist theories are that 'real' or significant change can only start with an economic change, and that therefore political struggle is of value only if it goes on in the work place, or, more limited still, in places where surplus value is produced. Our contention is that this position is wrong. We aim here briefly to show that the Pashukanis' position is economist, and secondly to show that this economist position does not correspond with the positions of Marx and Engels.

Pashukanis states that law is a bourgeois phenomenon only, intrinsic and specific to the capitalist mode of production. It is a form which has no place among the mechanisms of social control in non-capitalist formations except as an indicator of a nascent capitalism, or a vestige of a declining capitalist mode. Exponents of this view would anticipate that the bourgeoisie would be able to use law to strengthen and consolidate their emerging economic power, as the section about the transition from feudalism in Chapter 2 has shown; they would conceive it as an essential characteristic of the bourgeoisie that it should so generate and use those forms which alone Pashukanis characterizes as law. This theory, however, has little explanatory value when the forms of compromise and accommodation arrived at between the bourgeoisie and the feudal aristocracy are considered. Are the constitutional forms instated or reinstated by an aristocracy or a would-be absolute monarch (as in Prussia) also emanations of an emergent capitalist society? These can only be explained by a much closer analysis of the particular class structures and class struggles. Today too one might argue that Japan is ideologically and legally distinct, yet undeniably capitalist.

Marx' and Engels' empirical works are exemplars for such analyses. They show especially that the class in ascendance in a general sense, as retrospectively identified, need not be the class which is successful in a struggle at any single time or place. They show that in the real world there are always a multiplicity of classes co-existing, corresponding to different modes of production which exist in ascendance or decline in any social formation. Marx by and large considers in his political analyses the ruling class in conflict with pre-existing ruling classes and/or with workers or, most often in the extracts we have selected, with the peasantry. In the increasingly elaborate discussions about the working day in which Engels and Marx engage, a picture emerges of periods of uneasy truce between the two classes dominant in England at that time, the manufacturers and the landowners. Something like a 'power bloc' is thus formed,[3] although the authors do not in this context discuss the fractions of capital itself, which in Poulantzas' conception, also generate a tendency for the power bloc to split.

In these more complex formulations politics are made to matter. The argument that law is by its nature bourgeois is politically a negative one. It leads to the position that any legally backed achievement of the working class is in fact no more than a consolidation of bourgeois ideology in a bourgeois form—the law. At root this argument is a subtle variant of simple economic determinism.

Not only is the world much more complex than the economist position would allow, but also changes in relations of re-production, changes in the institutionalized forms of ideology and of politics which serve to reproduce the relations of production, are as appropriate as objects of class struggle as the relations of production themselves. Because the structure of ideology is integral to and constitutive of a particular social formation in its productive and re-productive relations, considerable changes can result if ideology is taken as the object of a successful struggle. The re-productive relations at the economic level, in the circuits of the re-production of capital, may be affected, as well as relations of re-production at the political and ideological levels. Indirectly changes in the relations of production may therefore be brought about.

Struggles with primarily ideological targets or objects may affect the members of classes as well as the structures themselves. Struggles against racism and sexism are immediate examples. Such struggles have value in their own right because of their capacity for transforming the life space of those involved or on whose direct behalf they are waged. We are not arguing that these struggles are important only if they affect some other social collectivity such as the working class. But success in such struggles could unify and strengthen the working class, and so help create the conditions necessary for the transformation of the relations of production.

In a similar way, the primary effectivity of the state is to ensure the re-production of the capitalist structure—of capital itself and of capitalist social relations—on both the economic and the ideological levels. The extent to which states have had to intervene to effect this re-production has varied between these two spheres. But at all times because of this special effectivity in the re-production of the formation it has been important for the subordinate classes to struggle to democratize zones of state activity.

In this chapter, therefore, we have organized the extracts to show not just the political uses of law. Some of these, such as legitimation and the constitution of concepts appropriate to a particular mode of production, such as property or contract, have been discussed in the preceding two chapters. Here we are more concerned with the struggles to gain the benefits of legal backing. These are, of course, struggles for political power, the success of which will be expressed in a legal outcome. Sometimes generalized political power is the immediate objective of these struggles. At other times, and today often, it is one of the means used to achieve an independently existing objective, such as, say, a shorter working day.

Our first section deals with the struggles of the former kind, in which political power *per se* is the object of struggle. Here we present extracts showing the uses of law by both feudal and bourgeois classes as a continuation of the struggles in which they were locked during the transition to capitalism. Thus the theme first expressed by Marx in "The Bill Proposing the Abolition of Feudal Obligations" (pp. 81–84), the theme of the importance of law to the bourgeoisie as a means of restructuring society, is picked up again here. As before, the emphasis is on political struggle, the outcome of which is not inevitable. A second theme reintroduced is that of legitimation (see pp. 221–225). The importance of securing a position of dominance constitutionally, i.e. by law, is the focus of these discussions. Class divisions and alliances, tactics and strategies, are also dealt with as Marx and Engels demonstrate empirically the ways in which legally backed gains may be achieved, and how they may on occasion be rendered ineffective.

Finally, discussions of working class struggles and working class successes are included. In these cases the object of struggle is less often political power. Rather the attempt described is to constrain the use of political power by others so as to secure an intermediate or more restricted objective. In this section are also included Marx' and Engels' rare theoretical statements about the effectiveness in improving the position of the working class in struggles to gain legal changes. Discussions about political strategies as such, the arguments, for example, in the meetings of the First International, have been excluded from this discussion by our rule to include only extracts which relate specifically to law.

The chapter concludes with a further eulogistic comment on the legal forms developed by the working class itself when it briefly held political power under the Paris Commune.

The Struggle for the Constitution

Perhaps the clearest exposition of the economy of constitutional rule, as opposed to any combination of economic power and force, is to be found in the discussions of the bourgeoisie in Prussia. In the first sentences of the opening extract, Marx indicates the need for "comfortable" and "low cost" rule, as well as victory. In the interests of achieving this objective, the Prussian bourgeoisie disowned its erstwhile allies, the people,[4] and forged an alliance with the Crown as representative of a feudal rump; subsequently, this rump of the medieval Estates, with the Crown as its figurehead, itself sought an alliance with the people, and though it achieved no more than their indifference, was none the less successful in ousting for a time the bourgeoisie from power. In all these manoeuvres, the claim to be the legally constituted authority was crucial. The people were at a disadvantage in establishing such a claim since there were no appropriate pre-existing forms of legality to which they could appeal. The basis of their too limited power and of their claim to legality was the revolution itself.

A most unsubtle but effective gerrymander is described in the piece from "The Eighteenth Brumaire". This again demonstrates the importance, at least to the participants, of substantiating a *legal* position. Considerable efforts were expended in achieving this. Part of the reason why legality was necessary is made clear in the following extract from "The Class Struggles in France". This presents a confusing picture of the bourgeoisie, itself divided into factions (not fractions in this case), each laying claim to legitimacy, and each prepared to use the subordinated classes, in particular the peasantry, as the exigencies of their internecine struggle required. The audience for legitimacy is other factions, as well as other classes. Law may be necessary simply because there is never a simple two-class situation in which one class controls the means of life and the other does not. In such a situation coercion would be so simple as to render politics and law unnecessary. But the world has never been like that. The struggle for legal backing must therefore be waged against other potentially dominant classes, and as part of the process whereby alliances with the subordinated classes are forged. This gives legalism an important ideological status, coupled with its status as a promise of political backing. Thus the subordinated classes can extrapolate it from the situations which gave birth and nourishment to it, and turn it to their own purposes. The use of law in this way by the working class and other subordinated classes is dealt with in the final section. Here what is shown is that constitutional law is additionally important for the ideological domination which it makes possible.[5]

In Switzerland too at this time the bourgeoisie was consolidating its position. Once more the necessary alliance of the bourgeoisie with one of the subordinated classes, here again the peasantry, is noted; more particularly in this extract the need of the bourgeoisie for centralization to achieve comparability of productive and marketing conditions is emphasized. The point is reiterated by Engels in relation to the German bourgeoisie. Control over the state here quite clearly means not only constitutional legitimation and legislative control, but also control over the state apparatuses, including, significantly, the judicial apparatuses. For Engels, control over judicial procedures necessitated *supplying the personnel* of justice: judges and jurors. This position, developed to the full in relation to other state apparatuses in the work of Miliband[6] stems directly from Engels' more humanist, thinker-based, conception of ideology. From such a position it becomes difficult to make sense of the fact that capitalist society may be strengthened by a broadening of the bases of recruitment to such positions, in fulfilment of its own ideology of equality. Marx' alternative position would allow the possibility of non-bourgeois personnel, but would find it difficult in terms of necessary transformation and strict reflexivity to account for the specific content of ideology at this level.

Above all, this section has demonstrated that empirically class struggles never take the form of simple diadic opposition. By its nature, because of the differing forms taken by capital in its circuits of expanded re-production, the bourgeoisie is divided into fractions. Marx himself in "The Class Struggles in France" engaged briefly in the contemporary ideological warfare against finance capital, the bearers of which were considered to be morally inferior to other capitalists (pp. 232–233). Furthermore, there are emergent or declining classes in any society, maybe in the process of transformation to capitalist forms, but still deriving from another mode of production. Their interests and affiliations are crucial in any real-life politics. Some of these, coexisting in contradiction, may be conceived as constituting a power bloc: that is how they appear from the standpoint of the subordinated classes. But the latter, to be effective, must also exploit their rivalries, just as the ruling classes themselves seek to turn peasants against workers, or to construct or eliminate ideological distinctions within a single class.

History proved wrong Engels' prediction as to the fate of the English constitution should the Corn Laws be repealed. But the argument by which he arrived at it remains important, if only because of the number of protagonists—three classes, one of them divided into two fractions—which it introduces. These are manufacturers, workers (also called the people), landowners and tenant farmers. Implicit here is the statement that having achieved constitutional legitimacy, necessarily in terms of the constitutive element of its ideology, individuated subject man, the bourgeoisie is then hoist with its own petard. The constitution defined for it the place and forms of political struggle with the outcomes of which it had to abide. This is not to argue that class struggle cannot perhaps even more importantly go on elsewhere: it is to argue that to deny defeat in its own arena would require the bourgeoisie to restructure its ideology, and that, given the constitutive and primary status of the component 'individual-man-as-subject' within bourgeois ideology, the resulting incongruence would have important repercussions on the economic level too—or could do, provided that the proletariat were prepared to seize its chance, and exploit such an ideological and political contradiction.

The Uses of Law

Both Marx' brief statement from "The Poverty of Philosophy" and Engels' much longer dialogue with Proudhon and his followers in "The Housing Question" indicate the dangers of treating law as autonomous, as by itself either a starting point or an end point of social change. The first piece makes the case that economic change may necessitate legal change: that economic socialization of labour is antecedent to and creates formally organized combinations, and the pressure for the legalization of such combinations. What Engels objects to are firstly, the reification of things which are non-material and legally constituted; and secondly and consequently, he objects to theorizing and to policy-making on the basis of a naïve and inadequate class analysis.[7]

As has been suggested, the way to proceed is to take as an object of struggle the desired change in condition. Legal changes are among many possible means which may be used separately, or more probably in combination in the achieving of that objective. If a legal fetish such as a title to real estate is taken as *in itself* a sufficient object of struggle, nothing materially will be gained by success. The workers could end up as so many weakling princes, with the ruling class as regent. Nationalization within the framework of capitalism may yield this result, if economic and political structures of relationships are not appropriately modified as well. If control over the material objects and perhaps contingent social relationships is taken as the object of struggle and the struggle is successful, this situation of nominal power and material impotence can not arise. But a legal change will be necessary for a successful outcome. In this example legal change is not appropriate as a final object of struggle, but as a means of attaining a material objective. As an intermediate object of a struggle, the true purpose of which is always kept in mind, the law is a correct target for the political action of the subordinated classes.

In another situation the permissible limits on a contract of employment might be appropriate intermediate objects of struggle. But nothing is achieved by a merely legal change: it is the use which is made of this in relation to the required change in conditions which matters. In this case if the legal change were treated as the final object of struggle the law would become an empty formula, a useless placebo.

It is not just legally constituted objects which may be fetishized. Indeed, Marx developed the concept in relation to an economically constituted object, the commodity, although it applies equally to interest, profit, wages and rent. Thus Engels argues that a correct analysis of the nature of rent is a prerequisite for adequate political struggle in this area.

But the appropriateness of an object of struggle, be it legal or economic, is not intrinsic to the object itself; it is given always by the material change required. Politics in the real world is time and project specific: its objects, both final and intermediate, must change with the structure and categories of the material world. Materialism must eschew as idealist any suggestion that there exists—in the realm of thought, since it has no other being—a universal political solution, a formula outside time because it is and has been permanent ideal truth. Such formulae, as Gramsci has cogently and caustically argued, can offer no practical guidance to real social classes engaged in material struggle.[8]

This analysis has extended beyond the extracts from Engels which we have presented. These texts, however, yield most of the little guidance we have in Marx' and Engels' works for a theorized distinction between reformist and other non-revolutionary political practice.

When he wrote "The Housing Question", Engels would presumably not have known the contents of Marx' letter to Bolte of just over a year earlier. In this Marx argues that economic efforts with the object of an eight-hour day backed by law constitute in their totality not an economic but a *political* struggle. His standpoint here is different from that from which he analyses in *Capital* the very same struggles for a shorter working day. There capital itself provides the standpoint: here the standpoint of the working class is adopted. In constructing his argument Marx defines political struggles and the political level of analysis. None the less he does not adequately develop the distinction between the economic and the political. In fact, he does little more than toss off some hints to one of his students as to how a theory of the political might be developed. The hints, however, are as yet unsurpassed for insight.

In the first of the three paragraphs cited, Marx states that the ultimate aim of working class struggles must be the conquest of political power in general. Next, however, he modifies this, arguing that a movement (a struggle) should be conceived as political if the working class is operating *as a class*, and the object of its struggle is its generalized interest. The two central sentences are reproduced again here, for they are crucial to an understanding of how Marx constituted the concept of class in articulation with both economic and political instances.

> . . . the attempt in a particular factory or even in a particular trade to force a shorter working day out of individual capitalists by strikes etc., is a purely economic movement. On the other hand the attempt to force through an eight hour etc. law is a *political* movement . . . that is to say, a movement of the *class* with the object of forcing its interests in a general form . . .

In this letter two criteria for *political* action are suggested. One is the generality of the object of struggle, in class terms; the second is the degree of organization of the class.

Particular and local struggles directed to economic or other objects are neither political nor class struggles as Marx here uses these terms. Recent contributors to a theory of politics would agree that such struggles are not class struggles. Both Hirst and Laclau, despite other differences in their positions, have pointed out that classes rarely if ever manifest themselves as such and that class members are rarely conscious of themselves as such.[9] But this may be to say no more than that the concept of class operates at a level of abstraction which cannot immediately be applied to the concrete. In addition, their lesson is that the intervention of the ideological at the moment of class action cannot be ignored for it is most often in the guise of the clash of ideologically constituted groupings that the contradictions of a social formation are fought out. To identify classes in a generalized sense requires a conceptual effort: it is possible to do this in theory regardless of the forms of organization in which such classes may appear. Nor is this to adopt an idealist position that a class existing in knowledge (theory) can bring about social change; changes can be known in class terms, but the subjects of change may indeed be ideologically constituted 'interest' groups or social and 'popular democratic' forces. The process involved is analogous to what Rancière[10] has described as the subjectivization of things: the process whereby in capitalist social formations, money lent really does yield interest. In some sense, money really is the subject of its own expansion; this process is the inverse and necessary corollary of the normal process of fetishism, whereby social relationships become objects or things. Interest groups are real in the sense that profit is real, and subjects at least in the sense that money is a subject. Thus it is possible, and indeed useful, to accept that isolated and particular struggles are not class struggles, at least in the immediate form of their appearance.

There is greater difficulty in accepting Marx' position that isolated struggles are not *political*. His position is internally consistent, for he constitutes the concept of the political at the level of generalized class action. But this would demote, say, the struggle of the residents of an area to achieve access to the London squares to a non-political activity. A struggle for a pay rise in one factory would likewise, from this standpoint, be deemed non-political.

The problem arises once again from the eliding of the immediately concrete and a more abstract level of analysis. If only those struggles are political which at a *concrete level* have a generalized object, such as a law reform, then plainly the struggles identified in the previous paragraph do not qualify. But if at a more abstract level, the isolated struggles can be identified as having a general class objective, they could none the less properly be conceived as political, in the same way as 'interest groups' might, at a higher level of abstraction, be capable of being conceived in class terms. For example, isolated incidents of arson occurred in the eighteenth century: perpetrators usually had no contact with each other. Certainly there was no class action towards a generalized objective. Yet these incidents are capable of being set together theoretically as a class protest and a political protest, at a level of abstraction above the immediate and concrete. It is the theorists' job correctly to identify both classes and political actions.[11] There is no way of distinguishing between class and other, political and other, struggles or movements so long as the distinction is forced at the particular level of analysis. When it is seen precisely as a distinction *between levels*, as Marx identifies it, then it becomes conceptually possible and useful.

Neither the concept of class nor the concept of politics suggested in this letter is static; nor should the lower level concept required to locate the forms in which struggle is concretely engaged be static. Classes and politics are conceived in dynamic terms, and their conception is necessary because of the concrete reality of struggle. The missing concept of the forms of struggle must also be dynamic, that is, must characterize the forms of organization by theorizing their activities and by the theorized objects of these activities. So a concrete theory of the relationship between politics and law, class action and legal change, can be developed.

Of the problems which remain for a further elaboration of the insights expressed in the 1871 letter to Bolte, one demands attention in this context. A practical problem of analysis for class members is how to identify among proposed legal changes those which represent the general class interest. But only political action can yield political solutions, and only a theorist integrally and actively related to a class and identifying 'interest' from this perspective could proffer a solution. This must be the domain of political debate; again we are reminded of the irrelevance of the timeless solutions of abstract science.[12]

How then does all this square with the discussion based on "The Housing Question"? There is no difficulty in rendering the positions consistent, for Marx' theoretical definition simply narrows the formulation that law is appropriate as an object of struggle provided that the real material object to be achieved is not lost sight of, that the legal formulae are not fetishized. Marx in fact both restricts and explains this formulation, by adding to it the requirement that the law taken as the object of struggle must be one which expresses the general class interest. The possibility of sectional laws is not totally excluded, but their mode of theorization remains arcane.

The exciting issues which this letter exposes must not be allowed to obscure its major import. While talking of the need for workers to organize as a class—to bring the concrete into line with the theoretical position, as one might say—he is also explicitly recommending organized action to push through single changes backed by law. So far is Marx from lambasting what has come to be known as reformism that here we find him most firmly advocating it!

Engels' early discussion of the use by the working class of the law and of the machinery of bourgeois democracy is placed to follow this letter because it is a straightforwardly empirical statement of the theoretical position we have just outlined. It would be false to attribute to the early Engels precognition of the elaborated theory of the letter to Bolte. But similarly it would be foolish to pretend that we can now absolve this theory from our minds when reading Engels' remarks. The later interpretation adds a richness to the earlier work which is only implicit in it. And since our primary purpose is to find lessons for now in the works of Marx and Engels, such a retrospective reading is not simply legitimate but also of greater value, for Engels' discussion of the Chartist successes yields just such contemporary lessons.

Twenty years on from "The Housing Question", Engels is found arguing euphorically for the inevitability of working class success. What pleases him, in this letter to Marx' son-in-law (pp. 241–242), is that the incipient political organization of the working class, as evidenced by the formation of the Independent Labour Party, is effectively forcing the Liberal Government to make concessions to the workers. Engels sees this as an attempt at trouble-shooting on the part of the government which is doomed to fail, since it involves increasing further still the political power of the working classes which will "naturally kick them out afterwards". Engels' ebullient good humour was unjustified, however. For, as a close reading of Marx' previous analysis might have warned, giving power to the workers was not the same as giving power to the working *class*. Engels' optimistic analysis falls into the classic humanist error of reducing the complex and abstract-material concept of class to a simple and crucially static aggregation of class 'members'. Power in the form of improved enfranchisement was ceded to working people, that is, to isolated individuals, whose 'political' power was thus as much potentially atomized as it was potentially generalized. Political power as conceived in the bourgeois concepts of man and politics was ceded to a wider range of people in improved electoral circumstances. But in practice, this frequently inhibited the manifestation of class power. Class objectives were often reduced to the separated objectives of securing the elections of particular candidates; meanwhile the material object of generalized class interests was liable to be lost sight of if formulated at all. Thus, there was created metonymic democracy, in which the processes of voting were seen as the totality.[13] This is not a statement against universal suffrage! It is a statement that universal suffrage under capitalism is not the same as working class political power. Engels, both here and elsewhere, comes dangerously close to operating *within* the conceptions of humanist, bourgeois–democratic ideology.

Our next selections present first Engels' and then Marx' discussions and descriptions of the struggles for the shorter working day and for guaranteed working conditions. Extracts from four texts are

included, while extracts from six others—the earlier writings of
Marx on the questions—are left out. The arguments are straightforward, requiring little exegesis. Points to note from Engels' two
longer discussions are as follows: first, the importance of the division
between landowning and manufacturing interests; second, the non-
isomorphic representation of this division in the two main parliamentary parties, especially in 1847; third, the importance of the
'image' of the manufacturers; fourth, the manifestation of the
political class struggles as a series of local struggles and deals at the
point of enforcement;[14] fifth, the workers' own shifting alliances
while remaining steadfast to their objective; sixth, the importance of
specific sets of circumstances or conjunctures such as temporary
fluctuations in market conditions—opportunism is avoided in
exploiting these by retaining fixity of purpose; and finally, Engels
notes that presenting issues, such as hours of work, remain under
capitalism as running sores. Conditions can be improved permanently or temporarily assuaged, but the problem of the working day
continues to exist. Only the revolution can dispel it. There is more
than a breath of Utopianism in Engels' remark (p. 249) that after the
proletarian revolution and the centralization of industry in the hands
of the state "those rivalries which today lie at the root of the
contradiction between regulation of working hours and industrial
progress will vanish . . .". In his last writing on the subject—indeed,
in the last comment upon the topic that either Marx or he produced—Engels notes not just the universality of the issue within
capitalism, but also the impact of universal suffrage on the course and
outcomes of the struggles. But in this case his characterization of the
power which the suffrage gives is consistent with his and Marx'
earlier theorization of the issue—the power exists in a relevant way
only if the representatives of the working class first, cooperate, and
second, identify correctly the class object of struggle, the generalized
class interest, although Engels calls it knowing "what is at issue".
Engels considered that a prolonged and painful struggle similar to
that of the English working class would not be necessary in order to
achieve a shortened working day in Germany or any country with
universal suffrage. And he was right.

The same set of points must be noted in Marx' analysis as were
listed above for Engels' longer contributions. The analysis in *Capital* I
differs markedly in style however, both from Marx' earlier writings

on the subject and from Engels' works. Politicians figure less frequently than classes and parties. He also shows the historic origins of the struggle, and locates the issue not just in the immediate economic context of the extraction of maximum surplus value, but also in the need to create, regulate and control a labour force—in the reproductive cycle of capital as well as in the productive moment. His sources are varied; his style polemical, ironic, clear, analytic, sophisticated and tough.

One new feature of this deceptively descriptive and in fact profound contribution is the analysis of the contribution of the professionals. The lawyers and factory inspectors, both for occupational reasons committed to the legislation, join forces against the manufacturers. But as the latter then controlled the magistracy in the relevant areas, the former achieved nothing (pp. 256–258). Surely this account of the inspectorate, coupled with a reading of their own accounts of their work, constitutes the starting point for the theorization of state agents in the class structure and struggle, a much neglected area of concern.

Readers interested in the development of Marx' thinking should follow up the cited extracts which we had no room to include; in these they will find a continuing and increasingly refined emphasis on the importance of class struggle, culminating in that presented here. Isolated and local occasions of struggle are political, and in this case *class* struggle, because they are particular manifestations of contest about an issue which has already been generalized. This is different from the situation in which an issue first emerges at a local level, antecedent to a generalization which may or may not take place in practice, and which may or may not be appropriate in theory.

"The irony of world history turns everything upside down", exclaims Engels in his introduction to "The Class Struggles in France". As has been noted twice before (pp. 112 and 208), Marx argued that the bourgeoisie, having established and fixed a political arena, is constrained by its own rules of legality, its own ideology. Although this constraint is not absolute, but is itself a function of political pressure, it means that there are moments when the workers achieve more by using the law than is possible even for the dominant classes. Means, like law, are created in order to be exploited, used, in political action. The working classes too can play this game, but neither side, least of all the working class whose conceptions and purposes are not embedded in the law, can afford to mistake the means for its real concrete objective.

We end with two extracts from "The Civil War in France" and Marx' first draft of it. They emphasize, as the extracts presented in Chapter 3 have already in part emphasized, the changed meaning and form of law in a workers' state. They offer, then, a glimpse of a condition, of an alternative conception of order, which could become part of the object of politics for the working classes.

Notes

1. Engels, F. Letters from London, I, *MECW* III, 381.
2. Pashukanis, E. B. (1951) General Theory of Law and Marxism, in *Soviet Legal Philosophy* (H. Babb and J. Hazard, eds.), pp. 111–225, Harvard University Press, Cambridge, Mass. *See also* Arthur, C. J. (1976) Towards a Materialist Theory of Law, *Critique*, 31–46; Kamenka, E. and Tay, A. (1970) The Life and Afterlife of a Bolshevik Jurist, *Problems of Communism* **29,** 72–79; Kamenka, E. and Tay, A. (1971) Beyond the French Revolution: Communist Socialism and the Concept of Law, *University of Toronto Law Journal* **21,** No. 2, 109–140,
3. Poulantzas, N. (1973) *Political Power and Social Classes*, New Left Books, London.
4. See Hill, C. (1975) *The World Turned Upside Down*, Penguin, Harmondsworth, for a discussion of a similar defection by the English bourgeoisie after the Civil War.
5. See also the discussion of legitimacy, Chapter 4, p. 111.
6. Miliband, R. (1973) *The State in Capitalist Society*, Quartet Books, London.
7. Cain has previously characterized this work as a diatribe against reformism, thus importing a concept which neither Marx nor Engels used. Both authors now regard this position as incorrect. Cain, M. (1974) The Main Themes of Marx' and Engels' Sociology of Law, *British Journal of Law and Society* **1,** No. 2, 136–148.
8. Gramsci, A. (1971) *Selections from the Prison Notebooks*, Lawrence and Wishart, London (for example, pp. 333–335, 434–436, 455 and 467).
9. Hirst, P. Q. (1977) Economic Classes and Politics, in *Class and Class Structure* (A. Hunt, ed.), Lawrence and Wishart, London; Laclau, E. (1977) *Politics and Ideology in Marxist Theory*, New Left Books, London (especially pp. 57–79).
10. Rancière, J. (1977) The Concept of Critique and the Critique of Political Economy, *Economy and Society* **5,** No. 3, 352–376
11. Although none of the researches is primarily concerned with such

incidents, evidence for this statement can be derived from Thompson, E. (1975) *Whigs and Hunters*, Allen Lane, London; Hay, D. (1975) Poaching and the Game Laws on Cannock Chase, and Thompson, E. (1975) The Crime of Anonymity, both in *Albion's Fatal Tree* (D. Hay *et al.*, eds.), pp. 189–253 and 255–308, Allen Lane, London.

12. These remarks lean heavily on Gramscian epistemology and Gramscian theory as to the place of the 'organic intellectual'. A complete discussion can be found in *Selections from the Prison Notebooks*, Lawrence and Wishart, London. Gramsci's epistemology is considered in Cain, M. (1977) Optimism, Law, and the State: A Plea for the Possibility of Politics, *European Yearbook of Law and Sociology*, Martinus Nijhoff, Amsterdam.

13. Marcuse, H. (1964) *One Dimensional Man*, Routledge and Kegan Paul, London (especially pp. 113–116). This gives the best analysis of the place of this myth in contemporary political science.

14. Collison has recently extended this discussion in relation to the enforcement of the Riot Acts. Collison, M. (1977) The State, the Law, and the Control of Labour in the Eighteenth Century. Mimeographed paper, BSA Annual Conference.

Extracts

The Struggle for the Constitution

MARX, The Bourgeoisie and the Counter-revolution, *Articles from NRZ*, 187.

Clearly the Prussian bourgeoisie now had only one duty—to settle itself comfortably in power, get rid of the troublesome anarchists, restore "law and order" and retrieve the profit lost during the storms of March. It was now merely a question of reducing to a minimum the *costs* of its rule and of the March revolution which had brought it about. The weapons which, in its struggle against the feudal society and the Crown, the Prussian bourgeoisie had been compelled to demand in the name of the people, such as the right of association and freedom of the press, were they not bound to be broken in the hands of a deluded people who no longer needed to use them to fight *for* the bourgeoisie and who revealed an alarming inclination to use them *against* the bourgeoisie?

The bourgeoisie was convinced that evidently only one obstacle stood in the way of its *agreement* with the Crown, in the way of a deal which the old state, which was resigned to its fate, and that obstacle was the people—*puer robustus sed malitiosus*, as Hobbes says. The *people* and the *revolution*!

The *revolution* was the *legal title of the people*; the vehement claims of the people were based on the revolution. The revolution was the bill drawn by the people on the bourgeoisie. The bourgeoisie came to power through the revolution. The day it came to power was also the day this bill became due. The bourgeoisie had to *protest* the bill.

Revolution in the mouth of the people meant: you, the bourgeois, are the *Comité du salut public,* the Committee of Public Safety, to whom we have entrusted the government in order that you should defend our interests, the interests of the people, *in face of* the Crown, but not in order that you should *come to an agreement with* the Crown regarding your own interests.

Revolution was the people's protest against an arrangement between the bourgeoisie and the Crown. The bourgeoisie that was making arrangements with the Crown *had therefore to protest* against the *revolution*.

MARX, *ibid.*, 182–183.

The *March revolution in Prussia* should not be confused either with the *English* revolution of 1648 or with the *French* one of 1789.

In 1648 the bourgeoisie was allied with the modern aristocracy against the monarchy, the feudal aristocracy and the established church.

In 1789 the bourgeoisie was allied with the people against the monarchy, the aristocracy and the established church.

The model for the revolution of 1789 (at least in Europe) was only the revolution of 1648; that for the revolution of 1648 only the revolt of the Netherlands against Spain. Both revolutions were a century ahead of their model not only in time but also in substance.

In both revolutions the bourgeoisie was the class that *really* headed the movement. The *proletariat* and the *non-bourgeois strata of the middle class* had either not yet evolved interests which were different from those of the bourgeoisie or they did not yet constitute independent classes or class divisions. Therefore, where they opposed the bourgeoisie, as they did in France in 1793 and 1794, they fought only for the attainment of the aims of the bourgeoisie, albeit in a non-bourgeois *manner*. The *entire French terrorism* was just a *plebian way* of dealing with the *enemies of the bourgeoisie*, absolutism, feudalism and philistinism.

The revolutions of 1648 and 1789 were not *English* and *French* revolutions, they were revolutions in the *European* fashion. They did not represent the victory of a *particular* social class over the *old political system*; they *proclaimed the political system of the new European society*. The bourgeoisie was victorious in these revolutions, but the *victory of the bourgeoisie* was at that time the *victory of a new social order*, the victory of bourgeois ownership over feudal ownership, of nationality over provincialism, of competition over the guild, of partitioning [of the land] over primogeniture, of the rule of the landowner over the domination of the owner by the land, of enlightenment over superstition, of the family over the family name, of industry over heroic idleness, of bourgeois law over medieval privileges. The revolution of 1648 was the victory of the seventeenth century over the sixteenth century; the revolution of 1789 was the victory of the eighteenth century over the seventeenth. These revolutions reflected the needs of the world at that time rather than the needs of those parts of the world where they occurred, that is, England and France.

MARX, *ibid.*, 188–189.

The Assembly sought to undo what had been done. It vociferously declared to the Prussian people that the people did not come to an agreement with the bourgeoisie in order to make a revolution against the Crown, but that the purpose of the revolution was to achieve an agreement between the Crown and the bourgeoisie against the people! Thus was the *legal title* of the revolutionary people annulled and a *legal basis* secured for the conservative bourgeoisie.

The legal basis!

Brüggemann, and through him the *Kölnische Zeitung*, have prated, fabled and moaned so much about the "legal basis", have so often lost and recovered, punctured and mended that "legal basis", tossed it from Berlin to Frankfurt and from Frankfurt to Berlin, narrowed and widened it, turned the simple basis into an inlaid floor and the inlaid floor into a false bottom (which, as we know, is the principal device of performing conjurors), and the false bottom into a bottomless trapdoor, so that in the end the legal basis has turned for our readers into the basis of the *Kölnische Zeitung*; thus, they could confuse the shibboleth of the Prussian bourgeoisie with the private shibboleth of Herr Joseph Dumont, a necessary invention of the *Prussian* world history with the arbitrary hobby-horse of the *Kölnische Zeitung*, and regard the legal basis simply as the basis on which the *Kölnische Zeitung* arises.

The *legal basis*, namely, the *Prussian legal basis*!

The *legal basis* on which Camphausen, the knight of the great debate, the resurrected phantom of the United Provincial Diet and the Assembly of conciliators, moved *after* the March revolution—is it the constitutional law of 1815 or the law of 1820 regarding the Provincial Diet, or the edict of 1847, or the electoral and agreement law of April 8, 1848?

It is none of these.

"Legal basis" simply meant that the revolution failed to gain firm ground and the old society did not lose its ground; that the March revolution was an "occurrence" that acted merely as a "stimulus" towards an "agreement" between the throne and the bourgeoisie, preparations for which had long been made within the old Prussian state, and the need for which the Crown itself had expressed in its royal decrees but had not, prior to March, considered as "*urgent*". In short, the "legal basis" meant that *after* the March revolution the bourgeoisie wanted to negotiate with the Crown on the same footing as *before* the March events, as though no revolution had taken place and the United Provincial Diet had achieved its goal without a revolution. The "legal basis" meant that the *revolution*, the legal title of the people, was to be ignored in the *contrat social* between the government and the bourgeoisie. *The bourgeoisie deduced its claims from the old Prussian legislation, in order that the people should not deduce any claims from the new Prussian revolution.*

Naturally, the *ideological cretins* of the bourgeoisie, its journalists, and such like, had to pass off this palliative of the bourgeois interests as the real interests of the bourgeoisie, and persuade themselves and others to believe this. The phrase about the legal basis acquired real substance in the mind of a *Brüggemann*.

See also **MARX**, *ibid.*, 197–199.

MARX, *ibid.*, 201–202.

Under the Brandenburg cabinet the Assembly of conciliators was ignominiously dispersed, fooled, derided, humiliated and hunted, and the *people*, at the decisive moment, remained *indifferent*. The *defeat* of the Assembly was the *defeat of the Prussian bourgeoisie*, of the *constitutionalists*, hence a *victory for the democratic party*, however dear it had to pay for that victory.

And the *imposed* constitution?

It had once been said that never would a "piece of paper" be allowed to come between the King and *his* people. Now it is said, there shall *only* be *a piece of paper* between the King and *his* people. The *real* constitution of Prussia is the *state of siege*. The imposed French constitution had only one article—the 14th, which invalidated it. Every article of the imposed Prussian constitution is an article 14.

By means of this constitution the Crown imposes new privileges—that is, upon *itself*.

It permits itself to dissolve the Chambers indefinitely. It permits ministers in the interim to issue any desired law (even those affecting property and so forth). It permits deputies to impeach ministers for such actions, but at the risk, under martial law, of being classed as "internal enemies". Finally, it permits itself, should the stock of the counter-revolution go up in the spring, to replace this nebulous "piece of paper" by a Christian-Germanic Magna Charta *organically* growing out of the distinctions of the medieval estates, or to drop the constitutional game altogether. Even in this case the conservative bourgeois would fold their hands and pray:

"*The Lord gave, and the Lord hath taken away; blessed be the name of the Lord!*"

The history of the Prussian middle class, and that of the German middle class in general between March and December shows that a purely *middle-class revolution* and the establishment of *bourgeois rule* in the form of a *constitutional monarchy* is impossible in Germany, and that the only alternatives are either a feudal absolutist counter-revolution or a *social republican revolution*.

MARX, The Eighteenth Brumaire of Louis Bonaparte, *MESW(3)* I, 438 and 440.

The parliamentary majority understood the weakness of its antagonists. Its seventeen burgraves—for Bonaparte had left to it the direction of and responsibility for the attack—drew up a new electoral law, the introduction of which was entrusted to M. Faucher, who solicited this honour for himself. On May 8 he introduced the law by which universal suffrage was to be abolished, a residence of three years in the locality of the election to be imposed as a condition on the electors and, finally, the proof of this residence made dependent in the case of workers on a certificate from their employers.

. . . .

The law of May 31, 1850, was the *coup d'état* of the bourgeoisie. All its conquests over the revolution hitherto had only a provisional character. They were endangered as soon as the existing National Assembly retired from the stage. They depended on the hazards of a new general election, and the history of elections since 1848 irrefutably proved that the bourgeoisie's moral sway over the mass of the people was lost in the same measure as its actual domination developed. On March 10, universal suffrage declared itself directly against the domination of the bourgeoisie; the bourgeoisie answered by outlawing universal suffrage. The law of May 31 was, therefore, one of the necessities of the class struggle. On the other hand, the Constitution required a minimum of two million votes to make an election of the President of the republic valid. If none of the candidates for the presidency received this minimum, the National Assembly was to choose the President from among the three candidates to whom the largest number of votes would fall. At the time when the Constituent Assembly made this law, ten million electors were registered on the rolls of voters. In its view, therefore, a fifth of the people entitled to vote was sufficient to make the presidential election valid. The law of May 31 struck at least three million votes off the electoral rolls, reduced the number of people entitled to vote to seven million and, nevertheless, retained the legal minimum of two million for the presidential election. It therefore raised the legal minimum from a fifth to nearly a third of the effective votes, that is, it did everything to smuggle the election of the President out of the hands of the people and into the hands of the National Assembly. Thus through the electoral law of May 31 the party of Order seemed to have made its rule doubly secure, by surrendering the election of the National Assembly and that of the President of the republic to the stationary section of society.

See also, MARX, *ibid*., 290–293.

MARX, The Class Struggles in France, *MESW(3)* I, 278–279.

The Hautpoul circular, by which the gendarme was appointed inquisitor of the prefect, of the sub-prefect and, above all, of the mayor, and by which espionage was organised even in the hidden corners of the remotest village community; the *law against the schoolteachers*, by which they, the men of talent, the spokesmen, the educators and interpreters of the peasant class, were subjected to the arbitrary power of the prefect, they, the proletarians of the learned class, were chased like hunted beasts from one community to another; the *bill against the mayors*, by which the Damocles sword of dismissal was hung over their heads, and they, the presidents of the peasant communities, were every moment set in opposition to the President of the Republic and the party of Order; the *ordinance* which transformed the seventeen military districts of France into four pashalics and forced the barracks and the bivouac on the French as their national *salon*; the *education law*, by which the party of Order proclaimed the unconsciousness and the forcible stupefaction of France as the condition of its life under the regime of universal suffrage—what were all these laws and measures? Desperate attempts to reconquer the departments and the peasants of the departments for the party of Order.

Regarded as *repression*, they were wretched methods that wrung the neck of their own purpose. The big measures, like the retention of the wine tax, of the 45 centimes tax, the scornful rejection of the peasant petitions for the repayment of the milliard, etc., all these legislative thunderbolts struck the peasant class only once, wholesale, from the centre; the laws and measures instanced made attack and the resistance *general*, the topic of the day in every hut; they inoculated every village with revolution; they *localised and peasantised the revolution*.

On the other hand, do not these proposals of Bonaparte and their acceptance by the National Assembly prove the unity of the two powers of the constitutional republic, so far as it is a question of repression of anarchy, that is, of all the classes that rise against the bourgeois dictatorship? Had not *Soulouque*, directly after his brusque message, assured the Legislative Assembly of his *dévouement* to order, through the immediately following message of *Carlier*, that dirty, mean caricature of Fouché, as Louis Bonaparte himself was the shallow caricature of Napoleon?

The *education law* shows us the alliance of the young Catholics with the old Voltairians. Could the rule of the united bourgeois be anything else but the coalesced despotism of the pro-Jesuit Restoration and the make-believe free-thinking July monarchy? Had not the weapons that the one bourgeois faction had distributed among the people against the other faction in their mutual struggle for supremacy again to be torn from it, the people, since the latter was confronting their united dictatorship? Nothing has aroused the Paris shopkeeper more than this coquettish *étalage* of Jesuitism, not even the rejection of the *concordats à l'amiable*.

See also MARX *ibid.*, 233–234; ENGELS, The Prussian Constitution, *MECW* VI, 64–67; ENGELS, Letter to Bebel, 18.11.1884, *Selected Correspondence 1846–1895*, 428–429.

ENGELS, The Movements of 1847, *MECW* VI, 524–525.

In 1847 these last enemies of the Swiss bourgeoisie were completely broken.

In almost all the cantons the Swiss bourgeoisie had had a pretty free hand in commerce and industry. In so far as the guilds still existed, they did little to hamper bourgeois development. Tolls within the country hardly existed. Wherever the bourgeoisie had developed to any considerable extent, political power was in its hands. But although it had made good progress in the individual cantons and had found support there, the main thing was still lacking, namely centralisation. Whereas feudalism, patriarchalism, and philistinism flourish in separated provinces and individual towns, the bourgeoisie needs for its growth as wide a field as possible; instead of twenty-two small cantons it needed *one* large Switzerland. Cantonal sovereignty, which best suited the conditions in the *old* Switzerland, had become a crushing handicap for the bourgeoisie. The bourgeoisie needed a centralised power, strong enough to impose a particular course of development on the legislation of the individual cantons and, by sheer weight of influence, to cancel out the differences in their constitutions and laws, to wipe out the vestiges of the feudal, patriarchal and philistine legislation, and energetically to represent the interests of the Swiss bourgeoisie in relation to other countries.

The bourgeoisie has won for itself this centralised power.

But did not the peasants also help in overthrowing the Sonderbund? Certainly they did! So far as the peasants are concerned, they will play the same part towards the bourgeoisie as they played for so long towards the petty bourgeoisie. The peasants will remain the exploited arm of the bourgeoisie, they will fight its battles for it, weave its calico and ribbons, and provide the recruits for its proletariat. What else can they do? They are owners, like the bourgeois, and for the moment their interests are almost identical with those of the bourgeoisie. All the political measures which they are strong enough to put through, are hardly more advantageous to the bourgeoisie than to the peasants themselves. Nevertheless, they are weak in comparison with the bourgeoisie, because the latter are more wealthy and have in their hands the lever of all political power in our century—industry. With the bourgeoisie, the peasantry can achieve much; against the bourgeoisie, nothing.

It is true that a time will come when the fleeced and impoverished section of the peasantry will unite with the proletariat, which by then will be further developed, and will declare war on the bourgeoisie—but that does not concern us here.

See also ENGELS, Letter to Spanish Federal Council, 13.2.1871, *MESC*, 315.

ENGELS, The Constitutional Question in Germany, *MECW* VI, 75–91.

The present political system of Germany is nothing more than a compromise between the nobility and the petty bourgeoisie, which amounts to resigning power into the hands of a third class: the bureaucracy. In the composition of this class the two high contracting parties participate according to their respective status; the nobility, which represents the more important branch of production, reserves to itself the higher positions, the petty bourgeoisie contents itself with the lower and only in exceptional circumstances puts forward candidates for the higher administration. Where the bureaucracy is subjected to direct control, as in the constitutional states of Germany, the nobility and petty bourgeoisie share in it in the same way; and that here also the nobility reserves to itself the lion's share is easily understood. The petty bourgeoisie can never overthrow the nobility, nor make itself equal to it; it can do no more than weaken it. To overthrow the nobility, another class is required, with wider interests, greater property and more determined courage: *the bourgeoisie.*

In all countries the bourgeoisie emerges from the petty bourgeoisie with the development of world trade and large-scale industry, with the accompanying free competition and centralisation of property. The petty bourgeoisie represents inland and coastal trade, handicrafts, manufacture based on handwork—branches of industry which operate within a limited area, require little capital, have a slow turnover and give rise to only local and sluggish competition. The bourgeoisie represents world trade, the direct exchange of products of all regions, trade in money, large factory industry based on the use of machinery—branches of production which demand the greatest possible area, the greatest possible capital and the quickest possible turnover, and give rise to universal and stormy competition. The petty bourgeois represents *local*, the bourgeois *general* interests. The petty bourgeois finds his position sufficiently safeguarded if, while exercising indirect influence on state legislation, he participates directly in provincial administration and is master of his local municipality. The bourgeois cannot protect his interests without direct, constant control of the central administration, foreign policy and legislation of his state. The classical creation of the petty bourgeoisie were the free cities of the German Reich, that of the bourgeoisie is the French representative state. The petty bourgeois is conservative as soon as the ruling class makes a few concessions to him; the bourgeois is revolutionary until he himself rules.

What then is the attitude of the German bourgeoisie to the two classes that share political rule?

While a rich and powerful bourgeoisie has been formed in England since the seventeenth and in France since the eighteenth century, one can speak of a German bourgeoisie only since the beginning of the nineteenth century. There were before then, it is true, a few rich shipowners in the Hanseatic towns, a few rich bankers in the interior, but no class of big capitalists, and least of all of big *industrial* capitalists. The creator of the German bourgeoisie was Napoleon. His continental system and the freedom of trade made necessary by its pressure in Prussia gave the Germans a manufacturing industry and expanded their mining industry. After a few years these new or expanded branches of production were already so important, and the bourgeoisie created by them so influential, that by 1818 the Prussian government saw that it was necessary to allow them protective tariffs. The Prussian Customs Act of 1818 was the first official recognition of the bourgeoisie by the government. It was admitted, though reluctantly and with a heavy heart, that the bourgeoisie had become a class indispensable for the country. The next concession to the bourgeoisie was the Customs Union. The admission of most of the

German states into the Prussian customs system was no doubt originally occasioned simply by fiscal and political considerations, but no one benefited from it as much as did the German, more especially the Prussian, bourgeoisie. Although the Customs Union here and there brought a few small advantages to the nobility and petty bourgeoisie, on the whole it harmed both groups still more through the rise of the bourgeoisie, keener competition and the supplanting of the previous means of production. Since then the bourgeoisie, especially in Prussia, has developed rather quickly. Although its advance during the last thirty years has not been nearly as great as that of the English and French bourgeoisie, it has nevertheless established most branches of modern industry, in a few districts supplanted peasant or petty-bourgeois patriarchalism, concentrated capital to some extent, produced something of a proletariat, and built fairly long stretches of railroad. It has at least reached the point of having either to go further and make itself the ruling class or to renounce its previous conquests, the point where it is the only class that can at the moment bring about progress in Germany, can at the moment rule Germany. It is already in fact the leading class in Germany, and its whole existence depends upon its becoming legally so as well.

.   .   .   .

And the propertyless, in common parlance the working, classes? We shall soon speak of them at greater length; for the moment it is sufficient to point to the division among them. This division into farm labourers, day labourers, handicraft journeymen, factory workers and lumpen proletariat, together with their dispersal over a great, thinly populated expanse of country with few and weak central points, already renders it impossible for them to realise that their interests are common, to reach understanding, to constitute themselves into *one* class. This division and dispersal makes nothing else possible for them but restriction to their immediate, everyday interests, to the wish for a good wage for good work. That is, it restricts the workers to seeing their interest in that of their employers, thus making every single section of the workers into an auxiliary army for the class employing them. The farm labourer and day labourer supports the interests of the noble or farmer on whose estate he works. The journeyman stands under the intellectual and political sway of his master. The factory worker lets himself be used by the factory owner in the agitation for protective tariffs. For a few talers the lumpen proletarian fights out with his fists the squabbles between bourgeoisie, nobility and police. And where two classes of employers have contradictory interests to assert, there exists the same struggle between the classes of workers they employ.

.   .   .   .

The factory owners are further divided into two sections: the one gives the initial processing to raw materials and sends them into trade half-finished, the other takes over the half-finished materials and brings them to market as finished commodities. To the first group belong the spinners, to the second the weavers. In Germany the first section also includes the iron producers.*

. . . to introduce newly invented techniques, to establish good communications, to obtain cheap machines and raw materials, to train skilled workers, requires an entire industrial system; it requires the interlocking of all branches of industry, sea-ports which are tributary to the industrial interior and carry on a flourishing trade. All this has long ago been proved by the economists. But such an industrial system requires also nowadays, when England is almost the only country that has no competition to fear, a complete protective system embracing all branches of industry threatened by foreign competition, and modifications to this system must always be made according to the position of industry. Such a system the existing Prussian Government *cannot* give, nor can all the governments of the Customs Union. It can only be set up and operated by the ruling bourgeoisie itself. And for this reason also the German bourgeoisie can no longer do without political power.

Such a protective system, moreover, is all the more necessary in Germany, since there manufacture lies in its death throes. Without systematic tariff protection the competition of English machinery will kill manufacture, and the bourgeoisie, petty bourgeoisie and workers hitherto maintained by it will be ruined. Reason enough for the German bourgeoisie to ruin what remains of manufacture rather with *German* machines.

Protective tariffs are therefore necessary for the German bourgeoisie and only by that bourgeoisie itself can they be introduced. If only for that reason, then, it must seize state power.

But it is not only by insufficient tariffs that the factory owners are hindered in the complete utilisation of their capital; they are also hindered by the *bureaucracy*. If in the matter of customs legislation they meet with indifference from the government, in their relations with the bureaucracy they meet with its most direct hostility.

The bureaucracy was set up to govern petty bourgeoisie and peasants. These classes, dispersed in small towns or villages, with interests which do not reach beyond the narrowest local boundaries, have necessarily the restricted horizons corresponding to their restricted mode of life. They cannot govern a large state, they can have neither the breadth of vision nor the knowledge to balance the different conflicting interests. And it was exactly at *that* stage of civilisation when the petty bourgeoisie was most flourishing that the different interests were most complicatedly intertwined (one need only think of the guilds and their conflicts). The petty bourgeoisie and the peasants cannot, therefore, do without a powerful and numerous bureaucracy. They must let themselves be kept in leading strings so as to escape the greatest confusion, and not to ruin themselves with hundreds and thousands of lawsuits.

* Here four pages of the manuscript are missing.

But the bureaucracy, which is a necessity for the petty bourgeoisie, very soon becomes an unbearable fetter for the bourgeoisie. Already at the stage of manufacture official supervision and interference become very burdensome; factory industry is scarcely possible under such control. The German factory owners have hitherto kept the bureaucracy off their backs as much as possible by bribery, for which they can certainly not be blamed. But this remedy frees them only from the lesser half of the burden; apart from the impossibility of bribing *all* the officials with whom a factory owner comes into contact, bribery does not free him from perquisites, honorariums to jurists, architects, mechanics, nor from other expenses caused by the system of supervision, nor from extra work and waste of time. And the more industry develops, the more "conscientious officials" appear—that is, officials who either from pure narrow-mindedness or from bureaucratic hatred of the bourgeoisie, pester the factory owners with the most infuriating chicaneries.

The bourgeoisie, therefore, is compelled to break the power of this indolent and pettifogging bureaucracy. From the moment the state administration and legislature fall under the control of the bourgeoisie, the independence of the bureaucracy ceases to exist; indeed from this moment, the tormentors of the bourgeoisie turn into their humble slaves. Previous regulations and decrees, which served only to lighten the work of the officials at the expense of the industrial bourgeoisie, give place to new regulations which lighten the work of the industrialists at the expense of the officials.

The bourgeoisie is all the more compelled to do this as soon as possible because, as we have seen, all its sections are directly concerned in the quickest possible increase of factory industry, and factory industry cannot possibly grow under a regime of bureaucratic harassment.

The subordination of the customs and the bureaucracy to the interest of the industrial bourgeoisie are the two measures with the implementation of which the bourgeoisie is most directly concerned. But that does not by any means exhaust its needs. The bourgeoisie is compelled to subject the whole system of legislation, administration and justice in almost all the German states to a thoroughgoing revision, for this whole system serves to maintain and uphold a social condition which the bourgeoisie is continually working to overthrow. The conditions under which nobility and petty bourgeoisie can exist side by side are absolutely different from the conditions of life of the bourgeoisie, and only the former are officially recognised in the German states. Let us take the Prussian status quo as an example. If the petty bourgeoisie could subject themselves to the judicial as well as to the administrative bureaucracy, if they could entrust their property and persons to the discretion and torpidity of an "independent", i.e., bureaucratically self-sufficient judicial class, which in return offered them protection against the encroachments of the feudal nobility and at times also against those of the administrative bureaucracy, the bourgeoisie cannot do so. For lawsuits concerning property the bourgeoisie requires at least the protection of publicity, and for criminal trials moreover that of the jury as well, the constant control of justice through a deputation of the bourgeoisie.—The petty bourgeois can put up with the exemption of nobles and officials from common legal procedure because his official humiliation in this way fully corresponds to his lower social status. The bourgeois, who must either be ruined or make his class the first in society and state, cannot do this.—The petty bourgeois can, without prejudice to the smooth course of his way of life, leave legislation on landed property to the nobility alone; in fact he must, since he has enough to do to protect his own urban interests from the influence and encroachment of the nobles. The bourgeois cannot in any way leave the regulation of property relationships in the countryside to the discretion of the nobility, for the complete development of his own interests requires the fullest possible industrial exploitation of agriculture too, the creation of a class of industrial farmers, free saleability and mobilisation of landed property. The need of the landowner to procure money on mortgage gives to the bourgeois here an opportunity and forces the nobility to allow the bourgeoisie, at least in relation to the mortgage laws, to influence legislation concerning landed property.—If the petty bourgeois, with his small scale of business, his slow turnover and his limited number of customers concentrated in a small area, has not found the miserable old Prussian legislation on trade too oppressive but has even been grateful for the bit of protection it provided, the bourgeois cannot bear it any longer. The petty bourgeois, whose highly simple transactions are seldom dealings between merchant and merchant, but almost always only sales from retailer or producer direct to consumer—the petty bourgeois seldom goes bankrupt and easily accommodates himself to the old Prussian bankruptcy laws. According to these laws, debts on bills are paid off from total assets before book debts, but customarily the whole assets are devoured by court costs. The laws are framed first of all in the interests of the judicial bureaucracy who administer the assets, and then in the interests of the non-bourgeois as opposed to the bourgeois. The noble in particular, who draws or receives bills on the purchaser or consignee of the corn he has dispatched, is thereby covered, and so are in general all those who have something to sell only once a year and draw the proceeds of that sale in a single transaction. Among those engaged in trade, the bankers and wholesalers are again protected, but the factory owner is rather neglected. The bourgeois, whose dealings are *only* from merchant to merchant, whose customers are scattered, who receives bills on the whole world, who must move in the midst of a highly complicated system of transactions, who is involved at every moment in a bankruptcy—the bourgeois can only be ruined by these absurd laws.—The petty bourgeois is interested in the general policy of his country only in so far as he wants to be left in peace; his narrow round of life makes him incapable of surveying the relations of state to state. The bourgeois, who has to deal or to compete with the most distant countries, cannot work his way up without the most direct influence on the foreign policy of his state.—The petty bourgeois could let the bureaucracy and nobility levy taxes on him, for the same reasons that he subjected himself to the bureaucracy; the bourgeois has a quite direct interest in having the public burdens so distributed that they affect *his* profit as little as possible.

In short, if the petty bourgeois can content himself with opposing to the nobility and the bureaucracy his inert weight, with securing for himself influence on the official power through his *vis inertiae*, the bourgeois cannot do this. He must make his class dominant, his interests crucial, in legislation, administration, justice, taxation and foreign policy. The bourgeoisie must develop itself to the full, daily expand its capital, daily reduce the production costs of its commodities, daily expand its trade connections and markets, daily improve its communications, *in order not to be ruined.* The competition on the world market compels it to do so. And to be able to develop freely and to the full, what it requires is precisely political dominance, the subordination of all other interests to its own.

That in order not to be ruined the German bourgeoisie requires political dominance *now*, we have shown above in connection with the question of protective tariffs and with its attitude to the bureaucracy. But the most striking proof of this is *the present state of the German money and commodity market.*

The prosperity of English industry in 1845 and the railway speculations to which it led had on this occasion a stronger effect on France and Germany than at any earlier lively period of business. The German factory owners did good business, which stimulated German business in general. The agricultural districts found a willing market for their corn in England. The general prosperity enlivened the money market, facilitated credit and attracted on to the market a large number of small amounts of capital, of which in Germany there were so many lying half idle. As in England and France, only somewhere later and in somewhat—*

MARX, The Class Struggles in France, *MESW(3)* I, 208.

Since the finance aristocracy made the laws, was at the head of the administration of the state, had command of all the organised public authorities, dominated public opinion through the actual state of affairs and through the press, the same prostitution, the same shameless cheating, the same mania to get rich was repeated in every sphere, from the Court to the Café Borgne, to get rich not by production, but by pocketing the already available wealth of others. Clashing every moment with the bourgeois laws themselves, an unbridled assertion of unhealthy

* Here the manuscript breaks off.

and dissolute appetites manifested itself, particularly at the top of bourgeois society—lusts wherein wealth derived from gambling naturally seeks its satisfaction, where pleasure becomes debauched, where money, filth and blood commingle. The finance aristocracy, in its mode of acquisition as well as in its pleasures, is nothing but the *rebirth of the lumpenproletariat on the heights of bourgeois society*.

See also MARX, The East India Company, *On Colonialism*, 50–51.

ENGELS, History of the English Corn Laws, *MECW* IV, 657–661.

Meanwhile, opposition to the Corn Laws had become organised. The industrial middle class, which had to pay its workers higher wages because of the increase in the price of corn, resolved to do its utmost to secure at any cost the abolition of these hated laws—the last survivals of the old dominance of the agricultural interests, which at the same time facilitated foreign competition against English industry. Towards the end of 1838, some of the leading Manchester manufacturers founded an anti-Corn Law association, which soon spread in the neighbourhood and in other factory districts, adopted the name of Anti-Corn Law League, started a subscription fund, founded a journal (the *Anti-Bread-Tax Circular*), sent paid speakers from place to place and set in motion all the means of agitation customary in England for achieving its aim. During its first years, which coincided with a four-years' slump in business, the Anti-Corn-Law League was extremely active. When, however, at the beginning of 1842, the business slump turned into a downright commercial crisis which threw the working class into the most atrocious poverty, the Anti-Corn-Law League became definitely revolutionary.

.   .   .   .

This great means in the hands of the manufacturers, by which they wished in 24 hours to bring together a meeting of 500,000 persons on the Manchester racecourse and to raise an insurrection against the Corn Laws, consisted in *closing down their factories*.

.   .   .   .

The Anti-Corn Law League, in order to furnish conspicuous proof that it had not been defeated by the failure of the insurrection, started a new large-scale campaign in 1843, with the demand for contributions from its members amounting to £50,000, and it amassed more than this sum in the course of a year. It began its agitation afresh, but it soon found itself compelled to seek a new audience. It always made a great boast that it found nothing more to do in the factory districts after 1843 and could therefore turn to the agricultural districts. But there was a snag to this. After the insurrection of 1842 it could no longer hold any public meetings in the factory districts without its representatives being most ignominiously driven from the platform and literally beaten up by the angry people whom it had so shamefully betrayed. Consequently, if it wanted to propagate its doctrines, it was compelled to go to the agricultural districts. Here the League was of some real service by arousing among the tenant-farmers a certain feeling of shame at their dependence hitherto on the landowners, and by making the agricultural class aware of more general interests.

.   .   .   .

If now one asks what has been the motive of this colossal movement, which has spread from Manchester to the whole of England and has carried with it the vast majority of the English middle class, but which—we repeat—has not received an atom of sympathy from the working class, it must be acknowledged that this motive is the private interest of the industrial and commercial middle class of Great Britain. For this class it is of the greatest importance to have a system which, as it believes at least, ensures it for all time a world monopoly of trade and industry by enabling it to pay just as low wages as its competitors and to exploit all the advantages that England possesses as a result of its 80 years' start in the development of modern industry. From this point of view the middle class alone, and not the people, benefits from the abolition of the Corn Laws. Secondly, the middle class demands this measure as a supplementary law to the Reform Bill. Through the Reform Bill, which introduced suffrage based on a property qualification and abolished the old electoral privileges of particular individuals and corporations, the monied middle class had come, in principle, to power. In reality, however, the landowning class still retained a considerable preponderance in Parliament since it sends there *directly* 143 members for the countries and *indirectly* almost all the members representing small towns, and is represented in addition by the Tory members from the towns. In 1841, this majority of the agricultural interest brought *Peel* and the *Tories* into the cabinet. The abolition of the Corn Laws would deal a fatal blow to the political power of the landowners in the Lower House, and hence in fact in the whole English legislature, since it would make the tenant-farmers independent of the landowners. It would proclaim capital to be the supreme power in England, but at the same time it would shake the English Constitution to its foundations; it would rob an essential constituent of the legislative body, viz. the landed aristocracy, of all wealth and all power, and thereby exert a different and greater influence on the future of England than many other political measures. Once again, however, we find that from this aspect too the abolition of the Corn Laws offers no advantage to the people.

See also ENGELS, The Internal Crises, *MECW* II, 372–373; ENGELS, The Corn Laws, *MECW* II, 380–382; ENGELS, On England, *Articles from NRZ*, 80–81; ENGELS, The Coercion Bill for Ireland, *MECW* VI, 445–447; MARX, Letter to Engels in Vevey, 17.8.1849, *MESC*, 44–45; MARX, The War Question, *On Ireland*, 67; MARX, Ireland's Revenge, *On Ireland*, 76; MARX, From Parliament, *On Ireland*, 77.

The Uses of Law

MARX, The Poverty of Philosophy, *MECW* VI, 209.

> "A workers' strike is *illegal*, and it is not only the Penal Code that says so, it is the economic system, the necessity of the established order. . . . That each worker individually should dispose freely over his person and his hands, this can be tolerated but that workers should undertake by combination to do violence to monopoly, is something society cannot permit." (Tome I, pp. 334 and 335.)

M. Proudhon wants to pass off an article of the Penal Code as a necessary and general result of bourgeois relations of production.

In England combination is authorised by an Act of Parliament and it is the economic system which has forced Parliament to grant this legal authorisation. In 1825, when under the Minister Huskisson, Parliament had to modify the law in order to bring it more and more into line with the conditions resulting from free competition, it had of necessity to abolish all laws forbidding combinations of workers. The more modern industry and competition develop, the more elements there are which call forth and strengthen combination, and as soon as combination becomes an economic fact, daily gaining in solidity, it is bound before long to become a legal fact.

Thus the article of the Penal Code proves at the most that modern industry and competition were not yet well developed under the Constituent Assembly and under the Empire.

Economists and socialists* are in agreement on one point: the condemnation of *combinations*. Only they have different motives for their act of condemnation.

ENGELS, The Housing Question, *MESW(3)* II, 314–315

> After what has been said above, we already know in advance how our Proudhonist will solve the great housing question. On the one hand, we have the demand that each worker have and own his own home in order that we may no longer be *below the savages*. On the other hand, we have the assurance that the two, three, five or tenfold repayment of the original cost price of a house in the form of rent, as it actually takes place, is based on a *legal title*, and that this legal title is in contradiction to "*eternal justice.*" The solution is simple: we abolish the legal title and by virtue of eternal justice declare the rent paid to be a payment on account of the cost of the dwelling itself. If one has so arranged one's premises that they already contain the conclusion, then of course it requires no greater skill than any charlatan possesses to produce the result, prepared

---

* That is, the socialists of that time: the Fourierists in France, the Owenites in England. F. E. [*Note to the German edition. 1885.*]

beforehand, from the bag and proudly point to unshakeable logic whose result it is.

And so it happens here. The abolition of rented dwellings is proclaimed a necessity, and couched in the form of a demand that every tenant be turned into the owner of his dwelling. How are we to do that? Very simply:

> "Rented dwellings will be redeemed. . . . The previous house-owner will be paid the value of his house to the last farthing. Whereas rent represents, as previously, the tribute which the tenant pays to the perpetual title of capital, from the day when the redemption of rented dwellings is proclaimed the exactly fixed sum paid by the tenant will become the annual instalment paid for the dwelling which has passed into his possession. . . . Society . . . transforms itself in this way into a totality of free and independent owners of dwellings."

The Proudhonist finds it a crime against eternal justice that the house-owner can without working obtain ground rent and interest out of the capital he has invested in the house. He decrees that this must cease, that capital invested in houses shall no longer yield interest; nor ground rent either, so far as it represents purchased landed property. Now we have seen that the capitalist mode of production, the basis of present-day society, is in no way affected hereby. The pivot on which the exploitation of the worker turns is the sale of his labour power to the capitalist and the use which the capitalist makes of this transaction, the fact that he compels the worker to produce far more than the paid value of his labour power amounts to. It is this transaction between capitalist and worker which produces all the surplus value afterwards divided in the form of ground rent, commercial profit, interest on capital, taxes, etc., among the diverse varieties of capitalists and their servitors. And now our Proudhonist comes along and believes that if we were to prohibit *one single variety* of capitalists, and at that of capitalists who purchase no labour power directly and therefore also cause no surplus value to be produced, from making profit or receiving interest, it would be a step forward! The mass of unpaid labour taken from the working class would remain exactly the same even if house-owners were to be deprived tomorrow of the possibility of receiving ground rent and interest.

ENGELS, *ibid.*, 319–321.

Proudhon, from his legal standpoint, explains the rate of interest, as he does all economic facts, not by the conditions of social production, but by the state laws in which these conditions receive their general expression. From this point of view, which lacks any inkling of the interconnection between the state laws and the conditions of production in society, these state laws necessarily appear as purely arbitrary orders which at any moment could be replaced just as well by their exact opposites. Nothing is, therefore, easier for Proudhon than to issue a decree—as soon as he has the power to do so—reducing the rate of interest to one per cent. And if all the other social conditions remain as they were, this Proudhonist decree will simply exist on paper only. The rate of interest will continue to be governed by the economic laws to which it is subject today, all decrees notwithstanding. Persons possessing credit will continue to borrow money at two, three, four and more per cent, according to circumstances, just as before, and the only difference will be that *rentiers* will be very careful to advance money only to persons with whom no litigation is to be expected. Moreover, this great plan to deprive capital of its "productivity" is as old as the hills; it is as old as—the *usury laws* which aim at nothing else but limiting the rate of interest, and which have since been abolished everywhere because in practice they were continually broken or circumvented, and the state was compelled to admit its impotence against the laws of social production. And the re-introduction of these medieval and unworkable laws is "to take the productivity of capital by the horns"? One sees that the closer Proudhonism is examined the more reactionary it appears.

And when thereupon the rate of interest has been reduced to zero in this fashion, and interest on capital therefore abolished, then "nothing more would be paid than the labour necessary to turn over the capital." This is supposed to mean that the abolition of interest is equivalent to the abolition of profit and even of surplus value. But if it were possible *really* to abolish interest by decree, what would be the consequence? The class of *rentiers* would no longer have any inducement to loan out their capital in the form of advances, but would invest it for their own account in their own industrial enterprises or in joint-stock companies. The mass of surplus value extracted from the working class by the capitalist class would remain the same; only its distribution would be altered, and even that not much.

In fact, our Proudhonist fails to see that already now, in commodity purchase in bourgeois society, no more is paid on the average than "the labour necessary to turn over the capital" (it should read, necessary for the production of the commodity in question). Labour is the measure of value of all commodities, and in present-day society—apart from fluctuations of the market—it is absolutely impossible that in the aggregate more should be paid on the average for commodities than the labour necessary for their production. No, no, my dear Proudhonist, the difficulty lies elsewhere. It is contained in the fact that "the labour necessary to turn over the capital" (to use your confused terminology) is simply *not fully paid for*!

· · · · · · · · · · · ·

And now it must have become clear even to the blindest that "the owner himself would be the first to agree to a sale because otherwise his house would remain unused and the capital invested in it would be simply useless." Of course. If the interest on loaned capital is abolished no house-owner can thereafter obtain a penny piece in rent for his house, simply because house rent [Miete] may be spoken of as rent *interest* [Mietzins] and because such "rent interest" contains a part which is really interest on capital. Sawbones is sawbones. Whereas the usury laws relating to ordinary interest on capital could be made ineffective only by circumventing them, yet they never touched the rate of house rent even remotely. It was reserved for Proudhon to imagine that his new usury law would without more ado regulate and gradually abolish not only simple interest on capital but also the complicated house rent [*Mietzins*] for dwellings. Why then the "simply useless" house should be purchased for good money from the house-owner, and how it is that under such circumstances the house-owner would not pay money himself to get rid of this "simply useless" house in order to save himself the cost of repairs—about this we are left in the dark.

After this triumphant achievement in the sphere of higher socialism (Master Proudhon called it suprasocialism) our Proudhonist considers himself justified in flying still higher:

> "All that still has to be done now is to draw some conclusions in order to cast complete light from all sides on our so important subject."

ENGELS, *ibid.*, 360–361.

But all the economic investigations into house rent will not enable us to turn the abolition of the rented dwelling into "one of the most fruitful and magnificent aspirations which has ever sprung from the womb of the revolutionary idea." In order to accomplish this we must translate the simple fact from sober economics into the really far more ideological sphere of jurisprudence. "The house serves as a perpetual legal title" to house rent, and *"thus it comes"* that the value of a house can be paid back in rent two, three, five or ten times. The "legal title" does not help us a jot to discover how it really "does come," and therefore I said that Mülberger would have been able to find out *how* it really "does come" only by inquiring how the house becomes a legal title. We discover this only after we have examined, as I did, the *economic* nature of house rent, instead of quarrelling with the legal expression under which the ruling class sanctions it. Anyone who proposes the taking of economic steps to abolish rent surely ought to know a little more about house rent than that it "represents the tribute which the tenant pays to the perpetual title of capital." To this Mülberger answers, "A description is one thing, an explanation another."

We have thus converted the house, although it is by no means everlasting, into a perpetual legal title to house rent. We find, no matter how "it comes," that by virtue of this legal title, the house brings in its original value several times over in the form of rent. By the translation into legal phraseology we are happily so far removed from economics that we now can see no more than the phenomenon that a house can gradually get paid for in gross rent several times over. As we are thinking and talking in legal terms, we apply to this phenomenon the measuring stick of right, of justice, and find that it is *unjust*, that it is not in accordance with the "conception of right of the revolution," whatever that may be, and that therefore the legal title is no good. We find further that the same holds good for interest-bearing capital and leased agricultural land, and we now have the excuse for separating these classes of property from the others and subjecting them to exceptional treatment. This consists in the demands: (1) to deprive the owner of the right to give notice to quit, the right to demand the return of his property; (2) to give the lessee, borrower or tenant the gratuitous use of the object transferred to him but not belonging to him; and (3) to pay off the owner in instalments over a long period without interest. And with this we have exhausted the Proudhonist "principles" from this angle. This is Proudhon's "social liquidation."

Incidentally, it is obvious that this whole reform plan is to benefit almost exclusively the petty bourgeois and the small peasants, in that it *consolidates* them in their position as petty bourgeois and small peasants. Thus "the petty bourgeois Proudhon", who, according to Mülberger, is a mythical figure, suddenly takes on here a very tangible historical existence.

ENGELS, *ibid.*, 369–370.

I rub my eyes in astonishment, I am reading Mülberger's disquisition through once again from beginning to end in order to find the passage where he says his redemption of the rented dwelling presupposes as an accomplished fact "the actual seizure of all the instruments of labour, the seizure of industry as a whole by the working people," but I am unable to find any such passage. It does not exist. There is nowhere mention of "actual seizure," etc., but there is the following on page 17:

> "Let us now assume that the productivity of capital *is really taken by the horns*, as it must be sooner or later, for instance, *by a transitional law which fixes the interest on all capitals at one per cent*, but mark you, with the tendency to make even this rate of interest approximate more and more to the zero point. . . . Like all other products, houses and dwellings are naturally also included within the purview of this law. . . . We see, therefore, from this angle that the redemption of the rented dwelling *is a necessary consequence of the abolition of the productivity of capital in general.*"

Thus it is said here in plain words, quite contrary to Mülberger's latest about-face, that the productivity of capital, by which confused phrase he admittedly means the capitalist mode of production, is really "taken by the horns" by a law abolishing interest, and that precisely as a result of such a law "the redemption of the rented dwelling is a necessary consequence of the abolition of the productivity of capital in general." Not at all, says Mülberger now. That transitional law "does not deal with relations of *production* but with relations of *circulation*." In view of this crass contradiction, "equally mysterious for wise men as for fools," as Goethe would say, all that is left for me to do is to assume that I am dealing with two separate and distinct Mülbergers, one of whom rightly complains that I "tried to make him say" what the other caused to be printed.

ENGELS, *ibid.*, 375.

But enough. If this polemic serves for nothing else it has in any case the value of having given proof of what there really is to the practice of these self-styled "practical" Socialists. These practical proposals for the abolition of all social evils, these universal social panaceas, have always and everywhere been the work of founders of sects who appeared at a time when the proletarian movement was still in its infancy. Proudhon too belongs to them. The development of the proletariat soon casts aside these swaddling-clothes and engenders in the working class itself the realisation that nothing is less practical than these "practical solutions," concocted in advance and universally applicable, and that practical socialism consists rather in a correct knowledge of the capitalist mode of production from its various aspects. A working class which knows what's what in this regard will *never* be in doubt in any case as to which social institutions should be the objects of its main attacks, and in what manner these attacks should be executed.

See also MARX, Report on Inheritance: Report of the General Council, 4th Annual Congress of the International Workingmen's Association, *The Critique of Capitalist Democracy*, 59–60.

MARX, Letter to F. Bolte, 23.11.1871, *MESC*, 328.

. . . The political movement of the working class has as its ultimate object, of course, the conquest of political power for this class and this naturally requires a previous organization of the working class developed up to a certain point and arising precisely from its economic struggles.

On the other hand, however, every movement in which the working class comes out as a *class* against the ruling classes and tries to coerce them by pressure from without is a political movement. For instance, the attempt in a particular factory or even in a particular trade to force a shorter working day out of individual capitalists by strikes, etc., is a purely economic movement. On the other hand the movement to force through an eight-hour, etc., *law*, is a *political* movement. And in this way, out of the separate economic movements of the workers there grows up everywhere a *political* movement, that is to say, a movement of the *class*, with the object of enforcing its interests in a general form, in a form possessing general, socially coercive force. While these movements presuppose a certain degree of previous organization, they are in turn equally a means of developing this organization.

Where the working class is not yet far enough advanced in its organization to undertake a decisive campaign against the collective power, i.e. the political power of the ruling classes, it must at any rate be trained for this by continual agitation against this power and by a hostile attitude toward the policies of the ruling classes. Otherwise it remains a plaything in their hands, as the September revolution in France showed, and as is also proved to a certain extent by the game that Messrs. Gladstone & Co. have been successfully engaged in England up to the present time.

See also MARX/ENGELS, The Communist Manifesto, *MECW* VI, 493; MARX, Wages, Prices and Profit, *MESW(3)* II, 73.

ENGELS, The Condition of the Working Class in England, *MECW* IV, 517.

Since the working-men do not respect the law, but simply submit to its power when they cannot change it, it is most natural that they should at least propose alterations in it, that they should wish to put a proletarian law in the place of the legal fabric of the bourgeoisie. This proposed law is the People's Charter, which in form is purely political, and demands a democratic basis for the House of Commons. Chartism is the compact form of their opposition to the bourgeoisie. In the Unions and turnouts opposition always remained isolated: it was single working-men or sections who fought a single bourgeois. If the fight became general, this was scarcely by the intention of the working-men; or, when it did happen intentionally, Chartism was at the bottom of it. But in Chartism it is the whole working-class which arises against the bourgeoisie, and attacks, first of all, the political power, the legislative rampart with which the bourgeoisie has surrounded itself. Chartism has proceeded from the Democratic party which arose between 1780 and 1790 with and in the proletariat, gained strength during the French Revolution, and came forth after the peace as the Radical party. It had its headquarters then in Birmingham and Manchester, and later in London; extorted the Reform Bill from the Oligarchs of the old Parliament by a union with the Liberal bourgeoisie, and has steadily consolidated itself, since then, as a more and more pronounced working-men's party in opposition to the bourgeoisie.

ENGELS, Letter to Paul Lafargue, 25.2.1893, *MESC*, 431–432.

The only country where the bourgeoisie still has a little common sense is England. Here the formation of the Independent Labour Party (though still in embryo) and its conduct in the Lancashire and Yorkshire elections have put a match to the government's backside; it is stirring itself, doing things unheard-of for a Liberal Government. The Registration Bill (1) unifies the suffrage for all parliamentary, municipal, etc., elections, (2) adds at least 20 to 30 per cent to the working-class vote, (3) removes the cost of election expenses from the candidates' shoulders and places it on those of the government. The payment of an honorarium to M.P.s is promised for the next session; and there are also a whole number of juridical and economic measures for the benefit of workers. Finally, the Liberals recognise that, to make sure of governing at the present time, there is nothing for it but to increase the political power of the working class who will naturally kick them out afterwards. The Tories, on the other hand, are behaving at the moment with unbounded stupidity. But once Home Rule is on the Statute Book, they will realise that there is nothing for it but to enter the lists to gain power, and to that end there remains but one means: to win the working-class vote by political or economic concessions; thus Liberals and Conservatives cannot help extending the power of the working class, and hastening the time which will eliminate both the one and the other.

ENGELS, The Condition of the Working Class in England, *MECW* IV, 459–464.

The ruinous influence of the factory system began at a early day to attract general attention. We have already alluded to the Apprentices' Act of 1802. Later, towards 1817, Robert Owen, then a manufacturer in New Lanark, in Scotland, afterwards founder of English Socialism, began to call the attention of the Government, by memorials and petitions, to the necessity of legislative guarantees for the health of the operatives, and especially of children. The late Sir Robert Peel and other philanthropists united with him, and gradually secured the Factory Acts of 1819, 1825, and 1831, of which the first two were never enforced, and the last only here and there. This law of 1831, based upon the motion of Sir J. C. Hobhouse, provided that in cotton mills no one under twenty-one should be employed between half-past seven at night and half-past five in the morning; and that in all factories young persons under eighteen should work no longer than twelve hours daily, and nine hours on Saturday. But since operatives could not testify against their masters without being discharged, this law helped matters very little. In the great cities, where the operatives were more restive, the larger manufacturers came to an agreement among themselves to obey the law; but even there, there were many who, like the employers in the country, did not trouble themselves about it. Meanwhile, the demand for a ten hours' law had become lively among the operatives; that is, for a law which should forbid all operatives under eighteen years of age to work longer than ten hours daily; the Trades Unions, by their agitation, made this demand general throughout the manufacturing population; the philanthropic section of the Tory party, then led by Michael Sadler, seized upon the plan, and brought it before Parliament. Sadler obtained a parliamentary committee for the investigation of the factory system, and this committee reported in 1832. Its report was emphatically partisan, composed by strong enemies of the factory system, for party ends. Sadler permitted himself to be betrayed by his noble enthusiasm into the most distorted and erroneous statements, drew from his witnesses by the very form of his questions, answers which contained the truth, but truth in a perverted form. The manufacturers themselves, incensed at a report which represented them as monsters, now demanded an official investigation; they knew that an exact report must, in this case, be advantageous to them; they knew that Whigs, genuine bourgeois, were at the helm, with whom they were upon good terms, whose principles were opposed to any restriction upon manufacture. They obtained a commission in due order, composed of Liberal bourgeois, whose report I have so often cited.

.   .   .   .

The result of this report was the Factory Act of 1833.

.   .   .   .

Meanwhile the agitation for the Ten Hours' Bill by no means died out among the operatives; in 1839 it was under full headway once more, and Sadler's place, he having died, was filled in the House of Commons by Lord Ashley and Richard Oastler, both Tories.

.   .   .   .

Oastler vigorously opposed the New Poor Law also, and was therefore imprisoned for debt by a Mr. Thornhill, on whose estate he was employed as agent, and to whom he owed money. The Whigs offered repeatedly to pay his debt and confer other favours upon him if he would only give up his agitation against the Poor Law. But in vain; he remained in prison, whence he published his Fleet Papers against the factory system and the Poor Law.

The Tory Government of 1841 turned its attention once more to the Factory Acts. The Home Secretary, Sir James Graham, proposed, in 1843, a bill restricting the working-hours of children to six and one-half, and making the enactments for compulsory school attendance more effective, the principal point in this connection being a provision for better schools. This bill was, however, wrecked by the jealousy of the dissenters; for, although compulsory religious instruction was not extended to the children of dissenters, the schools provided for were to be placed under the general supervision of the Established Church, and the Bible made the general reading-book, religion being thus made the foundation of all instruction, whence the dissenters felt themselves threatened. The manufacturers and the Liberals generally united with them, the working-men were divided by the Church question, and therefore inactive. The opponents of the bill, though outweighed in the great manufacturing towns, such as Salford and Stockport, and able in others, such as Manchester, to attack certain of its points only, for fear of the working-men, collected nevertheless nearly two million signatures for a petition against it, and Graham allowed himself to be so far intimidated as to withdraw the whole bill.

ENGELS, The English Ten Hours Bill, *Articles on Britain*, 96–108.

The history of the Ten Hours Bill provides a striking example of the path of development peculiar to the class contradictions in England and therefore deserves closer perusal.

It is common knowledge how the rise of large-scale industry brought in its wake a completely new, utterly shameless form of exploitation of the working class by the factory owners. . . . industrial exploitation at once engulfed the whole family, imprisoning it in the factory.

.   .   .   .

From an early stage the state was obliged to introduce measures to check the factory owners' utterly ruthless exploitation, which defied all postulates of a civilised society. However, these original legal restrictions proved highly inadequate and were soon obviated. It was not until fifty years after the introduction of large-scale industry, when industrial development had already taken firm root, not until 1833, that it was possible to enact an effective law, which at least put a stop to the most glaring excesses.

As early as the beginning of this century a group was formed under the leadership of a number of philanthropists, which campaigned for the legal restriction of the working day in the factories to ten hours. This group, which, under Sadler's leadership in the twenties and, after his death, that of Lord Ashley and Richard Oastler, continued agitating until the Ten Hours Bill was finally passed, gradually rallied to its banner, apart from the workers themselves, the aristocracy and all those sections of the bourgeoisie that were hostile to the factory owners. This association between workers and the most heterogeneous and reactionary elements of English society meant that the campaign for the Ten Hours Bill had to be conducted quite separately from the revolutionary campaign of the workers. The Chartists, of course, supported the Ten Hours Bill to a man; they were the most numerous and active participants at the meetings in support of the Ten Hours Bill and they put their press at the disposal of the Short-Time Committee. Yet not a single Chartist campaigned officially alongside the aristocratic and bourgeois advocates of the Bill or sat on the Short-Time Committee in Manchester. This committee consisted exclusively of workers and factory foremen. The workers concerned, however, were completely broken individuals, worn out by work, meek, God-fearing, respectable men, who were filled with pious horror at the very thought of Chartism and socialism, showed deep respect for Crown and Church and were too downtrodden to hate the industrial bourgeoisie; all they were still capable of was humble reverence for the aristocracy, who at least deigned to take an interest in their wretched plight. The working-class Toryism of these supporters of the Ten Hours Bill was the echo of the workers' original opposition to industrial progress, which was aimed at re-establishing the former patriarchal conditions, while its most active manifestations had gone no further than the smashing of machines. The bourgeois and aristocratic leaders of this group were just as reactionary as these workers. They were all without exception sentimental Tories, for the most part utopian visionaries, wallowing in reminiscences of the extinct patriarchal cottage-industry exploitation and its concomitant piety, homeliness, hidebound worthiness and its set patterns handed down from generation to generation. Their thick skulls reeled at the mere glimpse of industrial revolutionary ferment.

.   .   .   .

Whenever the question of the ten-hour working day became a focus of public interest, all sections of society whose interests had suffered as a result of the industrial revolution and whose livelihood was threatened by it gave their support to these elements. At such times the bankers, stockjobbers, shipowners and merchants, the landed aristocracy, the big landowners from the West Indies and the petty bourgeoisie rallied in ever larger numbers to the support of the Ten Hours Bill campaign.

The Ten Hours Bill provided an excellent meeting ground for these reactionary classes and factions to join forces with the proletariat against the industrial bourgeoisie. While the Bill served to hold down the rapid growth of the wealth and influence, social and political power of the factory owners, it brought the workers a purely material, even strictly physical benefit. It saved their health from too rapid deterioration. It did not, however, give them anything which might have made of them a threat to their reactionary fellow-campaigners; it neither brought them political power nor altered their social position as wage-workers. On the contrary, this campaigning for a ten-hour working day kept the workers permanently under the influence and to some extent under the actual leadership of these property-owning allies, a leadership from which they had been making increasing efforts to dissociate themselves ever since the Reform Bill and the rise of the Chartist movement. It was quite natural, particularly at the beginning of the industrial revolution, that the workers, engaged as they were in direct struggle against only the industrial bourgeoisie, should ally themselves to the aristocracy and other sections of the bourgeoisie, who did not exploit them directly and who were also opposing the industrial bourgeoisie. But this alliance contaminated the working-class movement with a considerable influx of reactionary elements, which is taking a long time to disappear; it gave rise to a significant increase in the influence of reactionary elements in the working-class movement, namely, those workers, whose branch of production was still at the manufactory stage and therefore threatened by industrial progress, as, for example, the hand-loom weavers.

It was therefore most fortunate for the workers that the Ten Hours Bill was finally put through in 1847, at a time of general turmoil, when all the old parliamentary parties were disintegrating and the new ones had not yet taken shape. The passing of this Bill was but one of a whole series of extremely confused parliamentary divisions, the results of which appeared to be determined by nothing other than chance and during which, apart from the convinced freetraders among the factory owners, on the one hand, and the fanatically protectionist landowners, on the other, no party voted in a consistent united fashion. This Bill was seen as a cunning blow, which the aristocracy, some of the Peelites and some of the Whigs had dealt at the factory owners, so as to take their revenge for the major victory the latter had won by repealing the Corn Laws.

The Ten Hours Bill not only satisfied an absolutely essential need of the workers by protecting their health to some extent from the frenzied exploitation of the factory owners, but also freed the workers from the association with sentimental dreamers, from the partnership with England's reactionary classes in general. Patriarchal rantings of the Oastlers and moving professions of sympathy from the Lord Ashleys fell on deaf ears, once the Ten Hours Bill ceased to be the point of their tirades. It was only then that the working-class movement started to concentrate its entire attention on the conquest of political power by the proletariat, as the primary means of revolutionising the whole of the existing society. Whereupon the aristocracy and reactionary sections of the bourgeoisie, but a short while ago allies of the workers, now started both violently opposing the working-class movement and allying themselves with the bourgeoisie with a similar fervour.

.   .   .   .

The industrial bourgeoisie, having once gained access to the field of parliamentary struggle after the Reform Bill, could not fail to win victory after victory. As a result of the restrictions on sinecures the financiers' aristocratic hangers-on were sacrificed to the industrial bourgeoisie, as were the paupers as a result of the Poor Law of 1833 and the financiers and landowners through the reduction of tariffs and the introduction of income tax, which did away with their tax privileges. These victories swelled the numbers of the industrialists' minions. Wholesale and retail trade became their tributaries and London and Liverpool began paying homage at the altar of free trade, the industrialists' Messiah. But with these victories their requirements and aspirations also grew.

.   .   .   .

At the present juncture the industrialists are campaigning for restrictions on state spending and on taxation and for the enfranchisement of that section of the working class on whom they can best rely. They are eager to bring new allies into Parliament in order to win direct political power for themselves all the faster: this alone will enable them to put an end to the now absurd but very costly traditional appendages of the English state machine, namely, the aristocracy, the church, the rotten boroughs and the semi-feudal legal system. There is no doubt that the now imminent new trade crisis, which seems bound to coincide with new major collisions on the Continent, will at least bring about this advance in England's development.

Yet amidst this series of uninterrupted victories of the industrial bourgeoisie reactionary groups succeeded in hampering its advance with the fetters of the Ten Hours Bill. The Ten Hours Bill was passed at a time marked neither by prosperity nor crisis, during one of those transition periods when industry is sufficiently embarrassed by the consequences of over-production as to be able to put in motion only a part of its resources and when the factory owners themselves do not allow their factories to work full time. At a moment such as this, when the Ten Hours Bill set limits to the competition between the factory owners themselves, only at such a moment, could it be tolerated. However, this moment was soon to make way for a new period of prosperity. The emptied markets demanded new supplies; speculation got under way once more, thus doubling demand and the factory owners could not produce enough. Now the Ten Hours Bill became an intolerable shackle for industry, which more than ever before required complete independence and freedom from all restrictions with regard to the disposal of all its resources. What was to become of the industrialists during the next crisis if they were not permitted to exploit to the full this short period of prosperity? The Ten Hours Bill had to be revoked. Since there was as yet insufficient support in Parliament to do this, ways would have to be found to obviate it.

The Bill set a ten-hour limit for the working day of young people under eighteen and all women workers. Since the latter and children make up the majority of factory workers, this meant that factories in general could work only ten hours a day. The factory owners, however, when the next wave of prosperity called for an increase in working hours, found a way out of the situation. As before, with regard to children under fourteen, whose working hours had been made subject to still stricter limits, so on this occasion they proceeded to engage some women and young people as relief and shift workers. Thus they were able to keep their factories running and adult employees working for as many as thirteen, fourteen and fifteen hours a day without a single individual, among those effected by the Ten Hours Bill, working for more than the statutory ten hours a day. This contravened the letter of the law to a certain extent, but the whole spirit of the law and the intention of its authors far more so. The factory inspectors complained while Justices of the Peace were divided among themselves and reached varying verdicts. The higher the wave of prosperity rose, the louder the industrialists protested against the Ten Hours Bill and against the intervention of factory inspectors. Sir George Grey, the Home Secretary, instructed the inspectors to close their eyes to the relay or shift system. Yet a good number of them did not let these instructions harass them, in the knowledge that they had the law behind them. Finally a much publicised case was brought before the Court of Exchequer which came out in favour of the factory owners. This verdict was tantamount to an abrogation of the Ten Hours Bill and the factory owners are once again unchallenged masters of their factories; in times of crisis they can keep their factories running two, three or six hours and during periods of prosperity thirteen or fifteen hours, while the factory inspector is no longer in a position to interfere. . . . .

Nevertheless the Ten Hours Bill is indispensable for the workers. For them it is a physical necessity. Without this Bill the whole of the present generation of English workers is doomed to physical collapse. Yet there is a tremendous gulf between the Ten Hours Bill which the workers are now demanding and the Ten Hours Bill which Sadler, Oastler and Ashley campaigned for and which was passed by the reactionary coalition of 1847. The Bill's short lifespan, its simple undoing—a mere court ruling, not even an act of Parliament, was required to revoke it—and the subsequent behaviour of their former reactionary associates have taught the workers what an alliance with reaction is worth. It has taught them how little they gain from the enactment of isolated, minor measures against the industrial bourgeoisie. It has taught them that the industrial bourgeoisie is so far the only class which at the present time is capable of providing their movement with leaders and that to obstruct its progressive mission would be fruitless. Despite their open hostility towards the industrialists, which has in no way been cooled, the workers are now much more inclined to support the latter in their campaign to achieve completely free trade, financial reform and an extension of the franchise, than to let themselves be rallied once more to the banners of the united forces of reaction by philanthropic mystification. They feel that their time can only come after the industrialists' energy has been completely spent and are thus responding to the right instincts in going out of their way to accelerate the process of development which will give the industrialists the power they seek and lead to their subsequent downfall. Meanwhile they do not forget that in doing so they are bringing their own, immediate enemies to power, and that they can only achieve their own liberation by overthrowing the industrialists and winning political power for themselves. The virtual annulment of the Ten Hours Bill has proved this to them once again most pointedly. The reinstatement of this Bill is futile without universal suffrage, and universal suffrage in England, two-thirds of whose population consists of industrial proletarians, implies exclusive political power for the working class, together with all those revolutionary changes in social conditions intrinsic to that power. The Ten Hours Bill which the workers are now calling for is therefore quite different from the one which the Court of Exchequer has just abrogated. It no longer represents an isolated attempt to cripple industrial progress, it is a link in a long chain of measures aimed at radically changing the whole of the present structure of society and gradually doing away with hitherto existing class contradictions. It is no longer a reactionary but a revolutionary measure for which they are campaigning.

The moment the confines of the world market become too narrow for the full deployment of all modern industry's resources, the moment this industry requires a social revolution in order that its potential may once more have free scope for action, the restriction of working hours ceases to be a reactionary measure or a brake on industrial progress. On the contrary such restrictions emerge of their own accord. The first result of the proletarian revolution in England will be the centralisation of large-scale industry in the hands of the state, in other words, in the hands of the ruling proletariat, and those rivalries which today lie at the root of the contradiction between regulation of working hours and industrial progress will vanish with the centralisation of industry. Thus the problem of the ten-hour working day, like all those which stem from the contradiction between capital and wage-labour, can be solved by one thing and one thing only—the *proletarian revolution*.

ENGELS, Marx's "Capital", *MESW(3)* II, 150–151.

The struggle for the fixing of the working day has lasted from the first appearance of free workers in the arena of history down to the present day. In various trades various traditional working days prevail; but in reality they are seldom adhered to. Only where the law fixes the working day and supervises its observance can one really say that there exists a normal working day. And up to now this is the case almost solely in the factory districts of England. Here the ten-hour working day (ten and a half hours on five days, seven and a half hours on Saturday) has been fixed for all women and for youths of thirteen to eighteen, and since the men cannot work without them, they also come under the ten-hour working day. This law has been won by English factory workers by years of endurance, by the most persistent, stubborn struggle with the factory owners, by freedom of the press, the right of association and assembly, as well as by adroit utilisation of the splits in the ruling class itself. It has become the palladium of the English workers, it has gradually been extended to all important branches of industry and last year *to* almost *all trades*, at least to all those employing women and children. The present work contains most exhaustive material on the history of this legislative regulation of the working day in England. The next North German Reichstag will also have factory regulations to discuss and in connection therewith the regulation of factory labour. We expect that none of the deputies that have been elected by German workers will proceed to discuss this bill without previously making themselves thoroughly conversant with *Marx's* book. *There is much to be achieved here.* The splits within the ruling classes are more favourable to the workers than they ever were in England, because *universal suffrage compels the ruling classes to court the favour of the workers*. Under these circumstances, four or five representatives of the proletariat are *a power*, if they know how to use their position, if above all they know what is at issue, which the bourgeois do not know. And for this purpose, Marx's book gives them all the material in ready form.

MARX, *Capital* I, 253–287.

The capitalistic mode of production (essentially the production of surplus-value, the absorption of surplus-labour), produces thus, with the extension of the working-day, not only the deterioration of human labour-power by robbing it of its normal, moral and physical, conditions of development and function. It produces also the premature exhaustion and death of this labour-power itself. It extends the labourer's time of production during a given period by shortening his actual lifetime.

But the value of the labour-power includes the value of the commodities necessary for the reproduction of the worker, or for the keeping up of the working-class. If then the unnatural extension of the working-day, that capital necessarily strives after in its unmeasured passion for self-expansion, shortens the length of life of the individual labourer, and therefore the duration of his labour-power, the forces used up have to be replaced at a more rapid rate and the sum of the expenses for the reproduction of labour-power will be greater, just as in a machine the part of its value to be reproduced every day is greater the more rapidly the machine is worn out. It would seem therefore that the interest of capital itself points in the direction of a normal working-day.

.   .   .   .

No doubt in certain epochs of feverish activity the labour-market shows significant gaps. In 1834, *e.g.* But then the manufacturers proposed to the Poor Law Commissioners that they should send the "surplus-population" of the agricultural districts to the north, with the explanation "that the manufacturers would absorb and use it up." "Agents were appointed with the consent of the Poor Law Commissioners. . . . An office was set up in Manchester, to which lists were sent of those workpeople in the agricultural districts wanting employment, and their names were registered in books. The manufacturers attended at these offices, and selected such persons as they chose; when they had selected such persons as their 'wants required', they gave instructions to have them forwarded to Manchester, and they were sent, ticketed like bales of goods, by canals, or with carriers, others tramping on the road, and many of them were found on the way lost and half-starved. This system had grown up unto a regular trade."*

.   .   .   .

What experience shows to the capitalist generally is a constant excess of population, *i.e.*, an excess in relation to the momentary requirements of surplus-labour-absorbing capital, although this excess is made up of generations of human beings stunted, short-lived, swiftly replacing each other, plucked, so to say, before maturity. And, indeed, experience

* Ferrand's speech in the House of Commons, 27th April, 1863 [*Original note—eds*].

shows to the intelligent observer with what swiftness and grip the capitalist mode of production, dating, historically speaking, only from yesterday, has seized the vital power of the people by the very root—shows how the degeneration of the industrial population is only retarded by the constant absorption of primitive and physically uncorrupted elements from the country—shows how even the country labourers, in spite of fresh air and the principle of natural selection, that works so powerfully amongst them, and only permits the survival of the strongest, are already beginning to die off. Capital that has such good reasons for denying the sufferings of the legions of workers that surround it, is in practice moved as much and as little by the sight of the coming degradation and final depopulation of the human race, as by the probable fall of the earth into the sun. In every stock-jobbing swindle every one knows that some time or other the crash must come, but every one hopes that it may fall on the head of his neighbour, after he himself has caught the shower of gold and placed it in safety. *Après moi le déluge!* is the watchword of every capitalist and of every capitalist nation. Hence Capital is reckless of the health or length of life of the labourer, unless under compulsion from society. To the out-cry as to the physical and mental degradation, the premature death, the torture of over-work, it answers: Ought these to trouble us since they increase our profits? But looking at things as a whole, all this does not, indeed, depend on the good or ill will of the individual capitalist. Free competition brings out the inherent laws of capitalist production, in the shape of external coercive laws having power over every individual capitalist.

The establishment of a normal working-day is the result of centuries of struggle between capitalist and labourer. The history of this struggle shows two opposed tendencies. Compare, *e.g.*, the English factory legislation of our time with the English Labour Statutes from the 14th century to well into the middle of the 18th. Whilst the modern Factory Acts compulsorily shortened the working-day, the earlier statutes tried to lengthen it by compulsion. Of course the pretensions of capital in embryo—when, beginning to grow, it secures the right of absorbing a *quantum sufficit* of surplus-labour, not merely by the force of economic relations, but by the help of the State—appear very modest when put face to face with the concessions that, growling and struggling, it has to make in its adult condition. It takes centuries ere the "free" labourer, thanks to the development of capitalistic production, agrees, *i.e.*, is compelled by social conditions, to sell the whole of his active life, his very capacity for work, for the price of the necessaries of life, his birthright for a mess of pottage. Hence it is natural that the lengthening of the working-day, which capital, from the middle of the 14th to the end of the 17th century, tries to impose by State-measures on adult labourers, approximately coincides with the shortening of the working-day which, in the second half of the 19th century, has here and there been effected by the State to prevent the coining of children's blood into capital. That which to-day, *e.g.*, in the State of Massachusetts, until recently the freest State of the North-American Republic, has been proclaimed as the statutory limit of the labour of children under 12, was in England, even in the middle of the 17th century, the normal working-day of able-bodied artisans, robust labourers, athletic blacksmiths.

The first "Statute of Labourers" (23 Edward III., 1349) found its immediate pretext (not its cause, for legislation of this kind lasts centuries after the pretext for it has disappeared) in the great plague that decimated the people, so that, as a Tory writer says, "The difficulty of getting men to work on reasonable terms (*i.e.*, at a price that left their employers a reasonable quantity of surplus-labour) grew to such a height as to be quite intolerable." Reasonable wages were, therefore, fixed by law as well as the limits of the working-day. The latter point, the only one that here interests us, is repeated in the Statute of 1496 (Henry VII.).

. . . .

Still, during the greater part of the 18th century, up to the epoch of Modern Industry and machinism, capital in England had not succeeded in seizing for itself, by the payment of the weekly value of labour-power, the whole week of the labourer, with the exception, however, of the agricultural labourers. The fact that they could live for a whole week on the wage of four days, did not appear to the labourers a sufficient reason that they should work the other two days for the capitalist.

. . . .

After capital had taken centuries in extending the working-day to its normal maximum limit, and then beyond this to the limit of the natural day of 12 hours, there followed on the birth of machinism and modern industry in the last third of the 18th century, a violent encroachment like that of an avalanche in its intensity and extent. All bounds of morals and nature, age and sex, day and night, were broken down. Even the idea of day and night, of rustic simplicity in the old statutes, became so confused that an English judge, as late as 1860, needed a quite Talmudic sagacity to explain "judicially" what was day and what was night. Capital celebrated its orgies.

As soon as the working-class, stunned at first by the noise and turmoil of the new system of production, recovered, in some measure, its senses, its resistance began, and first in the native land of machinism, in England. For 30 years, however, the concessions conquered by the workpeople were purely nominal. Parliament passed 5 Labour Laws between 1802 and 1833, but was shrewd enough not to vote a penny for their carrying out, for the requisite officials, &c.

They remained a dead letter. "The fact is, that prior to the Act of 1833, young persons and children were worked all night, all day, or both *ad libitum*."*

. . . .

A normal working-day for modern industry only dates from the Factory Act of 1833, which included cotton, wool, flax, and silk factories. Nothing is more characteristic of the spirit of capital than the history of

---

* Report of Inspector of Factories, 30th April, 1860, p. 50 [*Original note—eds*].

the English Factory Acts from 1833 to 1864.

The Act of 1833 declares the ordinary factory working-day to be from half-past five in the morning to half-past eight in the evening, and within these limits, a period of 15 hours, it is lawful to employ young persons (*i.e.*, persons between 13 and 18 years of age), at any time of the day, provided no one individual young person should work more than 12 hours in any one day, except in certain cases especially provided for. The 6th section of the Act provided: "That there shall be allowed in the course of every day not less than one and a half hours for meals to every such person restricted as hereinbefore provided." The employment of children under 9, with exceptions mentioned later, was forbidden; the work of children between 9 and 13 was limited to 8 hours a day, night-work, *i.e.*, according to this Act, work between 8.30 p.m. and 5.30 a.m., was forbidden for all persons between 9 and 18.

The law-makers were so far from wishing to trench on the freedom of capital to exploit adult labour-power, or, as they called it, "the freedom of labour," that they created a special system in order to prevent the Factory Acts from having a consequence so outrageous.

.   .   .   .

That same "reformed" Parliament, which in its delicate consideration for the manufacturers, condemned children under 13, for years to come, to 72 hours of work per week in the Factory Hell, on the other hand, in the Emancipation Act, which also administered freedom drop by drop, forbade the planters, from the outset, to work any negro slave more than 45 hours a week.

But in no wise conciliated, capital now began a noisy agitation that went on for several years. It turned chiefly on the age of those who, under the name of children, were limited to 8 hours' work, and were subject to a certain amount of compulsory education. According to capitalistic anthropology, the age of childhood ended at 10, or at the outside, at 11. The more nearly the time approached for the coming into full force of the Factory Act, the fatal year 1836, the more wildly raged the mob of manufacturers. They managed, in fact, to intimidate the government to such an extent that in 1835 it proposed to lower the limit of the age of childhood from 13 to 12. In the meantime the pressure from without grew more threatening. Courage failed the House of Commons. It refused to throw children of 13 under the Juggernaut Car of capital for more than 8 hours a day, and the Act of 1833 came into full operation. It remained unaltered until June, 1844.

In the ten years during which it regulated factory work, first in part, and then entirely, the official reports of the factory inspectors teem with complaints as to the impossibility of putting the Act into force. As the law of 1833 left it optional with the lords of capital during the 15 hours, from 5.30 a.m. to 8.30 p.m., to make every "young person," and "every child" begin, break off, resume, or end his 12 or 8 hours at any moment they liked, and also permitted them to assign to different persons, different times for meals, these gentlemen soon discovered a new "system of relays," by which the labour-horses were not changed at fixed stations, but were constantly re-harnessed at changing stations. We do not pause longer on the beauty of this system, as we shall have to return to it later. But this much is clear at the first glance: that this system annulled the whole Factory Act, not only in the spirit, but in the letter. How could factory inspectors, with this complex book-keeping in respect to each individual child or young person, enforce the legally determined work-time and the granting of the legal meal-times? In a great many of the factories, the old brutalities soon blossomed out again unpunished. In an interview with the Home Secretary (1844), the factory inspectors demonstrated the impossibility of any control under the newly invented relay system. In the meantime, however, circumstances had greatly changed. The factory hands, especially since 1838, had made the Ten Hours' Bill their economic, as they had made the Charter their political, election-cry. Some of the manufacturers, even, who had managed their factories in conformity with the Act of 1833, over-whelmed Parliament with memorials on the immoral competition of their false brethren whom greater impudence, or more fortunate local circumstances, enabled to break the law. Moreover, however much the individual manufacturer might give the rein to his old lust for gain, the spokesmen and political leaders of the manufacturing class ordered a change of front and of speech towards the workpeople. They had entered upon the contest for the repeal of the Corn Laws, and needed the workers to help them to victory. They promised, therefore, not only a double-sized loaf of bread, but the enactment of the Ten Hours' Bill in the Free-trade millennium. Thus they still less dared to oppose a measure intended only to make the law of 1833 a reality. Threatened in their holiest interest, the rent of land, the Tories thundered with philanthropic indignation against the "nefarious practices" of their foes.

This was the origin of the additional Factory Act of June 7th, 1844.

.   .   .   .

It has been seen that these minutiæ, which, with military uniformity, regulate by stroke of the clock the times, limits, pauses of the work, were not at all the products of Parliamentary fancy. They developed gradually out of circumstances as natural laws of the modern mode of production. Their formulation, official recognition, and proclamation by the State, were the result of a long struggle of classes. One of their first consequences was that in practice the working-day of the adult males in factories became subject to the same limitations, since in most processes of production the co-operation of the children, young persons, and women is indispensable. On the whole, therefore, during the period from 1844 to 1847, the 12 hours' working-day became general and uniform in all branches of industry under the Factory Act.

The manufacturers, however, did not allow this "progress" without a compensating "retrogression." At their instigation the House of Commons reduced the minimum age for exploitable children from 9 to 8, in order to assure that additional supply of factory children which is due to capitalists, according to divine and human law.

The years 1846–47 are epoch-making in the economic history of England. The Repeal of the Corn Laws, and of the duties on cotton and other raw material; Free-trade proclaimed as the guiding star of legislation; in a word, the arrival of the millennium. On the other hand, in the same years, the Chartist movement and the 10 hours' agitation reached their highest point. They found allies in the Tories panting for revenge. Despite the fanatical opposition of the army of perjured Free-traders, with Bright and Cobden at their head, the Ten Hours' Bill, struggled for so long, went through Parliament.

The new Factory Act of June 8th, 1847, enacted that on July 1st, 1847, there should be a preliminary shortening of the working-day for "young persons" (from 13 to 18), and all females to 11 hours, but that on May 1st, 1848, there should be a definite limitation of the working-day to 10 hours. In other respects, the Act only amended and completed the Acts of 1833 and 1844.

Capital now entered upon a preliminary campaign in order to hinder the Act from coming into full force on May 1st, 1848. And the workers themselves, under the pretence that they had been taught by experience, were to help in the destruction of their own work. The moment was cleverly chosen. "It must be remembered, too, that there has been more than two years of great suffering (in consequence of the terrible crisis of 1846–47) among the factory operatives, from many mills having worked short time, and many being altogether closed."*

. . . .

The manufacturers tried to aggravate the natural effect of these circumstances by a general reduction of wages by 10%. This was done, so to say, to celebrate the inauguration of the new Free-trade era. Then followed a further reduction of $8\frac{1}{3}\%$ as soon as the working-day was shortened to 11, and a reduction of double that amount as soon as it was finally shortened to 10 hours. Wherever, therefore, circumstances allowed it, a reduction of wages of at least 25% took place. Under such favourably prepared conditions the agitation among the factory workers for the repeal of the Act of 1847 was begun. Neither lies, bribery, nor threats were spared in this attempt. But all was in vain. Concerning the half-dozen petitions in which workpeople were made to complain of "their oppression by the Act," the petitioners themselves declared under oral examination, that their signatures had been extorted from them. "They felt themselves oppressed, but not exactly by the Factory Act."†

But if the manufacturers did not succeed in making the workpeople speak as they wished, they themselves shrieked all the louder in press and Parliament in the name of the workpeople. They denounced the Factory Inspectors as a kind of revolutionary commissioners like those of the French National Convention ruthlessly sacrificing the unhappy factory

* Report of Inspector of Factories, 31st October, 1848.

† "'Though I signed it [the petition], I said at the time I was putting my hand to a wrong thing.' 'Then why did you put your hand to it?' 'Because I should have been turned off if I had refused.' Whence it would appear that this petitioner felt himself "oppressed", but not exactly by the Factory Act.' loc. cit. p. 102 [Original note—eds].

workers to their humanitarian crotchet. This manœuvre also failed. Factory Inspector Leonard Horner conducted in his own person, and through his sub-inspectors, many examinations of witnesses in the factories of Lancashire. About 70% of the workpeople examined declared in favour of 10 hours, a much smaller percentage in favour of 11, and an altogether insignificant minority for the old 12 hours.

Another "friendly" dodge was to make the adult males work 12 to 15 hours, and then to blazon abroad this fact as the best proof of what the proletariat desired in its heart of hearts. But the "ruthless" Factory Inspector Leonard Horner was again to the fore.

.   .   .   .

The manufacturers began by here and there discharging a part of, in many cases half of, the young persons and women employed by them, and then, for the adult males, restoring the almost obsolete night-work. The Ten Hours' Act, they cried, leaves no other alternative.

Their second step dealt with the legal pauses for meals. Let us hear the Factory Inspectors. "Since the restriction of the hours of work to ten, the factory occupiers maintain, although they have not yet practically gone the whole length, that supposing the hours of work to be from 9 a.m. to 7 p.m. they fulfil the provisions of the statutes by allowing an hour before 9 a.m. and half an hour after 7 p.m. [for meals]."*

.   .   .   .

All these shifts naturally were of no avail. The Factory Inspectors appealed to the Law courts. But soon such a cloud of dust in the way of petitions from the masters overwhelmed the Home Secretary, Sir George Grey, that in a circular of August 5th, 1848, he recommends the inspectors not "to lay informations against mill-owners for a breach of the letter of the Act, or for employment of young persons by relays in cases in which there is no reason to believe that such young persons have been actually employed for a longer period than that sanctioned by law." Hereupon, Factory Inspector J. Stuart allowed the so-called relay system during the 15 hours of the factory day throughout Scotland, where it soon flourished again as of old. The English Factory Inspectors , on the other hand, declared that the Home Secretary had no power dictatorially to suspend the law, and continued their legal proceedings against the pro-slavery rebellion.

.   .   .   .

But what was the good of summoning the capitalists when the Courts, in this case the country magistrates—Cobbett's "Great Unpaid"—acquitted them? In these tribunals, the masters sat in judgment on themselves. An example. One Eskrigge, cotton-spinner, of the firm of Kershaw, Leese, & Co., had laid before the Factory Inspector of his district the scheme of a relay system intended for his mill. Receiving a refusal, he at first kept quiet. A few months later, an individual named Robinson, also a cotton-spinner, and if not his Man Friday, at all events related to Eskrigge, appeared before the borough magistrates of Stockport on a charge of introducing the identical plan of relays invented by

---

* Reports, etc. for 31st October, 1848, pp. 133, 134 [*Original note—eds*].

Eskrigge. Four Justices sat, among them three cotton-spinners, at their head this same inevitable Eskrigge. Eskrigge acquitted Robinson, and now was of opinion that what was right for Robinson was fair for Eskrigge. Supported by his own legal decision, he introduced the system at once into his own factory. Of course, the composition of this tribunal was in itself a violation of the law. These judicial farces, exclaims Inspector Howell, "urgently call for a remedy—either that the law should be so altered as to be made to conform to these decisions, or that it should be administered by a less fallible tribunal, whose decisions would conform to the law . . . when these cases are brought forward. I long for a stipendiary magistrate."*

The crown lawyers declared the masters' interpretation of the Act of 1848 absurd. But the Saviours of Society would not allow themselves to be turned from their purpose. Leonard Horner reports, "Having endeavoured to enforce the Act . . . by ten prosecutions in seven magisterial divisions, and having been supported by the magistrates in one case only. . . . I considered it useless to prosecute more for this evasion of the law."†

.   .   .   .

As on the stage, the same persons had to appear in turns in the different scenes of the different acts. But as an actor during the whole course of the play belongs to the stage, so the operatives, during 15 hours, belonged to the factory, without reckoning the time for going and coming. Thus the hours of rest were turned into hours of enforced idleness, which drove the youths to the pot-house, and the girls to the brothel. At every new trick that the capitalist, from day to day, hit upon for keeping his machinery going 12 or 15 hours without increasing the number of his hands, the worker had to swallow his meals now in this fragment of time, now in that. At the time of the 10 hours' agitation the masters cried out that the working mob petitioned in the hope of obtaining 12 hours' wages for 10 hours' work. Now they reversed the medal. They paid 10 hours' wages for 12 or 15 hours' lordship over labour-power. This was the gist of the matter, this the masters' interpretation of the 10 hours' law! These were the same unctuous Free-traders, perspiring with the love of humanity, who for full 10 years, during the Anti-Corn Law agitation, had preached to the operatives, by a reckoning of pounds, shillings, and pence, that with free importation of corn, and with the means possessed by English industry, 10 hours' labour would be quite enough to enrich the capitalists. This revolt of capital, after two years was at last crowned with victory by a decision of one of the four highest Courts of Justice in England, the Court of Exchequer, which in a case brought before it on February 8th, 1850, decided that the manufacturers were certainly acting against the sense of the Act of 1844, but that this Act itself contained certain words that rendered it meaningless. "By this decision, the Ten Hours' Act was abolished."‡ A crowd of masters, who until then had been

---

* Reports, etc. for the 30th April, 1849, pp. 21–22.
† loc. cit.
‡ Reports, etc. for the 30th April, 1850.

afraid of using the relay system for young persons and women, now took it up heart and soul.

But on this apparently decisive victory of capital, followed at once a revulsion. The workpeople had hitherto offered a passive, although inflexible and unremitting resistance. They now protested in Lancashire and Yorkshire in threatening meetings. The pretended Ten Hours' Act, was thus simple humbug, parliamentary cheating, had never existed! The Factory Inspectors urgently warned the Government that the antagonism of classes had arrived at an incredible tension. Some of the masters themselves murmured: "On account of the contradictory decisions of the magistrates, a condition of things altogether abnormal and anarchical obtains. One law holds in Yorkshire, another in Lancashire; one law in one parish of Lancashire, another in its immediate neighbourhood. The manu-facturer in large towns could evade the law, the manufacturer in country districts could not find the people necessary for the relay system, still less for the shifting of hands from one factory to another," &c. And the first birthright of capital is equal exploitation of labour-power by all capitalists.

Under these circumstances a compromise between masters and men was affected that received the seal of Parliament in the additional Factory Act of August 5th, 1850.

.   .   .   .

However, the principle had triumphed with its victory in those great branches of industry which form the most characteristic creation of the modern mode of production. Their wonderful development from 1853 to 1860, hand-in-hand with the physical and moral regeneration of the factory workers, struck the most purblind. The masters from whom the legal limitation and regulation had been wrung step by step after a civil war of half a century, themselves referred ostentatiously to the contrast with the branches of exploitation still "free." The Pharisees of "Political Economy" now proclaimed the discernment of the necessity of a legally fixed working-day as a characteristic new discovery of their "science." It will be easily understood that after the factory magnates had resigned themselves and become reconciled to the inevitable, the power of resistance of capital gradually weakened, whilst at the same time the power of attack of the working-class grew with the number of its allies in the classes of society not immediately interested in the question. Hence the comparatively rapid advance since 1860.

.   .   .   .

The reader will bear in mind that the production of surplus-value, or the extraction of surplus-labour, is the specific end and aim, the sum and substance, of capitalist production, quite apart from any changes in the mode of production, which may arise from the subordination of labour to capital. He will remember that as far as we have at present gone, only the independent labourer, and therefore only the labourer legally qual-ified to act for himself, enters as a vendor of a commodity into a contract with the capitalist. If, therefore, in our historical sketch, on the one hand, modern industry; on the other, the labour of those who are physically and legally minors, play important parts, the former was to use only a special department, and the latter only a specially striking example of labour exploitation. Without, however, anticipating the subsequent development of our inquiry, from the mere connexion of the historic facts before us, it follows:

First. The passion of capital for an unlimited and reckless extension of the working-day, is first gratified in the industries earliest revolutionised by water-power, steam, and machinery, in those first creations of the modern mode of production, cotton, wool, flax, and silk spinning, and weaving. The changes in the material mode of production, and the corresponding changes in the social relations of the producers gave rise first to an extravagance beyond all bounds, and then in opposition to this, called forth a control on the part of Society which legally limits, regulates, and makes uniform the working-day and its pauses. This control appears, therefore, during the first half of the nineteenth century simply as exceptional legislation. As soon as this primitive dominion of the new mode of production was conquered, it was found that, in the meantime, not only had many other branches of production been made to adopt the same factory system, but that manufacturers with more or less obsolete methods, such as potteries, glass-making, &c., that old-fashioned handicrafts, like baking, and, finally, even that the so-called domestic industries, such as nail-making, had long since fallen as completely under capitalist exploitation as the factories themselves. Legislation was, therefore, compelled to gradually get rid of its exceptional character, or where, as in England, it proceeds after the manner of the Roman Casuists, to declare any house in which work was done to be a factory.

Second. The history of the regulation of the working-day in certain branches of production, and the struggle still going on in others in regard to this regulation, prove conclusively that the isolated labourer, the labourer as "free" vendor of his labour-power, when capitalist production has once attained a certain stage, succumbs without any power of resistance. The creation of a normal working-day is, therefore, the product of a protracted civil war, more or less dissembled, between the capitalist class and the working-class.

.   .   .   .

It must be acknowledged that our labourer comes out of the process of production other than he entered. In the market he stood as owner of the commodity "labour-power" face to face with other owners of commodities, dealer against dealer. The contract by which he sold to the capitalist his labour-power proved, so to say, in black and white that he disposed of himself freely. The bargain concluded, it is discovered that he was no "free agent," that the time for which he is free to sell his labour-power is the time for which he is forced to sell it, that in fact the vampire will not lose its hold on him "so long as there is a muscle, a nerve, a drop of blood to be exploited." For "protection" against "the serpent of their agonies," the labourers must put their heads together, and, as a class, compel the passing of a law, an all-powerful social barrier that shall prevent the very workers from selling, by voluntary contract with capital, themselves and their families into slavery and death. In place of the pompous catalogue of the "inalienable rights of man" comes the modest Magna Charta of a legally limited working-day, which shall make clear "when the time which the worker sells is ended, and when his own begins." Quantum mutatus ab illo!

See also MARX, Moralising Criticism and Critical Morality, MECW VI, 333; MARX, On the Question of Free Trade, MECW VI, 456–457; MARX/ENGELS, The Holy Family, MECW IV, 14–18; MARX, The Clergy and the Struggle for the Ten Hour Day, Articles on Britain, 156–158; MARX, Inaugural Address of the W.I.A. MESW(3) II, 16; MARX, Report to the Brussels Congress, The First International and After, 99.

ENGELS, The Prussian Military Question, The First International and After, 142–143.

But there's the rub! The government knows and the bourgeoisie knows too that at the present the whole German workers' movement is only tolerated and will only survive as long as the government wishes. The government will tolerate the movement as long as its existence suits it, as long as it is in its interests for the bourgeois opposition to be confronted by new and independent opponents. As soon as the workers develop through this movement into an independent power, as soon as this movement poses a danger for the government, the matter will come to an end immediately. The way in which the government put an end to the agitation of the Progressives in the press, to their associations and meetings, may serve as a warning to the workers. The same laws, decrees and measures which were applied there can be used at any time against the workers to deal a death-blow to their agitation; this will happen as soon as this agitation becomes dangerous. It is crucially important for the workers to be clear on this point and not to become victims of the same illusions as the bourgeoisie in the New Era, who were likewise merely tolerated although they thought themselves in complete control of the situation. And anyone who imagines that the present government will lift the present restrictions on the freedom of the press, association and assembly, places himself outside the arena of rational discussion. But without the freedom of the press, and the freedom of association and assembly, no workers' movement is possible.

The present Prussian government is not so stupid as to cut its own throat. Should it happen that the force of reaction toss a few sham political concessions to the German proletariat as a bait—then, it is to be hoped, the German proletariat will answer with the proud words of the old Hildebrandslied:

> Mit gêrû scal man geba infâhân, ort widar orte.
> Gifts shall be accepted with the spear, point against point.

As for the *social* concessions which the reaction might make to the workers—shorter working hours in the factories, a better implementation of the factory laws, the right to form combinations, etc.—the experience of all countries shows that the reactionaries introduce such legislative proposals without the workers having to offer the least in return. The reactionaries need the workers but the workers do not need them. Thus, as long as the workers insist on these points in their own agitation they can count on the moment coming when reactionary elements will present these same demands merely in order to annoy the bourgeoisie; and as a result the workers will achieve a victory over the bourgeoisie without owing the reactionaries any thanks.

But if the workers' party has nothing to expect from the reactionaries except minor concessions, which they would gain anyway, without having to go begging—what can it expect, then, from the bourgeois opposition?

See also MARX, The Communism of the *Rheinischer Boebachter*, *MECW* VI, 228.

ENGELS, Introduction to "The Class Struggles in France", *MESW(3)* I, 202.

The irony of world history turns everything upside down. We the "revolutionists" the "overthrowers"—we are thriving far better on legal methods than on illegal methods and overthrow. The parties of Order, as they call themselves, are perishing under the legal conditions created by themselves. They cry despairingly with Odilon Barrot: *la légalité nous tue*, legality is the death of us; whereas we, under this legality, get firm muscles and rosy cheeks and look like life eternal. And if *we* are not so crazy as to let ourselves be driven to street fighting in order to please them, then in the end there is nothing left for them to do but themselves break through this fatal legality.

Meanwhile they make new laws against overthrows. Again everything is turned upside down. These anti-overthrow fanatics of today, are they not themselves the overthrowers of yesterday? Have *we* perchance evoked the civil war of 1866? Have *we* driven the King of Hanover, the Elector of Hesse, and the Duke of Nassau from their hereditary lawful domains and annexed these hereditary domains? And these overthrowers of the German Confederation and three crowns by the grace of God complain of overthrow! *Quis tulerit Gracchos de seditione querentes?* Who could allow the Bismarck worshippers to rail at overthrow?

Let them, nevertheless, put through their anti-overthrow bills, make them still worse, transform the whole penal law into indiarubber, they will gain nothing but new proof of their impotence. If they want to deal Social-Democracy a serious blow they will have to resort to quite other measures, in addition. They can cope with the Social-Democratic overthrow, which just now is doing so well by keeping the law, only by an overthrow on the part of the parties of Order, an overthrow which cannot live without breaking the law. Herr Rössler, the Prussian bureaucrat, and Herr von Boguslawski, the Prussian general, have shown them the only way perhaps still possible of getting at the workers, who simply refuse to let themselves be lured into street fighting. Breach of the constitution, dictatorship, return to absolutism, *regis voluntas suprema lex!* Therefore, take courage, gentlemen; here half measures will not do; here you must go the whole hog!

But do not forget that the German empire, like all small states and generally all modern states, is a *product of contract*; of the contract, first, of the princes with one another and, second, of the princes with the people. If one side breaks the contract, the whole contract falls to the ground; the other side is then also no longer bound, as Bismarck demonstrated to us so beautifully in 1866. If therefore, you break the constitution of the Reich, the Social-Democracy is free, and can do as it pleases with regard to you. But it will hardly blurt out to you today what it is going to do then.

See also MARX/ENGELS, Fictitious Splits in the International, *MESW (3)* II, 275.

MARX, First Draft of "The Civil War in France", *The First International and After*, 238–239.

The notaries, bailiffs, auctioneers, bum-bailiffs and other judicial officers making till now a fortune of their functions, transformed into agents of the Commune receiving from it fixed salaries like other workmen.

As the professors of the École de Médecine have run away, the Commune appointed a commission for the foundation of *free universities*, no longer state parasites; given to the students that had passed their examination, means to practise independent of doctoral titles (titles to be conferred by the faculty).

Since the judges of the *Civil Tribunal of the Seine*, like the other magistrates always ready to function under any class government, had run away, the Commune appointed an advocate to do the most urgent business until the reorganization of tribunals on the basis of general suffráge (*26 April*).

3. General Measures

Conscription Abolished. In the present war every able man (National Guard) must serve. This measure excellent to get rid of all traitors and cowards hiding in Paris (*29 March*).

Games of Hazard Suppressed (*2 April*). Church separated from state; the religious budget suppressed; all clerical estates declared national properties (*3 April*). The Commune, having made inquiries consequent upon private information, found that besides the old guillotine the *"government of order"* had commanded the construction of a new guillotine (more expeditious and portable) and paid in advance. The Commune ordered both the old and the new guillotines to be burned publicly on 6 April. The Versailles journals, re-echoed by the press of order all over the world, narrated that the Paris people, as a demonstration against the bloodthirstiness of the Communards, had burnt these guillotines! (*6 April*). All political prisoners were set free at once after the revolution of 18 March. But the Commune knew that under the regime of L. Bonaparte and his worthy successor the Government of Defence, many people were simply incarcerated on no charge whatever as political suspects. Consequently it charged one of its members—Protot—to make inquiries. By him 150 people were set free who, being arrested six months before, had not yet undergone any judicial examination; many of them, already arrested under Bonaparte, had been for a year in prison without any charge or judicial examination (*9 April*). This fact, so characteristic of the Government of Defence, enraged them. They asserted that the Commune had liberated all felons. But who liberated convicted felons? The forger Jules Favre. Hardly got into power, he hastened to liberate Pic and Taillefer, condemned for theft and forgery in the affaire of the *Étendard*. One of these men, Taillefer, daring to return to Paris, has been reinstated in his convenient abode. But this is not all. The Versailles government has delivered, in the Maisons Centrales all over France, convicted thieves on the condition of entering M. Thiers's army.

MARX, The Civil War in France—Address of the General Council, *MESW(3)* II, 227.

The great social measure of the Commune was its own working existence. Its special measures could but betoken the tendency of a government of the people by the people. Such were the abolition of the nightwork of journeymen bakers; the prohibition, under penalty, of the employers' practice to reduce wages by levying upon their work-people fines under manifold pretexts—a process in which the employer combines in his own person the parts of legislator, judge, and executor, and filches the money to boot. Another measure of this class was the surrender to associations of workmen, under reserve of compensation, of all closed workshops and factories, no matter whether the respective capitalists had absconded or preferred to strike work.

See also MARX, *ibid.*, 255.

MARX, *ibid.*, 223–224.

It is a strange fact. In spite of all the tall talk and all the immense literature, about Emancipation of Labour, no sooner do the working men anywhere take the subject into their own hands with a will, than uprises at once all the apologetic phraseology of the mouthpieces of present society with its two poles of Capital and Wages Slavery. . . The Commune, they exclaim, intends to abolish property, the basis of all civilisation! Yes, gentlemen, the Commune intended to abolish that class-property which makes the labour of the many the wealth of the few. It aimed at the expropriation of the expropriators. It wanted to make individual property a truth by transforming the means of production, land capital, now chiefly the means of enslaving and exploiting labour, into mere instruments of free and associated labour.—But this is Communism, "impossible" Communism! . . . .

The working class did not expect miracles from the Commune. They have no ready-made utopias to introduce *par décret du peuple*. They know that in order to work out their own emancipation, and along with it that higher form to which present society is irresistibly tending by its own economical agencies, they will have to pass through long struggles, through a series of historic processes, transforming circumstances and men. They have no ideals to realise, but to set free the elements of the new society with which old collapsing bourgeois society itself is pregnant.

Sources of Translations and Key to References Cited

Abbreviated source indicators, e.g. *MESW(3)* I, are in brackets beside the full title.

Engels, F. (1959). *Anti-Dühring*. Foreign Languages Publishing House, Moscow.

Marx, K. and Engels, F. (1972). *Articles from "Neue Rheinische Zeitung" 1848–49*, Progress, Moscow (*Articles from NRZ*).

Marx, K. and Engels, F. (1971). *Articles on Britain*. Progress, Moscow.

Marx, K. (1970). *Capital* I. Lawrence and Wishart, London.

Marx, K. (1974). *Capital* II. Lawrence and Wishart, London.

Marx, K. (1972). *Capital* III. Lawrence and Wishart, London.

Marx, K. and Engels, F. (1975). *Collected Works* I–IV. Lawrence and Wishart, London (*MECW* I–IV).

Marx, K. and Engels, F. (1976). *Collected Works* V–VI. Lawrence and Wishart, London. (*MECW* V–VI).

Marx, K. (1968). *On Colonialism*. Lawrence and Wishart, London.

Tumanov, V. (ed.) (1974). *Contemporary Bourgeois Legal Thought*. Progress, Moscow.

Moore, S. (ed.) (1957). *The Critique of Capitalist Democracy*. Paine Whitman, New York.

Marx, K. (1974). *The First International and After*. Penguin, Harmondsworth.

Marx, K. (1969). *Grundrisse*. Penguin. Harmondsworth.

Marx, K. and Engels, F. (1971). *On Ireland*. Lawrence and Wishart, London.

Marx, K. (1953). *Letters to Americans*. International Publishers, New York.

Marx, K. *The Poverty of Philosophy*. Foreign Languages Publishing House, Moscow.

Marx, K. and Engels, F. (1973). *The Revolutions of 1848*. Penguin, Harmondsworth.

Marx, K. and Engels, F. (1975). *Selected Correspondence*. Progress, Moscow.

Marx, K. and Engels, F. (1934). *Selected Correspondence 1846–1895*. Foreign Languages Publishing House, Moscow.

Marx, K. and Engels, F. (1969). *Selected Works* I and II. Progress, Moscow (*MESW(3)* I–II).

Marx, K. and Engels, F. (1970). *Selected Works* III. Progress, Moscow (*MESW(3)* I).

Marx, K. (1969). *Theories of Surplus Value* I–III. Lawrence and Wishart, London.

Index of Cited Works